THE RADICAL NOVEL RECONSIDERED

A series of paperback reissues of mid-twentieth-century U.S. left-wing fiction, with new biographical and critical introductions by contemporary scholars.

Series Editor
Alan Wald, University of Michigan

BOOKS IN THE SERIES

To Make My Bread *Grace Lumpkin*
Moscow Yankee *Myra Page*
The People from Heaven *John Sanford*
Salome of the Tenements *Anzia Yezierska*
The Great Midland *Alexander Saxton*
Tucker's People *Ira Wolfert*
Pity Is Not Enough *Josephine Herbst*
Burning Valley *Phillip Bonosky*
The Big Boxcar *Alfred Maund*
The World Above *Abraham Polonsky*
A World to Win *Jack Conroy*

A WORLD TO WIN

Photo by David Eppelsheimer

A WORLD TO WIN

JACK CONROY

Introduction by Douglas Wixson

UNIVERSITY OF ILLINOIS PRESS
Urbana and Chicago

© 1935, renewed 1963 by Jack Conroy
Reprinted by permission of Douglas Wixson,
literary executor for Jack Conroy
Introduction © 2000 by Douglas Wixson
All rights reserved
Manufactured in the United States of America
♾ This book is printed on acid-free paper.

Library of Congress Cataloging-in-Publication Data
Conroy, Jack, 1899–
A world to win / Jack Conroy ;
introduction by Douglas Wixson.
p. cm. — (The radical novel reconsidered)
Originally published: New York: Covici, Friede, © 1935.
With new introd.
Includes bibliographical references.
ISBN 0-252-06927-7 (pbk. : acid-free paper)
1. Labor movement—Fiction. 2. Homeless persons—
Fiction. 3. Working class—Fiction. 4. Brothers—Fiction.
I. Title. II. Series.
PS3505.O53W67   2000
813'.52—dc21   00-039218

p 5 4 3 2 1

CONTENTS

Introduction by Douglas Wixson   ix

A WORLD TO WIN

    Green Valley   9

    The Green Dragon   101

    Nothing to Lose   225

INTRODUCTION
Douglas Wixson

> But the People are ungrammatical, untidy,
> and their sins gaunt and ill-bred.
> —Walt Whitman

Seldom do workers speaking in their own voices appear in American literature.[1] Even rarer are workers who, as Richard Wright said, "write out of what life gives us in the form of experience."[2] It is not the unusualness of Conroy's achievement as worker-writer, however, that draws us to his work but its significance and value.[3] Jack Conroy (1898–1990) grew up in working-class milieus where, as Leslie Shepard says in a different context, "the world of literature remained largely a closed book. Working men dreamed of the beauty and wisdom locked away in the printed pages, and literacy seemed the key to a magic world."[4] The circumstances of his youth and early manhood and how he came to write are subjects that preoccupied Conroy throughout his life. He reminds us of the Russian writer Maxim Gorky (1868–1936).[5] Both authors wrote of factory workers, the dispossessed, those living on the margins of society. Gorky and Conroy were spokesmen for the industrial proletariat, figures associated with revolutionary movements, and outsiders by virtue of their personal histories, which gave them unique perspectives on literature and life. Like Gorky, Conroy requires standards of evaluation and critical methods different from those traditionally associated with canonical literature.[6]

The title of Conroy's second novel confounded radical critics. Mike Gold viewed Conroy's rising star and hoped for a proletarian novel that would set a course for the cultural vanguard.

The title, drawn from the Communist Manifesto, suggests a work more in line with the tenets of socialist realism than with midwestern literary traditions, whose resources of folklore and humor Conroy employed. Decreed as official artistic doctrine by Stalin in 1932, socialist realism aimed to engage writers as "engineers of the soul" who, in the words of Victor Terras, would render "a truthful depiction of that which leads life toward socialism."[7] Models frequently cited included Gorky's *Mother* (1906) and Aleksandr Fadeev's *Rout* (1927). Gorky and Fadeev, Soviet critics argued, had shown the way to socialism under the Communist Party's leadership, joining workers in the spirit of collectivism to form a new society. What critics found in Conroy's novel, however, thwarted these expectations.[8]

A World to Win turns proletarian conventions on end. Political consciousness comes finally to the antihero, Leo Turley, like a knock on the head. Conroy was temperamentally incapable of employing prescriptive conventions of any kind, in fact lampoons them. Leo is a foolish, naive, lumpish figure, boxed about by life, a failed economy, his employers, and his own thick-headedness. A most unlikely proletarian hero, he ultimately blunders into commitment. Like Huck Finn, Leo finally does the right thing in spite of himself. When we first encounter Leo's half brother, Robert, he is a simpering crybaby, enamored of precious writing and lured by bourgeois aspirations, a pale, thin, young man in contrast to his robust father, Terry, an improvident Irish itinerant worker.

Conroy had chosen "Little Stranger" as the title, expanding the novel from stories published in little magazines, including one with the same title that appeared in *A Year Magazine* (December–April 1933).[9] Shaping short stories into a novel was the method he had used in *The Disinherited,* lending it an episodic character in keeping with the "picaresque," as Daniel Aaron called it, nature of the story.[10]

Conroy was sensitive to the criticism that *The Disinherited* was loose-jointed and un-novel-like, as if there were ready-made patterns to follow in novel writing. Granville Hicks praised Conroy's first novel but noted, "Something is missing, for otherwise the reader would feel that the climax of the book followed inevitably from everything that had gone before." Proletarian writers should, he suggested, learn from bourgeois writers "about growth."[11] Other reviewers judged it as an autobiographical "first novel," praising it for its "rejection of special pleading . . . and of literary artifice."[12] Clifton Fadiman of the *New Yorker* seemed to concur: "This book has no particular form, being in this respect closely imitative of the life of the migratory worker who is its hero. But the atmosphere rings true. There is no forced proletarianism about it, nor is there that youthful Hemingway romanticism which sees the depressed worker merely as a picturesque tough."[13] The *Washington News* reviewer underscored the autobiographical nature of Conroy's first novel: "The book is what all first novels should be, and usually are, whether the author is out to sell Marx, or marbles. It is an unloading of accumulated memories, of personal passion, of impressions, beliefs, peoples who make up the background of the author's childhood."[14]

If Conroy had succeeded in pumping the fresh water of his youthful experiences into a "formless" but usable container, then where was he to go with a second novel? "Proletarian literature," Gold wrote in a "fan" letter to Conroy published in the *New Masses*, "is in its first crude beginnings in America. You are one of the leaders of this movement, and your book is an advance-guard skirmish in the great battle."[15] It was a heavy burden to carry alone. After reading Gold's "letter" and finding it paternalistic, Josephine Herbst advised Conroy, "Go your own way for god's sake."[16] It was good advice, but the stakes were very high, complicated by the expectations of publishers and critics and the financial burden of supporting his family, including three children who needed new shoes for the fall school term. The idea of casting his incomparable knowledge and experiences of working-class life into "novelistic" form seemed to be his only option. His agent, Max Lieber, wrote that Covici-Friede Publishers was anxious to see his manuscript and sent along an advance of $500. The Covici-Friede editors wanted the title changed to "A World to Win." After much sparring over the title, Conroy reluctantly yielded; he desperately needed the money. Lieber warned him that it "would give a lot of humorists an excellent opportunity to make quips."[17]

Through a semiautobiographical series of episodes in *The Disinherited,* Conroy exposed his young hero, Larry Donovan, to the bruising, often destructive, economic forces confronting dispossessed workers. It was the form Conroy knew best because it is the "form" of a worker's life. But to cast in conventional novel form the story he wanted to tell in his new book meant forcing the sprawling, untidy, vital material of working-class existence into a structure that risked missing the truth of the subject. He knew, however, that problems with the unfamiliar cultural coding inscribed in *The Disinherited* had led to confusion and critical misinterpretation. Perhaps by turning to more familiar literary techniques, he would attract a broader readership.

Sinclair Lewis, recipient of the Nobel Prize for literature in 1930, set out to write a novel of American labor. Completely thwarted, he abandoned the project. "Did he find it too ungrateful a subject?" a critic asked.[18] Labor offered extremely complicated issues and blurred lines of battle in Conroy's lifetime. The confusion of the labor movement itself, lacking coherency and a central purpose, was reflected in the difficulties that bedeviled worker-writers. Submitting his elusive subject to the structural features of proletarian fiction—for example, a conversion ending—Conroy hoped to find an appropriate form for his second novel *and* answer his critics. At the same time, his novel had to ring true to those who, like Conroy, had from necessity spent most of their working days in a factory, mine, or mill. This was the criterion he applied in his approving review of Robert Cantwell's *Land of Plenty,* and it was the one he imposed on his own writing.[19]

A World to Win offers us insights into the difficulties facing a worker-writer. Conroy delineated these in his address to the 1935 American Writers' Congress. "Everything," he said, "is confusing and we have so little in the way of precedent or example, we are hampered by cultural deficiencies, we are harried by the fear of unemployment when working and by bodily and mental fatigue. But we have something vital and new to communicate...."[20] Studying the genesis and evolution of *A World to Win* gives us insight into the *making* of radical literature by a working-class writer. Conroy traces the path of this evolution through Larry Donovan in the first novel and the dual figures of Leo and Terry in the second. The narrative progression in both involves the growth of consciousness and the acquisition of communicative skills. The *process* that Conroy dramatizes in *A World to Win* includes the material conditions of its production as well as the currents that flow together in shaping its content and form. Its significance lies both in permitting us to view ways that historical knowledge becomes personal knowledge and in revealing the role of form and style in portraying working-class experience.

A Worker-Writer's Résumé

Born in a coal-mining camp in northern Missouri on 5 December 1898, Conroy experienced the most important events in twentieth-century labor history: the early period of industrial unionization, workers' struggles for economic security and stability in the face of dehumanizing mechanization, the bitter conflicts fought and the gains won through collective bargaining in the 1930s, the erosion of these gains after World War II, and the decline of organized labor's political power. The son of an immigrant Irishman who had left his Jesuit studies to become a miner and subsequently a leader of his union local, Conroy had a thirst for learning and a talent for writing. Early events that spurred his social consciousness were the death of his father and two uncles in mine accidents, the abandonment of the mines by the companies exploiting them, and the subsequent breakup of the community itself. Monkey Nest coal camp, with its communal and oral traditions, dangerous work conditions, and frequent labor-management struggles, left a deep, lasting impression on Conroy. Although he worked in factory cities throughout the Midwest and later turned to writing and editing, in his heart he never left this tiny work community. The miners' warm camaraderie, union solidarity, and militant activism shaped his consciousness from an early age. His genius for, as we would say today, "networking" grew from the kinship relationships he knew in his family and among the miners, almost entirely immigrants, who were highly skilled labor aristocrats despite low pay and hazardous work conditions.

Apprenticed in the railroad shops in nearby Moberly, Missouri, at age thirteen, Conroy entered a well-organized and successful union, the Brotherhood of Railway Carmen, whose pride in craft, status in the community, and democratic traditions shaped his early working-class "education." At the age of fifteen, he was chosen to be the recording secretary of the union local, probably because he had read every book in the workers' library maintained by the Wabash Railroad and most of those in Moberly's Carnegie Library.

In 1921, Conroy took a leave of absence from the Wabash shops and enrolled at the University of Missouri. A deacon in the Methodist church, he seemed destined for a professional degree and middle-class status. He found his college experience intellectually stimulating but missed the camaraderie of the Wabash shops. Furthermore, he balked at the required military training then in effect. After a semester, he returned to his old job. Conroy could have remained in the shops and eventually become a foreman, but he came out, along with most of the other carmen, in the great railroad strike of 1922 in protest against the government's newly enacted antilabor legislation designed to reverse earlier gains. World War I had brought prosperity to the railroads under government administration and had won a forty-eight-hour week for workers. The strike froze the nation's major railroads, altering the lives of many people in profound ways and bestowing a legacy of bitterness and conflict for many years. The antilabor administration under Warren Harding, together with the 1921 business depression, weakened the railroad unions' bargaining power. National Guard troops were brought in to enforce a lockout, and by winter the strike had failed. Conroy joined thousands of workers, the uprooted "proletariat," seeking jobs in the auto factories of Toledo and Detroit.

Working day shifts at a Toledo auto factory, Conroy wrote poems and sketches at night for short-lived little magazines with such names as *The Northern Light, Pegasus,* and *Morada*. In 1929, he helped found the Rebel Poets organization, which connected isolated worker-writers and radical poets through its publication, the *Rebel Poet* (1931–32). But it was H. L. Mencken, the conservative, outspoken editor of the *American Mercury,* who gave Conroy the boost he needed as a young writer. Mencken published six of Conroy's short stories and sketches in the *Mercury,* together with the writings of such young writers as William Faulkner, Josephine Herbst, George Milburn, James T. Farrell, Ruth Suckow, and Albert Halper. Mencken valued Conroy's ear for workers' speech and lore. Conroy perceived in Mencken's iconoclastic editorship the possibility of creating a new system of literary production that reached out to working-class readers at the same time that it gave voice to the voiceless.

In the meantime, however, an economic and social crisis of unprecedented dimensions gripped the nation, paralyzing initiative and stranding workers released from factory and farm jobs. When Willys-Overland shut down temporarily in the late fall of 1929, Conroy and his family returned to Moberly. Soon after, Mencken published Conroy's story entitled "Hard Winter," portraying the plight of the unemployed workers on the eve of an economic debacle that eventually put seventeen million out on the street.[21]

In a new magazine, the *Anvil* (1933–35), Conroy sought to apply the same publishing formula he had devised earlier: a low-cost printer, cooperation on the part of contributors and friends, and a network of distributors, including newspaper kiosks, bookstores, and the Communist Party's Central Distribution Agency. In content, however, the *Anvil* was a radical departure from the *Rebel Poet*. Conroy sought to focus his publication on vigorous writing with social content, avoiding inflated revolutionary rhetoric and the theoretical hairsplitting of radical sectarianism.

The contributions reflected the verve and energy of its editor, who nurtured many an unknown talent en route to distinguished literary achievement. From an abandoned gas station in Alpine, Texas, Nelson Algren sent a chapter from the draft of his first novel, *Somebody in Boots* (1935). Erskine Caldwell submitted two stories dealing with racial injustice, too controversial for other magazine editors. Langston Hughes anticipated Ralph Ellison's *Invisible Man* in a short story satirizing Jim Crow education. Young radical writers, such as Meridel Le Sueur, Sanora Babb, and Paul Corey, published their early stories. A Chicago postal worker named Richard Wright published his poetry in the *Anvil*, his first contribution to a magazine of national circulation.

The idea that a literature of rough-hewn vigor and social content would attract a large working-class readership proved unduly optimistic. A democratic art, accessible to all the people and speaking to their concerns—an ideal espoused much earlier by Walt Whitman—competed on unequal footing with a growing commodity culture produced for mass consumption.

It is clear in retrospect that Conroy's aims were part of the tentative counterhegemonic cultural trends initiated in the 1930s, suppressed in the cold war era, and struggling for existence today in the face of multinational ownership of publishing houses and the slow attrition of small publishers. Conroy conceived of a decentralized, nonhierarchical system of literary production that would foster a voluntary alliance among diverse perspectives. Instead of adhering to the star system of authors, Conroy took chances with new writers, black, white, female, working and middle class, without practicing reverse discrimination. The guiding criteria were to have something vital to say and to communicate it to the reader effectively. A revolution was underway, anticipating the information society of today. It never quite penetrated the ruling hegemony of powerful interests, however; independent and brash, it lost the support of the cultural apparatus of the Communist Party, most importantly its distribution agency.

As editor of the *Anvil* and author of *The Disinherited* and *A World to Win,* Conroy was a celebrated figure by 1935. He was warmly received as one of the principal speakers at the first American Writers' Congress in New York City the same year. The Popular Front, however, represented a shift from a cultural movement focused on working-class issues to a broader-based invitation to all writers and artists to lend support in a common struggle against fascism. Joining the Works Progress Administration's Federal Writers' Project, first in St. Louis and then in Chicago, Conroy began a literary collaboration with the black novelist Arna Bontemps, while reviving the *Anvil* with Nelson Algren's assistance. The *New Anvil* (1939–40) helped give a start to little-known writers, such as Margaret Walker, Tom McGrath, Vincent Ferrini, and Frank Yerby. It failed, however, to keep pace with the changing reading tastes of a public growing prosperous in an economy bolstered by preparations for war. Conroy's other significant achievement with the Illinois Writers' Project was to collect occupational folklore, much of it from his own memory, which became the basis of a series of juvenile books, including the best-selling *Fast Sooner Hound,* coauthored by Bontemps.

A World to Win: Situation and Text

The Conroy family's fortunes had reached low ebb by the summer of 1934. Soaring temperatures burned crops and blistered city streets. Conroy moved the kitchen table outdoors beneath a shade trade, where he typed with work-calloused fingers the draft of his second novel. He worked for his brother-in-law's construction company, but contracts were few, and the men were frequently laid off. His wife, Gladys, came out on strike against the Brown Shoe Company.

Four years of economic crisis and drought conditions in the Midwest had forced debt-ridden farmers to give up their homes and seek jobs as migrant workers in the West. Industrial cities, including Detroit, Toledo, and St. Louis, witnessed massive layoffs of workers. Some two million homeless people were on the road, riding the rails and looking for work. By the winter of 1934, seventeen million were on relief. Three thousand workers marched on the Ford plant in Dearborn, Michigan, to demand jobs. When high-pressure water hoses failed to turn them back, gunfire and tear gas were used, leaving four workers dead and many more wounded. In Los Angeles, St. Louis, and elsewhere, the homeless erected shacks, elected a council and mayor, and called their makeshift villages Hooverville. To Conroy and other radicals, the capitalist system seemed near collapse. In some factory cities, there was fear of starvation. Most workers accepted any kind of work they could find to tide them over until things improved. Some yielded to despair; others turned to collective, even militant action.

Conroy made trips to St. Louis often in the early 1930s, staying with Gladys's brother, Charlie Kelly, a factory worker, and his wife. Organized labor was beginning to stir in the cities. By 1932, the Communist Party was organizing unemployed workers to take part in public demonstrations. When the city of St. Louis threatened to cut back the relief roles, the Party's unemployed movement undertook mass actions, culminating in the "July Riot" of that same year. As the mob moved to enter city hall, the police fired tear gas. Several of the jobless protesters picked up the gas bombs and hurled them back at the police. In the ensuing melee, the police shot a black unemployed worker named Ben Powell, who, according to the paper, was "said to have stood alone, heaving bricks at the policeman, near Thirteenth and

Market Streets."²² The incident found its way into *A World to Win* in the figure of Fatfolks.

Wage cuts and discriminatory practices against blacks, predominantly women, at the Funsten Nut Company brought workers out in May 1933. During this strike, Conroy saw mass demonstrations, including a large meeting at the Labor Lyceum, where black and white workers mingled and sang "Solidarity Forever." For Conroy, it was like the old days, when the unions had a voice in politics. Following the nutpickers' strike came the Amalgamated Clothing Workers' strike, the bakers' union strike, demonstrations of the unemployed in Hooverville, the Laclede Gas Workers' strike, and, several years later, the electrical workers' strike against Emerson Electric, in which a Communist organizer named Bill Sentner played a central role. It is this period of incipient labor struggle that informed Conroy's second novel, published in April 1935.

Against this political and economic background, *A World to Win* focuses on three main settings: the radical-activist "Workers' Center," patterned after the Vanguard Bookstore in St. Louis in a once-elegant mansion on the corner of Franklin and Grand; the "Green Dragon," a parodic version of the Blue Lantern Inn on the Mississippi riverfront, where wharf workers, artists, and bootleggers mixed in an atmosphere of cigarette smoke, jazz, and the smell of gin; and "Roosevelt Roost," the Hooverville that stretched for a mile along the levee. When prohibition was repealed in 1933, the romance of furtive locales with their cultivated cynicism and apolitical debates about aesthetics evaporated. Artists and writers gravitated to Stanley Radulovich's Little Bohemia on Commercial Alley in the riverfront warehouse district, where art and politics elicited spirited discussion. Conroy met with Wallie Wharton, Clark Mills, and others of his *Anvil* editorial staff. On occasion, they were joined by an aspiring young writer named Thomas Lanier Williams, better known as Tennessee Williams, who worked in the International Shoe Company plant in St. Louis. His father had sent him to work in the factory after he failed his military requirement at the University of Missouri and left without a degree in 1932. Williams's early stories and one-act plays, according to Allean Hale, reflect his exposure to Hooverville squalor, riverfront bohemian locales, labor strikes, and the company of radical activists, including Conroy.[23]

St. Louis was a lively place in the 1930s. A young artist named Joe Jones had stirred up public controversy by conducting his art classes for the unemployed on a sidewalk outside the old courthouse. Jones was an ardent Communist at the time, meeting frequently met with Sentner, leader of the Electrical Workers Union, in Little Bohemia. Conroy himself maintained contacts with a local Party district organizer named Alfred Wagenknecht, whom Conroy and Wallie Wharton called "Wagonwheels." Not a Party member, Conroy nonetheless supported its aims while satirizing its clumsy, heavy-handed methods. By the mid-1930s, there was a new optimism in the air, a sense that conditions were different, that people could change things and themselves through cooperative action. In the new Popular Front era, anticipated in the concluding episodes of *A World to Win,* artistic milieus were crossed with radical politics and labor activism in new hybrids, for the threat was no longer starvation but, as Algren put it, "somebody in boots" (fascism).[24]

In structure, Conroy's first novel, *The Disinherited,* resembles the antiformalist montage of the revolutionary Russian filmmakers Dziga Vertov and Sergei Eisenstein, with its retreat from individual characterization and its emphasis on the collective experience of working-class people. Montage methods are also employed in *A World to Win,* although the composition differs from *The Disinherited* in at least one crucial structural feature. In the earlier novel, Larry Donovan steers an uncertain course between half-formed ideals and the grim, bitter reality of the dispossessed, unsure where his loyalties lie. In *A World to Win,* this opposition is split between two half brothers, Leo and Robert Hurley, who, linked by childhood but divided by education and aspirations, are eventually reconciled through experience and the growth it provides. In both novels, the loose linking of episodes creates an openness in the text that defamiliarizes the commonplace and invites the reader's critical scrutiny. The ordinary is revealed as socially constructed; the author invites critical scrutiny.

If the rise of workers from their humiliation and passivity was the principal message of *A World to Win*, its value would be only historical. Conroy was obviously aware that a novel closely linked to contemporary events would quickly lose its significance and that he must create a form that both challenges and makes use of the features of a particular genre system. Leftist thinkers viewed the factory as a site of struggle between labor and capital, but Conroy knew that no theoretical framework adequately described factory work or workers' motives. He focused on cultural difference and on the mentality of the working class, the attitudes, values, and self- perceptions of individuals, as if he were writing about a subculture.

"People live in their social class," writes Joyce O. Hertzler, "intuitively, habitually, and *verbally*."[25] Conroy perceived that among workers, passivity and complacency are expressed in clichés, a dulling-down of language that speaks of alienation. Humor is a form of resistance and the desire for greater freedom of action, and grime and smoke are evidence of work, of jobs. These are some examples of cultural modes of symbolic behavior that enrich Conroy's writing and make it interesting. Exploring such modes, as Robert P. Baker suggests, "may provide a new definition of the working class."[26] Conroy described the bohemian and working-class milieus of St. Louis as he knew them in terms of linguistic and cultural difference.

In the 1930s, circumstances forced the homeless and hapless to surrender much of their individuality and personal ambitions, indeed pretensions, and submerge themselves among the nameless masses in search of work. Their real despair was concealed behind a mask of cynical humor and rough fellowship. Evidence of this appears throughout *The Disinherited* in the pranks and rude larks of workers who live on the edge of existence, fearing dismissal and destitution. We can measure Leo Hurley's own desperation in *A World to Win* to the extent that as things turn worse for him, his manner becomes evermore awkwardly comic. Such behavior is the nature of folk literature, as G. K. Chesterton points out in his famous essay on Charles Dickens. "And all over the world," Chesterton wrote, "the folk literature, the popular literature, is the same. It consists of very dignified sorrow and very undignified fun. Its sad tales are of broken hearts; its happy tales are of broken heads."[27]

The pitfalls facing the working-class writer in 1934 were many, as I have suggested. And within a year, new ones appeared. Conroy was anxious to avoid these and attract a broad readership. He took considerable risks. Characterization in *A World to Win* involves deliberate exaggeration and distortion, like Dickens's figures. Similarly, he employed the methods of parody to underscore lack of consciousness, obsessional behavior, and folk eccentricity. Leo, Terry, Martha, Robert, Kurt Leischer, and Monty Cass are at various times absurd, comic, tragic, moving. Leo blunders from trouble to trouble, never planning for the next day or sure what happened to him the previous day. He "thought bitterly of saying to hell with you, Dudley, and walking out of the room, catching a Red Ball [freight train] for the Coast and never coming back." For a time he turns "scissorbill," cooperating with his bosses at the expense of his fellow workers. *Scissorbill*, according to the eminent labor folklorist Archie Green, derived from "Wobbly" (Industrial Workers of the World) speech and was used "to ridicule a yokel, yahoo, or unclass-conscious worker."[28] The *Oxford English Dictionary* (1989) cites Conroy's use of the term in a humorous folk narrative he wrote entitled "Slappy Hooper, the World's Bestest Sign Painter."[29] Such a worker in proletarian fiction would hardly inspire humor, but Conroy's method is to hold up moral blindness to comic reflection.

The inhibitions of Martha Hurley, once a talented student of classical literature, find release in religious fanaticism. Conroy loved to parody formal speech, including fundamentalist sermons. A sermon "of indeterminate authorship," which he had heard as a boy in rural Missouri, is included in his collection entitled *Midland Humor*. His infallible ear for linguistic oddity and incongruity furnish most of the intertexts, including Preacher Epperson's sermons. The audience is eager to hear salacious details yet remains sanctimoniously censorious of Anna Leischer. Is this not Dickens's method?

Like Dickens's, Conroy's portrayals, alternating human frailty and folly without demeaning human dignity, have a theatricality about them. Robert Hurley has literary pretensions but little talent. His head is filled with the hopeless trash of genteel romance and fragments of Victorian poetry. He withers under Leo's contempt for his "unworthiness." Lured by the bohemian milieu of the Green Dragon in "St. Luke" (St. Louis), Robert is no more enlightened than his half brother concerning the world about him, except that the hard knocks of Leo's experience are better teachers than Robert's encounters with failed artists and society matrons who patronize them.

Terry Hurley is the figure of an improvident Irish immigrant worker, whose mismatch with Martha exaggerates their differences, which neither one is capable of resolving and only drives them further into their eccentricities. There is foolishness and hurt in these portrayals but no cruelty. Leo may have a deformed conscience, as Henry Nash Smith says of Huck Finn, but he also has a sound heart.[30] The characters stumble along a twisted path, and only Leo and Robert finally arrive at some mutual understanding, as if to reknit the bond they shared as children. For it is in the hollows and woods of Green Valley (northern Missouri) that they first discovered the wonder and wickedness of human behavior in their encounters with the murderer Hade Pollard, the misanthropic Kurt Leischer, and the grim reality of Monty's death in a mine disaster.

If Conroy, like Dickens, was able to evoke compassion and warmth toward his characters through caricature while underscoring his meanings, his use of parody was likewise successful in extracting humor from the gray, circumscribed lives he portrays. He delights in satirizing sentimental verse, for he had often heard "The Blind Child," "The Murderer," and other ballads recited in his childhood home in a time when the tattered pieces of Victorian-era gentility still decorated working-class homes. His mother was addicted to the sentimental novels of Mrs. E. D. E. N. Southworth and Mary Jane Holmes, who appeared regularly in such popular magazines as *Comfort* and *Hearth and Home.* Sentimental fiction and pulp novels, intended for a new readership of literate workers, sparked Conroy's imagination with their lurid characterizations, crude dialogue, and breathless suspense. Hade Pollard's gallows speech or the "House of the Hand" adventure in *A World to Win* could have been written for Beadle and Adams's list of cheap editions that workers snapped up eagerly.

"Whore! It was a beautiful word to Robert," Conroy writes, and a shocking word to Martha, who "clung desperately to the remnants of her gentility." Like Terry Hurley, Conroy had "nabbed Red Balls" and lived in hobo jungles during the times he searched for work. While Jim Tully and other writers of the "tramp school" viewed hobos as romantic figures, Conroy (and such radical writers as Nelson Algren and Tom Kromer) saw broken lives, criminals on the run, destitute workers, and "jockers" (pederasts), who preyed on homeless young boys. The colorfulness of their speech belies the sadness of men without attachments. "I mooched the stem," the hobo cook says, "and Dude there battered the privates. Most he got was a dimmer in cash at a time, and a few lousy vegetables"—which means roughly, "I looked for handouts in town and Dude knocked on the doors of homes. All we got from each solicitation was a dime in addition to some vegetables for our stew." Parody also serves to expose the false piety of the Holy Rollers and unveil the shallow intellectual posturing of the Green Dragon bohemians. Conroy even parodies himself. Nell's poem is taken from the poem "Tragedy" that Conroy published in a little magazine in 1927.[31] His early poems with their romantic yearning and genteel imitations caused him to wince years later; yet, following the example of southwestern humorists, he saw comic potential in their inflated style.

Conroy's parodic excursions include the speech of the youthful radicals Sol Abraham and Alan Vass, who dabble in Marxist theory, and the black worker Fatfolks, the closest to a real heroic figure in *A World to Win*, who catches gas bombs in a strike and throws them back at the police. Larger pieces of parodic writing appear as intertexts, such as Danny Maupin's contribution to "Western" pulp magazines, the preacher's sermon defending the America First Vigilantes in "Roosevelt Roost" (Hooverville), and Bishop Taylor's funeral sermon. Conroy dialogizes these fragments representing different speech genres not only for comic purposes but also because they reflect the social diversity of his workers' verbal experiences. These intertexts play off against one another, representing interpenetrating points of view that tempt the hearer while containing warnings. The fragmented heteroglossia (social speech types) is the counterpart of the fragmented world of depression-era workers within which Leo and Robert make their way.

Conroy's stylistic method is best described by Mikhail Bakhtin's concept of dialogism, in which different speech genres compete, relativizing one another in a mixed, polyphonic carnival of voices representing the diverse aggregate of social relationships.[32] The narrative mode of Conroy's writing contrasts sharply with the flat, colorless "objective" style of Edward Anderson's *Hungry Men* (1935), for instance, and the idiosyncratic lyricism of Edward Dahlberg's *Bottom Dogs* (1930). The diversity of social speech types reflects working-class heterogeneity. Like Bakhtin's "carnivalesque," the cultural forms show an attraction to "the eccentric, the surprising, the bizarre; misalliances, the reunion of opposites; profanation and debasement."[33]

The conflict between Robert and Leo is manifested in their differing speech. Robert's is stilted, livresque, precious; changes in his diction trace his evolution as he gains experience. The various intertexts undermine the narrator's authority. High and low levels of speech are inverted; ungrammatical usage, vulgarisms, and "impurities" are coupled with characters whose ethical impulses are commendable, while purity of diction and formal learning are obstacles to clear thinking. The shifting of stylistic registers, linked with mimetic narration of seemingly irrelevant details, moves readers from a sentimentalizing concern for the poor to a contemplation of the social and political conditions that characterize jobless workers and alienated artists.[34]

The comic inversions of carnivalized language and folk humor in *A World to Win* support a grotesque realism of unsavory behavior, irreverent parody, and grim description as Conroy's figures bump up against the concreteness of an everyday world. In the rootless, proletarian world that Leo is forced by circumstances to inhabit, Conroy discovers and portrays a pervading folk sensibility, at times crude, comic, subversive, and blasphemous. It is, needless to say, a terrible existence. Leo and his family face starvation again and again. In the grotesque episode of Anna's death, the comic mode suddenly slips its parodic mask, revealing the poignancy of Leo's silent grief.

Conroy was aware that, as Terry Eagleton writes, "power structures are estranged through grotesque parody."[35] Folk consciousness, as Bakhtin clarified in his study of Rabelais, overturns the language of orthodoxy and officialdom. Concerns of a higher order are reduced to material, bodily functions. Death, sexuality, eating, and so forth are affirmed through comic, empathetic identification. The rootless flow of events, the fragmented experience of Leo and Robert, is represented by the competing "voices" of the text, a kaleidoscopic interplay of utterances that conflict and will not be resolved. Conroy depicts the living inferno of worker's existence as a condition of slow suffocation, symptomatic of which is the grinding poverty of beans, unwashed clothes, leaking roofs, broken-down cars, and spiritless, clichéd language. For Robert, it is experiencing the "not-life" of the Green Dragon, mooching off Nell's salary, pretending to write, steering clear of commitment.

INTRODUCTION xxvii

We know that this frozen world is finally breaking up when Leo and Robert utter fresh thoughts in vigorous language, as if they inhabited new linguistic space. "Some time we'll go down to the city halls ever'where," Leo says, anticipating Tom Joad's *prise de conscience* ("Wherever they's a fight so hungry people can eat, I'll be there."), "and we'll go inside t' stay. We won't never come out no more, and then women won't have t' die in ditches like my Anna did." Leo and Robert find temporary refuge with the Hungarian worker Joe. "It is good to be here," Robert muses. "It will be good to move. My body and my mind have been numbing from disuse, like a foot planted on the floor too long."

Reception and Further Reflections

In her review of *A World to Win* for *New Masses*, appearing soon after its publication, Meridel Le Sueur, a close ally in Conroy's efforts, suggested that Conroy had fallen victim to the "seductiveness of bourgeois literature and its forms" in the new novel. He had abandoned the "clear, muscular prose and the compelling incident of his first book, for the involved past-tense narrative style of this new book."[36] Jerre Mangione's review in the *New Republic* was of a similar vein: Conroy had tried to write a "novel"; he should have stuck with storytelling.[37] Robert Forsythe (a.k.a. Kyle Crichton), one of the most perceptive critics on the left, argued that proletarian writers "are clinging to a form which does not fit them." A proletarian writer who seeks to portray the needs of the worker effectively, Forsythe said, should dispense with the novel form altogether.[38] Most critics agreed that Conroy's extraordinary talents, exhibited in what Le Sueur called "his disinherited style," evident in individual episodes of *A World to Win,* were weakened by the novel's structure.[39]

For a time in the 1930s, it seemed that working-class writers would produce their own very different kind of art. As both writer and editor, Conroy was in the forefront of this incipient movement. Ripples from these attempts profoundly influenced artists and writers of backgrounds and education foreign to working-class experience, including William Carlos Williams, Aaron Copeland, Frank Capra, Ralph Ellison, Saul Bellow, and many others who achieved lasting renown. It was inevitable, George Orwell said, that a writer of the working class would in educating himself write "in the bourgeois manner, in the middle-class dialect." "So long as the bourgeoisie are the dominant class, literature must be bourgeois."[40]

"In the Thirties the relation of the working class to literature," Frank Kermode writes in *History and Value*, "was an urgent practical issue and not merely a problem of academic Marxist theory, as it is now."[41] Questions of form and content of working-class literature are no longer the subjects of debate in public forums that they were in the 1930s, yet interest continues to grow among publishers and scholars to recover and advance the legacy of radical literature, so that when the focus shifts again, that legacy will be available.

What, then, is now useful to us in the fragmented legacy of a contested time and the expressions of those who lived it? The "people who do not write" still perform the world's labor, which is increasingly displaced to third world countries and immigrant populations. In the Age of Information, what prospects exist for them to express themselves? Who among writers today is dedicated, as Conroy was, to give voice to the voiceless? Nothing has changed in the sense that Ralph Waldo Emerson once expressed it: "Men live by truth and stand in need of expression."

Notes

I thank Alan Wald, editor of the series, and the editors at the University of Illinois Press for their help in revising this essay.

1. Robert S. McElvaine, "Workers in Fiction: Locked Out," *New York Times Book Review*, 1 Sept. 1985, 1, 19. Walter Rideout, *The Radical Novel in the United States, 1900–1954* (Cambridge, Mass.: Harvard

INTRODUCTION   xxix

University Press, 1954), reminds us that Conroy's *World to Win* had the "distinction of being one of the relatively few proletarian novels written by a working-class author" (182). Literary anthologies published in the 1930s and 1940s often included radical writers. See, for instance, Cleanth Brooks, R. W. B. Lewis, and Robert Penn Warren, eds., *American Literature: The Makers and the Making* (New York: St. Martin's, 1973), which excerpted Conroy's *Disinherited*.

2. Richard Wright, *White Man, Listen!* (Garden City, N.Y.: Doubleday, 1957), 145.

3. Frank Kermode, *History and Value* (Oxford: Clarendon, 1988), discusses the question of value in political fiction and calls for new methods of interpretation and assessment. Recent critical efforts to deal with a diversity of cultural practices are serving to break down hierarchical, elitist critical standards. See, for example, Cary Nelson, *Repression and Recovery: Modern American Poetry and the Politics of Cultural Memory, 1910–1945* (Madison: University of Wisconsin Press, 1989); Russell J. Reising, *The Unusable Past: Theory and the Study of American Literature* (London: Methuen, 1987); Barbara Johnson, *A World of Difference* (Baltimore: Johns Hopkins University Press, 1987); Alan M. Wald, *The Responsibility of Intellectuals: Selected Essays on Marxist Traditions in Cultural Commitment* (Atlantic Highlands, N.J.: Humanities, 1992); Barbara Foley, *Radical Representations: Politics and Form in U.S. Proletarian Fiction, 1929–1941* (Durham, N.C.: Duke University Press, 1993); Terry Eagleton, *Literary Theory: An Introduction* (Oxford: Basil Blackwell, 1983); Thomas Kent, *Interpretation and Genre: The Role of Generic Perception in the Study of Narrative Texts* (Lewisburg, Pa.: Bucknell University Press, 1986); John Guillory, *Cultural Capital: The Problem of Literary Canon Formation* (Chicago: University of Chicago Press, 1993); and Marcus Klein, *Foreigners: The Making of American Literature, 1900–1940* (Chicago: University of Chicago Press, 1981).

4. Leslie Shepard, *The History of Street Literature: The Story of Broadside Ballads, Chapbooks, Proclamations, News-Sheets, Election Bills, Tracts, Pamphlets, Cocks, Catchpennies, and Other Ephemera* (Newton Abbot, England: David and Charles, 1973), 64.

5. J. Hoptner, critic for the *Philadelphia Record*, wrote that "Conroy can be called, without disparagement to either, the Gorki of America" ("Workers' Side of Depression Given by Jack Conroy," *Philadelphia Record*, 28 Nov. 1933).

6. George Bisztray, *Marxist Models of Literary Realism* (New York: Columbia University Press, 1978), discusses Gorky's views on the distinction between production and creation, for instance, and the primacy of work. These furnish pertinent guideposts in understanding Conroy's achievement as writer and editor.

7. Victor Terras, ed., *Handbook of Russian Literature* (New Haven, Conn.: Yale University Press, 1985), 429.

8. John Chamberlain, reviewer for the *New York Times,* compared *The Disinherited* with Valentine Kataev's *Time, Forward!* Critics, including the Book of the Month Club's Dorothy Canfield, familiarized themselves with Soviet proletarian literature because they expected American writers to take cues from the Soviet experience despite differences, as Chamberlain said, of "social structure" ("Book of the Times," *New York Times,* 22 Nov. 1933, 97).

9. Other Conroy stories reshaped into the novel were "Hoover City," *International Literature* 3 (July 1933): 46–49; "Down in Happy Hollow," *Anvil* 10 (Mar. 1935): 7–10, 26; and "For Men Must Work," *Midland Left* 1 (Feb. 1935): 14–19.

10. Daniel Aaron, introduction to *The Disinherited,* by Jack Conroy (1933; reprint, New York: Hill and Wang, 1963), xii.

11. Granville Hicks, "Revolution and the Novel," *New Masses,* 15 May 1934, 24.

12. Margaret Wallace, "Proletarian without Benefit of Propaganda," *New York Times Book Review,* 26 Nov. 1933, 89.

13. Clifton Fadiman, "Books," *New Yorker,* 2 Dec. 1933, 88.

14. H.B., "Jack Conroy Writes of Mine Folk in New Proletarian Novel," *Washington News,* 18 Nov. 1933, n.p.

15. Michael Gold, "A Letter to the Author of a First Book," *New Masses,* 9 Jan. 1934, 25–26.

16. Herbst to Conroy, 8 Jan. 1934, Newberry Library. John Dos Passos concurred: "For God's sake, don't let them make a literary gent out of you . . ." (Letter to Conroy, n.d., Newberry Library).

17. Lieber to Conroy, 19 Dec. 1934, Newberry Library.

18. William Soskin, *New York Evening Post,* 17 Nov. 1933.

19. Jack Conroy, "Robert Cantwell's 'Land of Plenty,'" in *The Jack Conroy Reader,* ed. Jack Salzman and David Ray (New York: Burt Franklin, 1979), 268.

20. Jack Conroy, "The Worker as Writer," ibid., 221.

INTRODUCTION xxxi

21. Jack Conroy, "Hard Winter," *American Mercury* 22 (Feb. 1931): 129–37.

22. *St. Louis Globe*, 13 July 1932, 1.

23. Allean Hale, "Tom Williams, Proletarian Playwright," *Tennessee Williams Annual Review*, no. 1 (1998): 13–22.

24. Robert Logsdon, interview with author, 10 Apr. 1984; Jack Conroy, interviews with author, 1980–88; Paul Dennis Brunn, "Black Workers and Social Movements of the 1930s in St. Louis" (Ph.D. diss., Washington University, 1975); Myrna Fichtenbaum, *The Funsten Nut Strike* (New York: International Publishers, 1992); Douglas Wixson, *Worker-Writer in America: Jack Conroy and the Tradition of Midwestern Literary Radicalism, 1898–1990* (Urbana: University of Illinois Press, 1994); Nelson Algren, *Somebody in Boots* (New York: Vanguard, 1935).

25. Joyce O. Hertzler, *A Sociology of Language* (New York: Random House, 1965), 366.

26. Robert P. Baker, "Labor History, Social Science, and the Concept of the Working Class," *Labor History* 14 (Winter 1973): 100.

27. G. K. Chesterton, *Charles Dickens* (New York: Schocken Books, 1965), 245.

28. Archie Green, *Calf's Head and Union Tale: Labor Yarns at Work and Play* (Urbana: University of Illinois Press, 1996), 33.

29. Jack Conroy, "Slappy Hooper, the World's Bestest Sign Painter," in *A Treasury of American Folklore: Stories, Ballads, and Traditions of the People*, ed. Benjamin A. Botkin (New York: Crown, 1944), 548.

30. Henry Nash Smith, "A Sound Heart and a Deformed Conscience," in *Mark Twain: A Collection of Critical Essays*, ed. Henry Nash Smith (Englewood Cliffs, N.J.: Prentice-Hall, 1963), 83–100.

31. Jack Conroy, "Tragedy," *Northern Light* 1 (Aug.–Sept. 1927): 111.

32. Mikhail Bakhtin, *The Dialogic Imagination*, ed. Michael Holquist, trans. Caryl Emerson and Michael Holquist (Austin: University of Texas Press, 1981).

33. Mikhail Bakhtin, *Rabelais and His World*, trans. Helene Iswolsky (Cambridge, Mass.: MIT Press, 1968), 79.

34. David R. Sewell, *Mark Twain's Languages: Discourse, Dialogue, and Linguistic Variety* (Berkeley: University of California Press, 1987), explores the dialogism in Twain's writing.

35. Terry Eagleton, *Walter Benjamin, or, Towards a Revolutionary Criticism* (London: NLB, 1981), 145.

36. Meridel Le Sueur, "Join Hand and Brain," *New Masses*, 9 July 1935, 25. Granville Hicks in a series of articles entitled "Revolution and the Novel" published in *New Masses*, in early 1934, urged proletarian writers to look to the "bourgeois" novel for technique.

37. Jerre Mangione, "Where Fiction Falters," *New Republic*, 4 Sept. 1935, 109.

38. Robert Forsythe, "Down with the Novel," *New Masses*, 16 Apr. 1935, 29.

39. Le Sueur, "Join Hand and Brain," 25. Contemporary reception of *A World to Win* was complicated by (1) misinformed ideas of proletarian literature (see, for example, Henry Hazlitt, "Literature and the 'Class War,'" *Nation*, 19 Oct. 1932); (2) the overblown praise of inferior novels, such as Clara Weatherwax's *Marching, Marching!* and (3) the Communist Party's attempt to orchestrate critical response.

40. George Orwell, "The Proletarian Writer: Discussion between George Orwell and Desmond Hawkins," in *The Collected Essays, Journalism, and Letters of George Orwell*, vol. 2, ed. Sonia Orwell and Ian Angus (New York: Harcourt, Brace and World, 1968), 41–42. Orwell seems influenced here by William Empson's views on proletarian literature, spelled out in *Some Versions of Pastoral* (New York: New Directions, 1974). Empson finds no measures appropriate to working-class expression other than those he knows from his study of classical literature.

41. Kermode, *History and Value*, 35.

Bibliography

Jack Conroy's papers, including manuscripts, extensive correspondence, photographs, magazines, and newspaper clippings, are in the Conroy archive at the Newberry Library, Chicago. Some five thousand books from his personal library are housed in the Jack Conroy Room at the Moberly Community College, Moberly, Missouri.

Selected Works by Jack Conroy

Anyplace But Here. Coauthored with Arna Bontemps. 1966. Reprint, Columbia: University of Missouri Press, 1995.

INTRODUCTION xxxiii

The Disinherited. 1933. Reprint, Columbia: University of Missouri Press, 1992.
The Fast Sooner Hound. Coauthored with Arna Bontemps. Boston: Houghton Mifflin, 1942.
The Jack Conroy Reader. Edited by Jack Salzman and David Ray. New York: Burt Franklin, 1979.
Midland Humor: A Harvest of Fun and Folklore. New York: Current, 1947.
Sam Patch, the High, Wide, and Handsome Jumper. Coauthored with Arna Bontemps. Boston: Houghton Mifflin, 1951.
Slappy Hooper, the Wonderful Sign Painter. Coauthored with Arna Bontemps. Boston: Houghton Mifflin, 1946.
They Seek a City. Coauthored with Arna Bontemps. Garden City, N.Y.: Doubleday, Doran, 1945.
The Weed King and Other Stories. Edited and with an Introduction by Douglas Wixson. Westport, Conn.: Lawrence Hill, 1985.
A World to Win. New York: Covici-Friede, 1935.
Writers in Revolt: The Anvil Anthology. Coedited with Curt Johnson. New York: Lawrence Hill, 1973.

Reviews of *A World to Win*

Adamic, Louis. "Nothing to Lose." *Saturday Review of Literature,* 11 May 1935, 12, 14.
Algren, Nelson. "A World to Win." *Windsor Quarterly* 2 (Fall 1935): 73.
Brewster, Dorothy. "On the Seamy Side." *Nation,* 22 May 1935, 607.
Cantwell, Robert. "A World to Win." *New Outlook,* June 1935, 58.
Crissey, James. "Probing America in Fiction." *Frontier and Midland* 1 (Fall 1935): 74–75.
Gold, Michael. "Change the World." *Daily Worker,* 29 Jan. 1934, 143.
———. "A Letter to the Author of a First Book." *New Masses,* 9 Jan. 1934, 25–26.
Gregory, Horace. "A World to Win." *New York Herald-Tribune Books,* 19 May 1935, 12.
Hansen, Harry. "The First Reader." *New York World-Telegram,* 24 Apr. 1935.

Le Sueur, Meridel. "Join Hand and Brain." *New Masses,* 9 July 1935, 25.

Mangione, Jerre. "Where Fiction Falters." *New Republic,* 4 Sept. 1935, 109.

Marsh, F. T. "The Class Conscious." *New York Times Book Review,* 5 May 1935, 7, 18.

Other Sources

Aaron, Daniel. *Writers on the Left.* New York: Oxford University Press, 1961.

Alt, John. "Beyond Class: The Decline of Industrial Labor and Leisure." *Telos* 28 (Summer 1976): 55–80.

Baker, Robert P. "Labor History, Social Science, and the Concept of the Working Class." *Labor History* 14 (Winter 1973): 98–103.

Bodnar, John. *Workers' World.* Baltimore: Johns Hopkins University Press, 1982.

Brunn, Paul Dennis. "Black Workers and Social Movements of the 1930s in St. Louis." Ph.D. diss. Washington University, 1975.

Fichtenbaum, Myrna. *The Funsten Nut Strike.* New York: International Publishers, 1992.

Foley, Barbara. *Radical Representations: Politics and Form in U.S. Proletarian Fiction, 1929–1941.* Durham, N.C.: Duke University Press, 1993.

Forsythe, Robert. "Down with the Novel." *New Masses,* 16 Apr. 1935, 29.

Green, Archie. *Calf's Head and Union Tale: Labor Yarns at Work and Play.* Urbana: University of Illinois Press, 1996.

Green, James R. *The World of the Worker.* New York: Hill and Wang, 1980.

Hazlitt, Henry. "Literature and the 'Class War.'" *Nation,* 19 Oct. 1932, 361–63.

Hicks, Granville. "Revolution and the Novel." *New Masses,* 15 May 1934, 23–25.

Hoggart, Richard. *The Uses of Literacy.* Boston: Beacon, 1961.

Kermode, Frank. *History and Value.* Oxford: Clarendon, 1988.

Klein, Marcus. *Foreigners: The Making of American Literature, 1900–1940.* Chicago: University of Chicago Press, 1981.

INTRODUCTION

Nelson, Cary. *Repression and Recovery: Modern American Poetry and the Politics of Cultural Memory, 1910–1945*. Madison: University of Wisconsin Press, 1989.

Orwell, George. "The Proletarian Writer: Discussion between George Orwell and Desmond Hawkins." In *The Collected Essays, Journalism, and Letters of George Orwell*. Vol. 2. Edited by Sonia Orwell and Ian Angus. New York: Harcourt, Brace and World, 1968.

Rideout, Walter. *The Radical Novel in the United States, 1900–1954*. Cambridge, Mass.: Harvard University Press, 1954.

Vincent, David. *Bread, Knowledge and Freedom*. London: Europa Publications, 1981.

Wald, Alan M. *The Responsibility of Intellectuals: Selected Essays on Marxist Traditions in Cultural Commitment*. Atlantic Highlands, N.J.: Humanities, 1992.

Wixson, Douglas. "Black Writers and White! Jack Conroy, Arna Bontemps, and Interracial Collaboration in the 1930s." *Prospects: An Annual of American Cultural Studies* 23 (1998): 401–30.

―――. *Worker-Writer in America: Jack Conroy and the Tradition of Midwestern Literary Radicalism, 1898–1990*. Urbana: University of Illinois Press, 1994.

A WORLD TO WIN

for ROBERT MINOR

"*These, seeing mankind going mad,
cried out, blew the sirens, knocked
on the factory doors.*"
—Joseph Freeman.

PART ONE: *GREEN VALLEY*

CHAPTER ONE

Martha Darrell was startled the first time the headlights of an eastbound freight train stabbed into the darkness of her upstairs rooms as she stood naked beside her bed. She grabbed her clothing and clasped it about her. Then she reassured herself that the window was too high to permit anybody either on the ground or aboard the train to see her. She stared down curiously at her own body, as though she had never seen it before. She was a lonely girl (well, not even a girl anymore, she thought sadly) living alone in the house inherited from her father, Marcus Anthony Darrell, sometime professor of English at Boone University, whose seat was Probstville, thirty miles away. Nobody ever came to see Martha save Decie, the Negro maid, who cooked the meals, cleaned the rooms, and washed clothes every Monday. Martha was past 29, and she supposed folks were calling her an old maid already.

When the headlights' beam struck her naked figure like a blow, Martha felt a pleasurable warmth after the first fright, a mild exultation. The light pierced through the window like a sword for about a minute, then the engine swung around a curve and the train rumbled and clanged down grade toward the river. For a long time Martha managed to be undressing just at the time the eastbound manifest rounded the bend and sent a shaft of light roving into second-story windows. Martha leaned over the sill, first glancing cautiously up and down the street to see that nobody was abroad, and watched the approaching engine, the lights sweeping in a broad swath across the fields, and veering around toward her room. She was excited by the thunderous roar and the shriek of the whistle for the crossings of the town. Then she sprang back into the room, planted her feet wide apart and extended her arms. She gasped and moaned, only to drop red-faced and exhausted on her bed the moment the train had passed.

She told herself that she wasn't really "bigotty," as the people of Green Valley said. She was the daughter of Marcus Anthony Darrell, the author of no less than a dozen books and monographs, and she had not intended to live in Green Valley until tiny wrinkles began to radiate from her eyes and from the corners of her mouth. She did not particularly dislike the people of the town, most of them sawmill hands, coal miners and woodchoppers and their families. But they were of a different world. Ten years ago Martha had sent her first story to the *Atlantic Monthly*, and was not very much depressed when it came back. She would be patient; she could wait steadfastly as many of the immortals had. For ten years she had sent out her stories, poems and essays to the *Atlantic Monthly*, to *Harper's Weekly*, and to *Century*, and they always came back. If one lingered, she was feverish with hope. But of late the little, precious world she had cloistered within Professor Darrell's library and the rooms and environs of the aging house was palling on her. The leather-bound volumes in the library exuded a smell she came to associate with death, and the odor followed her wherever she went. She left the grounds infrequently, but when she did she fancied that passersby sniffed at her and her bookish stench. The spiders spun their webs thicker in the high corners of the ceilings, while in almost every room mice had gnawed through the wainscoting and scampered and squealed nightly in search of food or pleasure.

She had never worried about her looks or her future,

but as she realized that her change of life was not far away at the rate the years were flying and that her monthly flow would cease forever some day, she thought more and more about men and whether their passions rose when they saw her. Her face was not beautiful, she knew, but she told herself that her intellect gave her features an air of distinction. Her eyes were too small and too pale and her nose was too large. She was slender to the point of angularity. Her upper lip pursed like a bird's beak above her thick lower, and her upper teeth protruded, but not too prominently, she consoled herself. She smirked at herself, and switched her hips a bit before the mirror.

The sawmill hands and woodchoppers loafed on benches outside the Palace Billiard Parlor, and sometimes bantered the girls as they passed. When Martha walked by, they reddened, averted their eyes and remained silent, or, at best, mumbled a commonplace greeting. The moment she had passed, she felt their eyes on her back and sensed the hunger these idlers felt for all women. She hated them for their fumbling timidity, their mice-glances attempting to peer stealthily beneath and through her skirts. Once she heard a muttered remark, and a gale of laughter, punctuated by the "kyah! kyah! kyah!" of Hycie Stook, the Negro racker and cue boy, who was also the current lover of Decie.

"Make Hycie tell you what the men in front of the billiard parlor said about me," she ordered Decie that evening.

The next morning Decie could scarcely suppress her giggles, but tried to look sober and indignant when she felt Martha looking at her.

"Well, what did they say?" Martha demanded.

"Said y'all sho' was purty. Said y'all should oughter have a beau, purty as y'all is," Decie said, rolling her eyes evasively.

"They *did not*! Tell me the truth, now. Don't be mealy-mouthed. I shan't be angry, no matter what they said."

"I don't know whut kind o' min's dem men got! Tch!

Tch! I'se 'shamed on all o' 'em. You know whut dat triflin' Bud Ellis 'lowed? 'Lowed y'all must 've swapped runnin' gears wid a shitepoke and got hornswaggled outen de butt!'"

"What else? Don't hold anything back!"

"Well, somebody, Hycie didn't rec'lect who, 'lowed yo' hinder parts looked like two sody crackers stuck together."

"What else?" The blood was hammering in Martha's head, and she gripped the table to steady a trembling in her legs.

"Dat's all, and dat's a fack, Miss Marthy! But it's a God's plenty, effen yo' asks me. Does 'pear dem loafers 'd fin' somethin' bettah t' do dan bla'gyard 'bout decent ladies." Decie wagged her head and clucked her tongue, but burst into audible titters as soon as Martha left the room. Martha had always imagined that the natives despised her for her high and mighty airs, but she could not bear to think they were laughing at her.

Martha didn't pass the billiard parlor after that. She sent Decie after groceries, and stayed in her room two days writing a poem about a girl crucified on a cross of loneliness and misunderstanding. But the poem came back, as did her nature article, *Wild Life and Wild Flowers Near Home*. She noticed that the calf bindings of some of the books in the library were beginning to crack badly, and when she opened a volume of the *Encyclopædia Britannica* she squeaked to see a short brown worm curled inside the front cover. She could not get interested in reading. Time had been when she had read the *Atlantic Monthly* eagerly, even the factual articles were morsels she rolled reverently about in her mind, attempted to fix them and make them hers permanently.

"It is barely eight years since street railroads have outgrown the horse-car period, and have required the use of the word 'interurban' to describe the enlargement of their field."

She did not file this item away in a cubicle of her memory. It did not matter any more, for there was nobody to tell about such things since her father died. And she was growing tired of writing and writing without ever seeing her work in print.

At the University all the boys had been very formal and very aloof. Co-educational institutions were still a bold experiment in the Mississippi Valley, and the nice boys were apparently afraid of the girls. "The male of the species refuses to mingle with his fellow students of the fair sex," reported the Boone Scroll, the college literary magazine.

Martha remembered leaning from her window in the dormitory to watch the boys strolling past in the moonlight, arms locked together behind, singing the school song she had composed:

> "Yes, we'll e'er revere thee, love thee,
> As we brave life's stormy sea.
> Duty's ear shall ever hear thee,
> Dear old Varsity!"

One of the singers threw back his head, shaking his long hair free, and for a moment looked Martha squarely in the eye. "The author and the singer face to face. I wonder if he knows it. No! How could he? Capricious Fate, how unfathomable thy whims!" she muttered theatrically to herself. The singer and his comrades paced down the campus, out of her sight, out of her life forever, she mused resentfully.

That belonged to the past, along with her picture in the school annual, and the class prophecy, delivered by a classmate she had never seen since, in which each member of the class was mentioned. "The crystal clouds again, and what shapes do I see emerging as it clears? Lo! 'Tis our winsome classmate, Martha Darrell, now a Boston bluestocking, editor of the *Atlantic Monthly,* and authoress of the literary sensation of the decade, *Fate's Double Turning, or Life's Accolade.* Who is that standing beside her, holding a cooing, chubby infant in his arms? 'Tis none other than Merlin Bishop, who is now the Mayor of the

Hub of the Universe and the proud husband of the talented novelist and editress."

She had flushed; Merlin grumbled angrily.

Years were long in the old house, bought by Professor Darrell after he had retired from the professorship at Boone. Property was cheaper in Green Valley than in Probstville, and the professor was not rich. He had saved some of his salary, but it had never been high, and the royalties from his books dwindled year by year. He had written his last eighteen years before his death.

Year after year Martha was obliged to gnaw at the principal of her scant hoard. She compared herself to the cat and its partner, the mouse, who hid a pot of fat beneath the altar of a church. First it was "top off"—some money to buy shingles and paint; then, within a few years, "half gone"; and "empty" not far away.

She no longer knew anybody at Boone, and the horse and buggy that Professor Darrell had driven about the countryside had long ago been sold.

She began to be plagued by terrifying dreams of men, but woke to find herself alone and a-sweat in her bed. She waited each night for the headlights of the train as a girl waits for her sweetheart or a bride for her husband. She would become morose and tearful after the hot flash of ecstasy she felt while the light poured over her naked body. She was obsessed by strange whims which at times convinced her that she was losing her reason. She had driven two large nails in the wall as far apart as her extended arms could reach, and sometimes she spread wide her arms and caught the nails between her fingers as though she was spiked to a cross she had outlined on the wall paper. When the white hot light struck her, she tried to feel Christ's agony and fancied that the shaft of the headlight was a sword piercing her again and again.

In spite of her desperate and pious resolutions, she thought more and more about men, and often she drew Drake's *History of Greece* from the shelves in the library and examined curiously the engravings of discus throwers and wrestlers. But the eyes of the ancient men were as dull and as sad as those of a dead fish. The books cracked in the middle, showing the meshy and age-stained fabric that held the backs of the pages together, and the musty smell became stronger every day. Martha knew that it was sinful to be thinking of men the way she did. She prayed for moral strength, and read the Bible, but she restlessly turned the pages until she found passages like this:

"My beloved put in his hand by the hole of the door, and my bowels were moved for him.

"I arose to open to my beloved; and my hands dripped with myrrh, and my fingers with sweet smelling myrrh, upon the handles of the lock.

"I opened to my beloved; but my beloved had withdrawn himself, and was gone: my soul failed me when he spake: I sought him, but I could not find him; I called him, but he gave me no answer."

This was in winter when days were short and nightfall early. Toward the end of spring and at the beginning of the hot days of summer, the train rumbled past before nightfall with the headlights unlit.

CHAPTER TWO

After dusk the Darrell house was lonely with the dark spreading out from the corners of the rooms and down from the high ceilings. The great trees in the yard made it gloomy even when the sun was high and bright.

At nine o'clock Martha had been long abed, and she hesitated and shivered when the door bell buzzed "brrr! brrr! brrr!" and kept it up. At last she crept down stairs and turned the knob. A short, bandy-legged man, with a whimpering child in his arms, stood on the stoop. He had his foot upraised to kick the door as Martha opened it. He was bareheaded, and the stiff night breeze worried his long red hair from side to side.

"Are ye deaf?" demanded the stranger. "This is Missus Darrell's lodging house, I take it. Have ye room fer a tired and heart-broken man and a sick bye?"

"This is *Miss* Darrell's house, sir, but it's not a lodging house, and I have room for no one. Good night!"

She prepared to shut the door, but the Irishman stuck his foot against the jamb, his blue eyes pleading as a dog's or an Irishman's can.

" 'Tis only a divil in human form c'd cod a man wi' a sick child and niver a place t' lay its head or his own the night," he said desperately. "A lengthsome bugger down the strate, right ferninst the pool room, he told me t' come here. Said you was inquirin' about lodgers. It's a dozen o' places I been to a'ready, and it's iver the same song and dance. They're afeared o' me, and afeared o' the bye and his sickness. Sure, it's nawthin' worse nor the drizzlin' scours, and well I know it."

Martha knew that one of the billiard parlor loafers had been playing a joke on her and on the stranger. The more she looked at the Irishman, the more she liked his bold manner, the resolute and unabashed cock of his head, and the salty and exotic flavor of his tongue.

"Bring the child in," she said, and led the way to a tufted sofa in the library.

The boy's lips were cracked and dark with fever, and his breath smelled sickly sweet. The Irishman laid the child down, and began rubbing his own arms to restore the circulation. He had been carrying his burden a long time. Martha left the room to fetch a glass of water.

"What's his name?" Martha asked when she came back.

"Leo. Leo Augustus Hurley, tho it's niver meself w'd be after wishin' sich a handle on the youngun. 'Twas his mither, the whorin' slut!"

(Oh! Oh! I should order this ruffianly blackguard out of the house this instant!) Martha often thought in the manner of *Prose Selections by Mrs. Sigourney*, and *A Fireside Garland of Choice Literature*, collected by the Rev. Jefferson Paul, two volumes in the library.

But she justified her definite inclination to let the Irishman stay by reasoning that the child needed help. He was a stranger, and I took him in, she thought.

"Where *is* his mother?" she asked.

"Last I seen of 'er was in Seattle betune the sheets wi' a big curly-headed brute of a logger. Sure, I caught 'em right in the act!"

"What did you do?" (Heavens! What a question! No decent woman would listen a minute to such talk, let alone ask such questions, she thought.)

"I pitched a silver dollar on the bed and told him some things is cheap if you get 'em fer nawthin'. Told him t' take the dollar and go down t' Slue-Foot Bessie's and get himself somethin' good on me. After that I walked out wi' Leo and only the clothes to our backs. Got a deevorce wi' no trouble at all, at all. Rode the freights, bearin' to'rds the east, not carin' where I might land. Leo tuk sick, and off we dropped. Lucky, too, I'm here t' tell ye."

"I don't see how I can . . ." Martha began to protest.

"If ye leave 'im lay here till I can fetch a doctor, I've the money t' pay, niver fear," broke in the Irishman. "Terry Hurley has made his own way in this hard world sence he was past yellerin' his didies. I sailed the seas, man and bye, I wurrked in the mines and among the big trees, but not a damned cint do I owe a blessed soul. That purty little black-eyed bitch in Seattle made me no more nor a baby in 'er hands, and I, fool that I was, I—I thought it c'd last fer keeps, and me rovin' days was over. It's not the life o' Riley that home bodies might guess. Sure, I'd like t' settle down in a snug berth like thisun, away from the storms."

That was the way Terry Hurley came to Green Valley, and before he had been in the town a week he had a job at the sawmill and swore he would never leave till he was carried feet foremost to the burying ground at Walnut Grove church. "Plant me closest t' yer dad, the old Perfessor. I'll be after takin' a long chat wi' the old gent when I'm laid out t' cool fer me last, long slape," Terry told Martha.

Leo's fever soon left, and his skinny body fattened till he looked his six years. He played very quietly in the yard, never bothering Martha with questions or noise. Each evening he might be seen peering through the pickets to greet Terry with a "Hi, poppy!" shortly after the five o'clock whistle at the sawmill blew. "Ain't he a buster? Fat as a pig!" Terry would say to the other sawmill workers with whom he happened to be walking.

Terry was never like a stranger in the house, and almost from the first he would throw an arm boisterously about Martha, squeeze her breasts tightly and kiss her loudly. She remonstrated feebly and clawed half-heartedly at his hands. Sometimes he playfully nipped her inner thighs with his blunt, strong fingers, but he stopped to apologize and to soothe her when she trembled and wept violently.

"I fergit meself; I ain't been used t' a good woman like

you around," Terry told her. "Ye'll make a gintleman out o' me yit. Don't run me away t' go t' the divil ag'in."

Martha never thought of the locomotive headlights even when winter came around again. She heard the train go past, saw the headlights sweep around the curve, but stayed down stairs with Terry. He sat about smoking or "coddling" apples on the top of the heating stove. The apples sizzled and the juice browned the polish, but Martha did not mind. There was something reassuring in the solid cut of the man, his unruffled self-reliance. The mice gnawed in the walls and scampered and squeaked behind the books in their cases, and she found a nest behind Gibbon's *Decline and Fall of the Roman Empire*. The nest had been manufactured from bits of paper chewed off the pages and there were some naked, squirming babies. Martha set traps and found a cat that was a good mouser. Again she loved the house and was proud of it. With a rag tied on the end of a broom she swabbed the ceilings, sweeping down spider webs and the celled clay nests of mud wasps.

" 'Tis too cold fer a man and a woman t' slape alone in the same house. Slape wi' me t' night, and we'll be married a-Saturday," Terry told her calmly one night.

"Oh, I couldn't! I *won't*! I can't! What kind of a woman do you think I am? Would you want to marry a woman who would go to bed with a man not her husband?"

"If I was the man, I would. I'll be makin' Terry a cozy bed in the liberry ferninst the fire, and I'll be a-comin' up the stairs right after ye."

Martha resolved to lock her door, to tell him that things had gone far enough—too far—and that he must go packing. But when she heard him mounting the stairs determinedly, she moved over in her bed. She turned her back, and begged him in a low voice to blow out the kerosene lamp flame. She lost her shame in the terrible ecstasy that flooded her at the touch of his hand.

The next morning she was snivelling, and she cast reproachful looks at Terry as she cooked his breakfast and prepared his lunch. He remained masterful and unabashed, and strode off to work with his head cocked jauntily and high.

When they were married Saturday, nobody was surprised.

It was not long before morning nausea and the course of the moon told Martha that she was pregnant. Her face became pinched and sallow, and she was petulant most of the time. But at night she lay fingering her belly, trying to imagine she could feel a foot or elbow prodding within. It would be a boy, she decided, and would grow into a great man—a great writer. The heritage of intellect from Professor Darrell and herself, who could have been a great writer, too, under happier circumstances and with freedom from her stultifying environment, would rise above and conquer the grosser blood of Terry, the Irish boomer. The fire she had nurtured so long in secret burned out in a few weeks of indulgence; she had grown to dread the prospect of sleeping with Terry and feeling his hot, hairy body next to her or above her. A bit later and the expected little stranger would give her a good excuse for a separate bed. Her breasts swelled for the milk, and her hips broadened as she neared her time.

"Looks like a fresh Jersey; two quarts to the tit," Terry said admiringly, tweaking a nipple, and slapping her lustily and appreciatively across her widening buttocks. Martha shrank from these familiarities now, but reflected pensively that she had no legitimate right to be insulted by them.

"You'll cause a cancer that way," she warned, covering her breasts with her hands.

The child Leo never strayed beyond the picket fence surrounding the house and garden. He tunnelled in the ground and played at coal mining, solemnly rode a broomstick around and around the house or aimed a wooden gun at imaginary redskins behind the currant bushes, shouting: "Bang! Bang! You're dead, you Injun varmint!" At first Martha tried to keep him clean, changing his clothing three or four times a day, but as her limbs grew sluggish and her head drowsy, as the skin tautened across her stomach and made it difficult for her to stoop, she allowed him to run free all day. Terry scrubbed him before bedtime.

"You get lonesome, don't you?" Martha would say to Leo as she watched him playing in the yard. "Did you know there's a little stranger coming to our house to live? Would you like to have a little stranger to play with?"

"I don't care," Leo answered. He had never been conscious of loneliness, but he was so often reminded of the anticipated arrival of the little stranger that he began asking: "When will the little stranger get here to play with me?"

On the night the little stranger arrived, Terry led Leo into the library and told him to stay there until he was called. Leo sat thinking of Martha's pale and tear-stained face, contorted in agony, as he had seen it last, of her restless hands, now clasping her heavy stomach, now gripping the arms of her rocking chair. He heard somebody drive a buggy into the yard; a horse nickered and stamped, and the front door opened and closed. The sound of feet bounding up the stairs, and Martha moaning low and piteously at first, then her wild, high, and free screaming. Leo was scared so badly that he wanted to run out of the library, but he didn't know where to go. At length he fell asleep on the lounge, and when he awoke sunlight was making stars on the cracked and drawn window shades.

Terry came in and took Leo up stairs to see the little stranger, red faced and puckered, rooting away avidly at Martha's breast.

"Here he is," said Martha, smiling weakly and proudly. "What do you think of your little brother, Leo?"

Leo was disappointed.

"Sure is red!" he grumbled. "Better watch 'im when he gets a little bigger. Looks like he might be an Injun—might skelp us all in our sleep."

"His name's Robert Browning Hurley. That's the name I set my heart on as soon as I knew he would bless our home with his presence. And he's going to be a great writer, like his grandfather—like I wanted to be.

> "Low in the manger,
> Dear little stranger. . . ."

she sang gaily. She rolled her eyes toward Terry. He did not like the name, but he kept silent. Bob was not so bad. He would be Bob in the man's world he must move in; the Browning part would not last long.

The next day Leo was rummaging in a clothes closet to find his knife in a pair of soiled overalls he had taken off the day before. He was startled to find a bundle of sheets, horribly clotted and stained with blood. Decie spied him and ran quickly to haul him out of the closet by his collar.

"Heah! Who tol' *you* t' go pokin' around in theah? Min' yo' own bizness, will yo'? Get out o' heah!"

Leo's mind held the mystery and terror of the little stranger's arrival, the discovery of the sheets, in a dark corner for a long time.

CHAPTER THREE

In Happy Hollow and on the hills encircling it the trees with tall, straight boles had been cut long ago for mine props and timber. Some of them had been hewed into railroad ties. The second growth of hickory and scrub oak grew as thick as the hair on a dog's back, and Leo and Robert found it a fine place to play hide and seek and redskin and cowboy. A corduroy road made of oak and elm poles with the bark on wound through the hollow, first on one side of the creek, then on the other. Coal wagons from the drift mines down the valley and from the smaller tributaries of Happy Hollow creaked along the road, the drivers cursing and lashing their teams, the horses' shoes ringing loudly on the tough wood of the road. Leo and Robert liked to pretend that the coal wagons were wagon trains crossing the prairie, with the boys in the role of bloody savages lying in ambush on the hills. They skulked from tree to tree, sometimes shying stones at the drivers, who swore thunderously and shook their blacksnake whips.

It was in Happy Hollow that Robert and Leo first saw Monty Cass, the murderer.

Splashing down the creek with their breeches rolled high, the rank-smelling blue mud of the bottom squirting up between their toes and staining the water, they found Monty kneeling by the side of the stream, prodding a dry land terrapin with a stick. The terrapin had drawn its feet and legs beneath its shell.

"Derned critter won't crawl fer love or money when it knows you want it to," Monty told the boys disgustedly. "Some way 'r other, it tickles me like all get-out t' see one o' them scoundrels take out a-crawlin' and a-stretchin' his neck."

He gave up his teasing of the terrapin, and rose to his feet. At one time he had been a tall man, but a mine accident had caved his chest in, stooped his shoulders, and raised a hump on his back. He spoke in wheezing gasps, his voice dying in a metallic rasping. He had the long, lean face, straight nose and protruding ears of the farmers thereabout, descendants of the pioneers, but there were blue lumps under the skin on his face where sharp chips of coal had burrowed. Many of the farmers in the vicinity opened small "drift" mines, dug horizontally under the hills, in the winter after the heavy work of harvesting was over. These dilletantes were bitterly hated by the miners who had no other source of income—Irish, Italian, and Polish interlopers, overflow from the mines of Pennsylvania and Illinois.

A forelock of Monty's heavy, graying hair dropped persistently over his right eye. He had a habit, when preoccupied, of thrusting the end of the forelock behind his ear.

The boys splashed down the creek, while Monty trotted along the bank, eyeing them brightly and slyly.

"Come down t' the shack, boys. I'll show you a real live horse-hair snake, longest and fullest o' life I ever seed."

Leo and Robert had often heard it said that a horsehair, left in water when the signs of the Zodiac were auspicious, would, after a certain period, become a snake. The boys were anxious to find out the truth or falsity of the assertion.

Monty led them down an abandoned road that ran up a ravine. Saplings as thick as broomsticks had grown up in the center, and the ruts worn by the heavy wheels of coal wagons were filling with the fallen and rotten leaves of autumn after autumn. Monty climbed a blue slag heap before the timbered mouth of a "slope" mine. "Watch y' selfs!" he cautioned. In some places live fire was eating under the crust of slag, and a leg plunging into it would be badly burned before it could be withdrawn. The heavy scent of sulphur and a dank wind from the mouth of the "slope" smote the boys as they reached the summit of the slag heap. The blacksmith shanty was standing, and Monty paused beside the door, waiting for the boys.

"Come in and make yerselfs at home," he invited.

Inside, the rusty anvil was being used for a seat, and a rude table had been built of unplaned oak boards. Pans and a skillet depended from nails hammered in the wall, and a small cot with a corn shuck mattress filled one end of the shack. The boys sat down on the cot, and the shucks rustled harshly. Monty turned to a corner and began searching in a heap of rusty picks and tin cans.

"Well, I declare!" exclaimed Monty, trying to look astonished, "Reckon when I pitched that pick I was a-sharpenin' over here yestiddy I busted the jar and let the water out offen the snake. 'Twas jist as lively as a chipmunk, and here 'tis dead as a mackerel, stiff as a board." He picked up an ordinary horse hair beside a broken fruit jar and regarded it ruefully.

"Never was no snake in the first place. I wasn't born yesterday," Leo jeered. He was fifteen now, and had learned a few things. "Come on, Bob, let's go," Leo said.

"Wait! Wait!" begged Monty, grinning sheepishly. "Reckon that's a hoss on *me*! Sure, I'll own up, it was only a snide about the horse hair snake. I ast ever'body that come this way fer a month, and you two's the first one t' even feel cur'ous t' come and take a peep. It was wantin' somebody t' talk to, mainly. About the man I killed. I killed a man. I ain't braggin' about it, no more am I sorry. I mean I'm sorry I *had* t' kill him, but I *had* to. Wa'n't no way out o' it. If 'twas t' do over, I'd do the same. But I wish t' the good Lord it had never happened."

The words poured from him in a torrent, as though he wanted to say as much as he could before the boys ran away, as though he was accustomed to seeing people run away before he had his say.

"Don't be a-skeered o' me, boys! Fer Jesus' sake,

amen! I wouldn't no more harm ary hair on yer head no more than I would my poor old mother's. Won't you set a while and leave me talk t' you? I'll tell you where t' find a den of polecats where you c'n lay in a bush and watch 'em friskin' around like kittens. Ain't *nothin'* on God's green earth purtier 'n a baby polecat, ain't nothin' more cunnin' and ful o' ginger. This is gospel from now on, I'll swear on a stack o' bibles high as yan white oak. . . ."

The boys had started to their feet and were edging uneasily toward the door. Monty paused for breath, and picked up two powder cans, setting them side by side.

"Set down! Set down!" he urged. He feverishly poked his forelock behind his ear, only to have it fall limply over his eye again. The boys were afraid to refuse, and sat stiffly on the kegs, peering furtively at their feet to see whether the madman had a fuse attached to blow them to kingdom come.

"Got t' get it straight in my own noggin," began Monty, flinging his leg over the anvil and resting his hip against the horn. "I go around talkin' t' myself about it, and that's why folks thinks I've got bats in my belfry. When I seed Jess Gotts a-layin' there breathin' his last, with my pick buried in his head, and the red blood and grey brains blubberin' out o' his skull, I was sure heartsick and sorry. Hearin' his wife and kid hollerin' and screamin' didn't help none, either. That was back in the days when the union was stronger, before they busted it with the gun-totin' deppities from St. Luke and chased the organizers clean out o' these hollers. If the union hadn't been so strong, I'd 've got my neck stretched or life in the pen. The jury had some union men on it, and I got off with twenty-five years. I was a model prisoner, and inside o' twelve years, back I come. But sometimes I wisht they had stretched my neck in the first place. They blackballed me in all the tipple mines, and nobody don't want me a-workin' even in their dog holes where you got t' wiggle back t' the face like a snake crawlin' on his belly. I start a slope o' my own ever' fall, but I hate t' go t' town, people always makin' hard and cur'ous eyes at me. So I don't sell much coal, but it don't take much fer me t' live when I c'n put up wild blackberries an raise a little garden and a hog 'r two fer my meat. It's the lonesomeness hurts me most. I took a notion t' go into Green Valley one night and see one o' these here movie pitchers. 'Twas 'bout a murderer, and he was allers a-bein' ha'nted by the ghost o' the man he killed, and he was allers a-seein' 'Thou Shalt Not Kill' spelled out right in front of 'im. I been imaginin' things sence, and danged if I don't see them words a-spellin' out against the trees on yan hill or in the crick when I'm a-fishin'. Heer'd somebody a-prowlin' around here at night, and took a shot to'rds 'em. Somethin' squealed like a rabbit, and I've 'lowed sence it might 've been that wild girl, Anna Leischer, that lives up Butler Holler. Her father, that blasphemin' old Dutchman, he leaves 'er go anywheres she wants and she roams at night more 'n day time.

"She used t' sashay around that hill there, and tease me. I had most forgot about women, but I got t' studyin' how nice it would be t' get 'er in the shack here. I offered 'er all kinds of purties, but she only laughed and shied puff balls at me. I got along ver' well without even thinkin' what a woman was like till *she* got t' horsin' around.

"I was right in killin' Jess because he was a scab. The way the miners has been treated sence the union was busted w'd make even a blind man see that. Scabs take the bread and butter from the mouths o' widders and orphans. So they got t' be fought.

"Nobody can't say I aimed t' kill Jess when he tried t' pass the picket line that mornin'. I only wanted t' keep 'im away.

" 'Jess, don't go! Jess, be a white man!' I coaxed 'im, as nice as I knew how. I'd been a-strikin' three weeks, and purty ga'nt under the belt. I had a wife and a kid then, as happy a home as ever you clapped eyes on. They dusted out when I was sent up t' the pen; God knows where they are or what a pass they've come to.

" 'Jess, don't stick no knife in yer brothers' back,' I pled as pitiful as I c'd, willin' and anxious t' do anythin' or say anythin' t' touch his heart and cause him t' dump the water out o' his water deck and turn back from the tipple.

"What I'll allers stick to long as the breath o' life's in me is that it wasn't Monty Cass hittin' Jess Gotts with a pick; it was a union man hittin' a scab, and such things 's got t' be. I brang the pick along mostly t' skeer the scabs, but never aimed t' hit one with it. Leastways, not the sharp end of it.

"When he wouldn't lis'en to me, and walked off to'rds the mine, I run after 'im and hit 'im. It sure was a horrible feelin' in my arm, in my head and in my stummick when I felt the pick point dig right into his brain.

"I stood right there while they fetched his woman and kid, and them a-pawin' and a-sobbin' over 'im, and I never felt much sorry till that.

"If I could dust out o' here som'eres t' where the union is still alive and strong, it wouldn't be so bad. But seems like I took roots here in this holler, seems like this is where I'll cash in my chips."

"Let's not go past Monty's," Leo said two weeks later as the two boys made their way down the hollow. "He'll nail us again and talk our heads off."

They had seen Monty several times since their first encounter with him, and each time he had managed to hold them for an hour or so. They skirted the hill opposite Monty's ravine. They heard and felt the dull rumble of a blast under their feet as they descended toward the corduroy road.

"Somebody under here. Maybe it's Davy and the goblins," said Robert who was always trying to invest every situation with romance garnered from fairy stories.

"Maybe. More likely somebody tryin' to get a few more chunks of coal out of the hill. Been a dozen mines in it a'ready."

They were dismayed to see Monty leaning against a mining car at the foot of the hill and drinking in noisy gulps from a tin syrup bucket. He had taken possession of an old, presumably worked-out, slope mine this time, and was trying to clean up the fallen rocks and dirt, bale out the water, and replace the rotted timbers with sound ones. A large shepherd dog stood nearby, barking excitedly at the mouth of the mine.

"He ain't used t' hearin' the shots," Monty explained, as he took the bucket from his face and wiped his mouth with the sleeve of his overall jacket. "Boy! I struck it rich this time fer true. Rover here run a rabbit back in this old slope, and I follered back there. A four-foot vein o' the purtiest coal ever laid under these hills, and I seen a world of it. Don't know why the devil and Tom Walker somebody give it up, but that's not *my* funeral. Don't even hafta pay no royalty! This land belongs t' the Jones heirs, and they ain't been seen or heerd of in these parts fer years. They 'lowed all the coal was gone offen their land, and it's so poor a rabbit has t' pack his lunch t' get acrost it."

He sat down and poked his forelock behind his ear time and again. His shirt was open, and Robert saw his caved-in chest with the cruel weals across it. It always made him sick. Monty wiped the sweat off his face, and fanned himself with his miner's cap. His lard oil torch smoked close to the entrance of the slope. He was in a high humor.

> "Oh, I eat when I'm hungry,
> And I drink when I'm dry.
> If a tree don't fall on me,
> I'll live till I die!"

he sang.

"I jist put in a shot. Coal'll be a little red fer a load 'r two, but back there a few feet it'll be black as a crow and burn like a pine knot. Soon's the smoke clears out a mite, I'm goin' back there t' see what the shot's done. 'Fraid I set it a little toein'. Can't allers tell jist *how* coal 'll shoot. No two pieces of coal shoots alike; it's a God's fact."

"Can we go back, too?" asked Leo. The boys had never been to the face of the coal in any of the slopes, though they had crawled inside the mouth to the gate set across the rails to keep intruders out. Sometimes rocks fell with splashing noises in water far back in the mine, and the boys ran out to the sunlight, making a bright square of the mouth, with their hearts thumping. Icy drops of yellow sulphur water were distilled on the poles that timbered the roof, and the boys winced when globules trickled onto their heads and down their necks.

"No, better not. I ain't afraid fer myself. I've worked in the mines, man and boy, fer thirty odd years. But if somethin' sh'd happen t' a greenhorn, I'd feel t' blame. I do aim t' take you back, boys, soon 's I git 'er in apple-pie shape. Looks like the smoke 's cleared out considerable. I'll jist ease back and see how the land lays."

He shook his lard oil torch till the flame brightened. The boys watched the light recede into the mine like a fading star, heard Monty's hobs ring on the rails, then a faint shout of exultation: "Boy! purtiest shootin' coal I've seen in a month o' Sundays. Knocked some o' the props loose, tho. . . ."

His voice ascended to a terrified yell, and the light died suddenly. A mighty whoosh of cold and foul air rushed out of the mine and set the leaves a-trembling on bushes for a hundred feet around. At the same time there was a tremendous rumbling and grinding and the staccato cracking of timbers.

"God A'mighty! He's buried!" Leo shouted.

A weak moaning could be heard after the noise of the cave-in subsided. Clouds of dust were belching from the mouth of the mine.

"He's still alive! Run like hell for help. I'll go back and see if I can help him any," Leo told Robert. "Run on, you little fool! Are you paralyzed? For Christ's sakes!" Leo gave Robert a shove that sent him running mechanically down the slag heap, then ran inside the tool shed to look for a torch. He found one, and some matches in a tobacco tin.

The torch shed a wan light, and Leo felt along cautiously with his feet. It seemed to him that his feet were detached from his head and acting independently. His shins struck against the rails and the ends of the cross ties.

When he reached the cave-in, he saw that the whole passage way was blocked and daylight filtering down through the dust motes in the air. The roof had caved in to the grass roots. Leo shouted Monty's name, and heard a muffled answer, but it was hard to tell its direction. The shepherd bounded down the slope, his bark booming and echoing. He sniffed beneath the edge of a huge rock and began barking more loudly. Leo knelt and saw Monty's wild eyes shining beneath the rock. He was so frightened that he dropped the torch and it was sputtering out when he righted it just in time.

"It was a union man killin' a scab, not Monty Cass stickin' a pick in Jess Gotts' head and makin' a widow and an orphan. People oughter see it that-a-way," Monty wheezed painfully. "I c'n see you, boy! Don't leave me alone! Scoot me some water back here. You c'n do it in the deck o' my dinner pail, over by the wall. It's pressin' closer, squshin' me right in the muck same 's a man would mash a worm under his foot."

Leo tried to pass the water deck of Monty's dinner pail under the rock, but there was not room. He seized a rock and bent down the edges. Blood was gushing from Monty's mouth and nose, and it splashed in the water, dyeing it red, before he could gulp a swallow. He did not notice, and plucked avidly at the water with his lips. He could not move his head or use his hands to tilt the deck.

"Might get a prop—might ease up on me if you c'n get a prise under the aidge," gurgled Monty. "I been in most as bad scrapes and got out. When I got my chest caved in . . . God A'mighty, Son o' God, Jesus! If you got mercy like preachers claims, lift yer million-ton foot offen me and let me breathe! . . ."

The shepherd climbed up the heap and barked at the daylight. Leo called sharply for him to come down. It didn't seem right for the dog to be jumping on the heap that covered Monty. Like as if that little extra weight would make any difference. I must be going crazy, thought Leo.

He found a long prop, but didn't understand just how to use it. He was afraid that Monty was getting out of his head.

"Some folks don't understand union principles. In them days it was a fight fer more props and better air, fer wash houses so's a man c'd scrub some o' the black offen him before startin' home. . . . I didn't kill you, Jess Gotts; I killed a scab. That's different. . . ."

"Here's the prop. You hear me? Here's the prop. But I don't know how to use it. Can you hear me?"

"Sure I kin. Get a good bite under the aidge. I mean stick it back fur 'nough so 's the aidge won't break off, but not too far. Then raise it up purty high and stick a chock fer a heel under the prop fur back as it 'll go. Hardest rock r' wood you kin find fer a heel. Then heave all you got on the fur end. If you might prise it up jist a *little*, ease it offen me so 's I c'd breathe, then fetch help. . . ."

Leo found a billet of oak wood for a heel, selected a thick part of the rock, and threw all his weight on the end of the prop. To his joy, the rock slowly lifted five or six inches.

"Doin' good! Doin' good! Keep it up!" Monty called.

Leo felt himself lifted and hurled through the air like a stone from a sling. He thudded against the heap, and saw the prop cocked in the air before him, the edge of the rock skinning down the bark. When he leaped down, the rock had settled so low that he could not even see underneath.

"Oh, God! He's a goner! I killed him!" Leo yelled to himself. He ran frantically around the heap and noticed something he had not seen before. Monty's foot and ankle were protruding. What if I could yank him out? thought Leo, grabbing the foot. It wabbled loosely on the ankle and the gritting of bones sickened Leo. As he lifted Monty's foot, dark blood poured out of the shoe.

It was Leo's first grim contact with the violent aspects

of a world he knew he was destined to share. He was cut out for it; had never learned much at school. He belonged with those men who had their fingers clipped off by whirling saws in the sawmill where his father worked, with trainmen roasted and scalded in the telescoped debris of train wrecks. Violence, death, backbreak. It was tacitly understood at home that Robert must go to college. He was to be coached for the world of his grandfather, a world of soft hands, clean faces, and good clothes. Robert was bright in his studies; Leo didn't see the necessity of having a good education for the kind of work he was manifestly fated for. And books made his head ache. He knew what to do when Monty was under the cave-in. Robert would never learn such things if he lived to be a hundred. Books didn't teach anybody such things. It had to be *in* you. By God, it's only the men who *do* things who count, after all. Sitting on the piled up rock and dirt above Monty's body, Leo began building around him a wall of defensive dignity and a sense of importance that was to grow year by year.

He lay back and began sobbing, but he stopped when he heard the rescue party stumbling down the slope. Robert had been afraid to come inside with them.

CHAPTER FOUR

Leo and Robert did not like to linger near the head of the hollow where Monty had been killed. They found an interesting spot a mile down the creek where Butler Hollow branched off from Happy Hollow. This was the gypsy camp, where one caravan after another rested to allow their horses to feed on the luxuriant wild grasses.

The gypsies camped near a large spring and soaked their wagon wheels in the pools in the creek bed. They were horsetraders, but the farmers were wary of them. The gypsies were supposed to know ways of covering up the defects of worn-out plugs fit only for the bone yard until they looked and performed for the moment like spirited thoroughbreds. The women wore gaudily flowered dresses, necklaces of coins about their necks, and heavy earrings. They drove into Green Valley to tell fortunes. Hitching their horses, they systematically visited each house, offering to reveal the past, present and future for cash or for anything they could use. They sometimes threatened to curse those who refused them. The townspeople feared the reputed potency of a gypsy's curse. The gypsies, both men and women, stole anything they could make away with, even spiriting away whole haystacks from the farmers' fields. But the farmers were afraid to complain to the authorities. The legend ran that a farmer who had informed on a band of gypsies had had all his stock poisoned and his house and barn burned, the whole family perishing in the flames.

The gypsies were more fun for Robert and Leo than the coal haulers. The boys lay on their bellies on the hilltop and peered for hours at the gypsies below. The women bared their enormous and pendulous brown breasts and suckled their young; they squatted unconcernedly to relieve their kidneys and bowels, their long and brilliantly colored dresses held high. Sometimes they shed their clothing and bathed in the pools near the camp. Most of the women were fat and shapeless, but Robert, now almost nine, watched them with eager curiosity. Leo breathed heavily at times as he stared at the naked women. He writhed on the ground and looked so queer that Robert was frightened. Often Leo ordered Robert to lie where he was without turning his head, then ran into the deeper woods. He came back slowly and told Robert they must be getting along home.

The gypsies cooked in black iron pots suspended by tripods over open fires fed with fallen limbs off the trees. It was all so mysterious and strange to hear the gypsies muttering and laughing, the babies wailing and the mothers singing, and the horses neighing and stamping. The gypsies had only to snap brittle branches underfoot, no chopping at tough poles, or packing coal. Robert and Leo envied them. It was a more exciting sight after nightfall. The bonfires flickered to illumine the dark faces, the vans with crude but vivid pictures of landscapes, the heads of horses or dogs, painted on their sides.

Dark came early in the aisles between the trees, and the boys ran home quickly when they realized how long they had stayed.

CHAPTER FIVE

"It's in there. It *was* in there, anyway," Robert sobbed. "I saw him pitch it in through the window. I was going to bring it home, and we would've made a pet of it. But Dogface Epperson he—he took it away from me, and he belted me a good one when I tried to get it back. Then he went in the house with it and came back with his daddy's razor. And . . . oh, it was awful!—he cut its throat, slashed it clear across, and threw it in the church window. There's the blood on the weatherboarding. See? It was such a cute little kitten, white as a snow ball, all but its black feet like tiny shoes."

"This is the window he throwed it in at?" asked Leo.

"That's the one, all right. Maybe it's dead now."

The Holy Roller Church was a sagging frame building. Its single room held a number of hard pine benches, an ordinary kitchen table for an altar, and a rheumatic melodeon. There were cabalistic charts, daubed in bright colors on the walls. These charts were a revelation of the Holy Scriptures, and neatly figured out all that Saint John found incomprehensible on the Island of Patmos. The windows were stained only with cheap white house paint, and the plastered walls were grimy with soot and smoke that belched from the pot-bellied stove.

"Give me a boost," commanded Leo. It was at times like this that he felt his superiority over Robert. When he became discouraged over the low grades he was making in school and was reminded of the "excellent" marks on Robert's report card, he fell sullenly silent, but cherished in the back of his head such incidents as this.

Robert hoisted him high enough to reach the window

sill, and Leo lifted the sash. Leo was afraid of the dark interior, but he would not let Robert know.

Almost every night Harry Epperson, the pastor of the church, could be heard bellowing pleas or threats at the unsaved, or, "the gift of tongues" having fallen upon him, mouthing unintelligible gibberish. The elect of the church called themselves "saints," and often expressed their exuberance by dancing violently for hours at a time. Pastor Epperson was reputed to be a divine healer; the sick and crippled were brought to him. He had not yet healed anybody, but he always explained that his failure was due to lack of faith on the part of the patient. In the old days the church building had been in the hands of the "Shouting Methodists," it passed from them to the Holiness, and finally to the sect called by its adherents The Pentecostal Church of the Nazarene. The amused—or outraged, as the case might be—natives called the Nazarenes "Holy Rollers." When the nights were fine in the summer and fall, girls and their fellows and even sedate householders gathered stealthily around the church to listen, giggling and whispering, to the hubbub inside. The bolder ones peered through the windows now and then. Some of the "saints," struck by the power of the Holy Ghost, might be lying prone on the floor, surrounded by praying and envious acolytes, others whirling like dervishes, or hoofing it like vaudeville dancers.

"Praise Him!"

"Yes, Lord!"

"Come, Jesus! Come, Jesus!"

"Have your way, Lord!"

"Thy will, not mine, Lord!"

"Jesus! Jesus! Jesus. Whoooooo! Hallelujah! Whoooo!"

Pastor Epperson darted here and there like a water bug on a mill pond, now plopping down to pray, now whooping shrilly as he cleared two benches in an agile leap, or— infrequently—struck by the "power" and reclining stark on the floor, in the center of a knot of sweating and shouting female "saints." It was charged by skeptics that he often cocked a sly eye as the sister "saints" squatted about him, but the faithful knew that this canard was false. Pastor Epperson, at such times as he measured his length on the floor, was in a divine trance, far away from the world, and in direct communication with God. He muttered to himself: "Yes, Lord! I understand, Jesus! It shall be done! Praise Thy holy name! Whoooooeee! *ashanagi maheesha mahio heeshana hyshen a lia genoa! Whoooooeeee!*" his voice ascending to a shout as he spat forth the words in the "unknown tongue." And after the "power" had lifted he smiled wanly, as he fancied Christ would have done, or Mary lying in the manger with the Savior on her arm and the cows staring reverently. Pastor Epperson would rub his face and shake his head till his long hair veiled his eyes. Then he'd relay to his gaping flock the burning messages of God. The Holy Rollers snapped up every word, and tried to hold it on their minds till it was graven there for keeps.

Robert glanced furtively around as Leo wriggled through the window. After a bit, Leo reappeared.

"Here it is, poor little feller," said Leo, holding up the kitten. The animal's throat gaped rawly, and it was meowing huskily. "It's a goner, sure as shootin'," Leo said soberly. "Purty little feller. It woulda made a dandy pet. I'll hafta put it out o' its misery now."

Suddenly he smashed the kitten's head against the window sill. There was a sickening crunch and a last piteous yelp. Leo flung the kitten to the ground, where it lay quivering, blood gushing afresh from its slashed throat, from its mouth, nose, and bulging, glazing eyes.

"Cry baby! Cry baby! Dear Little Stranger! Dear Little Stranger, born in a manger!" Leo taunted.

Then he said more seriously: "It's better off dead. I don't like t' see things suffer no more 'n you, but you don't help it none by bawlin' like a calf. That don't ease its poor throat none. Now I'll find Dogface and sock 'im so hard his shirt tail 'll roll up his back like a window blind."

He spat on his hands and hitched his trousers determinedly. Leo was small, wiry, dark and alert, like his "spiggoty" mother, Terry said. Robert was plump, blonde and rosy, always stumbling over his own feet. "Fall all over yerself, awk'ard," Leo would say to him scornfully when he tripped over something. Leo was continually defending Robert against the other boys, but he kept reminding him that every tub should rest on its own bottom. Robert would travel in a roundabout way home from school to keep out of the way of bullies who had snatched off his cap and trampled it in the mud, or inflicted even worse indignities, such as "taking it out and spitting on it." Leo marched into the very jaws of trouble as resolutely as the noble Six Hundred. When he was very angry, he laughed hysterically, and he liked to think and to say that this trait was indicative of a reckless courage. But he could not keep his legs from shaking when a fight was in prospect.

The boys found Dogface Epperson in a vacant lot near the church pulling the legs off grasshoppers and saying to them sternly: "Spit terbaccer juice, and I'll let ya go! Spit terbaccer juice, why don't ya?"

He was a head taller than Leo, but slow-witted and not especially pugnacious. He gratified his sadistic strain by torturing animals, birds or insects, but when he could he would inveigle a small boy into a coal shed or privy to inflict something peculiar and terrifying upon him. Robert could never get it straight in his head, but Dogface had done something horrible to Wally Hull. Wally's parents had been obliged to take him to the doctor about it, and Pastor Epperson beat Dogface so soundly that he limped for a week. "That's what comes from him leading himself around all the time. It's softened his brain," Robert heard Martha say to Terry, but he was as much in the dark as ever. He had an earache, and often probed in his ear with his finger, jerking it out with a pop to smell the end of it. He was afraid that his brain was softening, too. He worried about it long after Leo had curled into a rainbow and was sawing wood fit to kill. It was said that Dogface had cut the bottom out of his right trousers pocket, not only for his own convenience in school and even when walking on the street, but to play a joke on girls by inviting them to feel for candy. Dogface often leaned against the sunny side of the schoolhouse, a rapt look on his pan, his right hand thrust deep into his pocket. "Guess what I got a-holt of and I'll give you a bite of it," he'd tell the small boys who came near.

As Leo and Robert drew near, Dogface rose to his feet, and a sullen, belligerent look settled on his hatchet-sharp face. He could feel the seismal tremors of impending danger. Leo looked at him steadily, but was afraid that Dogface could notice his treacherous legs quivering.

"Well, why ya standin' there shiverin' like a dog hockeyin' peach seeds? What you skeered of?" Dogface jeered.

"Not you, nor any of yer kin. You can't hardly stand without leanin' ag'in something. If you don't quit floggin' yer dummy, the undertaker's gonna have a job. You ain't takin' kittens away from Little Stranger when you tangle horns with me."

"Stand there pickin' yer nose and eatin' it, you bigstand-up-and-bawl-fer-buttermilk! I'll knock a string o' farts out o' you as long as a grapevine."

They measured one another up and down, up and down, for a few moments, then Leo leaped nimbly forward and landed a blow squarely on Dogface's nose. The blood squirted, and Dogface ran bellowing toward home, stanching his nose with his sleeve.

"My daddy'll cook *your* goose! My daddy'll cook *your* goose!" Dogface shouted as he heeled it. "Wait and see, smart aleck!"

"What does he mean?" asked Robert worriedly. He was afraid of Pastor Epperson, as were most of the other Green Valley boys.

"Don' know. Don' care," Leo answered, but he was not easy in his mind and the sight of Dogface's blood pouring over his clothes had made him want to vomit.

"You been wantin' t' see The Hand," he said to Robert. "So we're goin' out there. Ain't nothin' to it. Ain't nobody ever seen no hand stick up out o' the water. Ain't no such thing as spooks."

Leo was in no hurry to get home, for he feared he might find Pastor Epperson there to enter a complaint with Martha or Terry. The boys left the town behind and followed the corduroy road that wound through Happy Hollow. When they passed near the spot where Monty Cass had been buried, Leo said, wagging his head dolefully: "Poor Monty! Reckon what you'd 'a' done in my shoes, seein' him squashed same as a ripe tomato?"

Robert had heard this before, and he knew that Leo was not so sorrowful about Monty as he was determined to impress his superior resource in a crisis upon his half-brother, the dear little innocent stranger, who couldn't go to the crapper, Leo often sneered, without asking somebody to unbutton his pants.

When they reached the clearing a half-mile past the neck of Butler Hollow, which was one of the several smaller valleys branching off Happy Hollow, Leo strode boldly toward the old house in the center of the weed-grown plot. It was a two-story frame structure, almost all the many-paned windows stoned out, the weatherboarding warped off, and the laths with the petrified plaster showing through them. The chimney had fallen and some of the bricks had crashed through the roof, others had slid to the ground. Weeds had seeded for many years in the clearing, and the dry stalks rattled harshly as the boys pushed through. "Stick tights"—the barbed pods of a low-growing plant—clung to their clothing and stung their legs.

Leo walked boldly to a window and thrust his head inside, sniffing inquisitively the dank odor of wet plaster and rotting wood. The floor was covered so thickly with fallen plaster and decayed leaves that small plants, spindly and yellow from wanting the sun, had rooted precariously there.

"It's at the back where you see The Hand—in the well," Leo said, turning from the window, his voice dropping almost to a whisper.

At the rear there were a few ancient apple trees spotted by fungi shaped like slices of liver, but the buck bushes and hickory sprouts were getting the best of it. Under the apple trees three or four weathered gravestones were tilted this way and that, none of them pointing straight towards the sky. And it seemed to Robert that the cistern, its curb built of flat sand stones, leaped ominously toward them. He stared at the warped and rotted oak planks covering the top, and imagined a white and dripping hand clawing its way through a crack.

"Let's go back. I don't want to see," he whimpered, pulling at Leo's arm.

"Some of 'em buried right here. Some of 'em that Hade Pollard murdered," said Leo solemnly, pointing at the gravestones, and not heeding Robert's agitation.

It had been twenty-five years since Hade Pollard, mad with jealousy because he fancied his wife loved the hired hand and was making a cuckold of her lawful wedded husband, who, God knows, had never let her suffer or neglected his family duties, but had rung the bell nine times to get six boys and three girls—seven children living and two dead—arose in the night, strangled his wife and split with an axe the skulls of his hired man and of the three children still at home. Then he had thrown all the bodies in the cistern and taken to the woods, which at that time retained much of their primitive fastness. He lived on roots and bark, but hunger at last drove him to a village, where he was recognized and apprehended. He confessed, and asked only sufficient time to get right with his maker before his neck was stretched. He was hanged on a scaffold erected on his own farm, near where the boys now stood, and hundreds of people jammed the clearing. Some had been travelling for days in wagons, afoot and on horseback, and the affair assumed the aspect of a holiday. The annual camp meetings at Dobson's Grove never attracted a larger crowd, even when Texas Taylor, the silver-tongued singer and evangelist, held his protracted meeting.

Hade mounted the scaffold praising God and blessing

the audience and the sheriff, who stood nearby, nervously fingering the knotted rope and holding the black hood fearfully as though he expected it to bite him.

"I want t' say t' all you folks, and 'specially t' the young folks," Hade said clearly and steadily just before the hood was fitted on his head and the light blotted from his eyes forever. "You want t' walk in the ways of Jesus, bless His name, and don't ever you stray down the pleasure paths of sin Old Scratch would derned well like fer you t' be a-travellin'. Oh, he kin make it sound mighty sweet and temptin'; he's got the most persuadin' ways a body could meet. I listened t' the old devil and done his biddin' when he whispered in my ear on a dark night right nigh this spot, and he has brought me to my death before you in disgrace and shame, but not in sin, praise His name who shed His blood on Calvary, for my sins has been washed whiter than snow, yes, whiter than wool and fleece, friends. I've been washed in the precious blood of the lamb. Do the biddin' of Jesus, friends and neighbors, and you'll never stand where I'm a-standin' now. I'm ready now, Mr. Sheriff, and may God bless you. Goodbye and good luck to one and all. . . ."

When the trap was sprung, ten women in the throng fainted and many vomited or burst into hysterical weeping or laughter. A doctor stood by, heavy hunting-case watch in hand, as Hade's legs writhed more weakly and soon stiffened to quietude. The farmers began hitching up for the drive home—it was a two days' journey for some. Many had brought their children from afar, believing that the youngsters might receive a moral lesson that would stick with them for life and serve as a deterrent when temptations reared.

Nobody lived in the house after the murders and the hanging, and it was said to be haunted. The most common phenomenon was a long feminine hand rising out of the water in the cistern and beckoning to the onlooker, who— the legend ran—was inevitably seized with an uncontrollable impulse to leap in the well.

Leo and Robert leaned gingerly over the curb and tried

to adjust their eyes to the gloom of the depths. Then Leo climbed onto the top.

"Hold me if I start to jump," Robert said. He was snivelling with fear and excitement.

Robert thought a long shaft of sunlight piercing through the cracks in the top looked like a hand. Leo began backing off, grumbling that The Hand was a fake. Robert saw his eyes dilate with horror as he pointed a finger at Robert or beyond him.

"Look out behind you!" Leo yelled, and jumped so violently that the brittle boards gave way beneath him. He plunged eight feet to splash in the black water.

Robert did not move. He wanted to run, or to shriek, or to help Leo somehow, but he did nothing. A girl with long hair flying dashed by him and knelt beside the well.

"Get that pole," she shouted. "Oh, *can't* you move, you little ninny? I'll get it myself!"

She fetched a tough oak pole that had once served as a chicken roost and poked it down into the well.

"Catch it! Catch it, and hold onto it and the rocks, too. I can't pull up all your weight," she called down to Leo.

Leo emerged dripping from the well, and stared curiously and angrily at the girl.

"What d' ye mean by wavin' yer hand out o' that window in such a funny way, and the rest of ya nowheres in sight, like as if ya was only a hand?" Leo demanded.

The girl was dark enough to be a gypsy, but her face was rather broad and heavy. Her hair was long, black and uncombed, her feet bare. She could not have been more than fifteen, but the contours of her breasts and hips were those of a woman.

"I scared you out of your wits," the girl snickered. "I bet you believe in The Hand. You thought I was a ghost."

"Bet I didn't. Bet you a million dollars ag'in a plugged penny! I told Little Stranger it was a fake, didn't I, Bob?"

"Sure," Robert assented. He was still uneasy about the place, and nothing would suit him better than to get away from it.

"Bet you're scared to go into the house. I'm not. I go

into the house and even upstairs all the time. I've got a playhouse up there. Want to see it?"

"Sure!" Leo said. "Come on, Little Stranger, watch out The Hand don't reach out o' that well and pull you in."

"What makes you call him Little Stranger?" the girl asked. "He's not a stranger to you, I know. I've seen you with him lots of times."

"Our ma—well, *my* stepmother, really by rights—used t' call him that t' me before he was hatched out on a stump where a crow had dropped him," Leo explained. "Whereabouts did you ever see us before?"

"Watching the gypsies, hunting birds with sling shots, gigging bull frogs. Oh, lots of places and lots of times. I saw you when you ran off to the woods by yourself, too," she giggled, rolling her eyes and stuffing her cheek with her tongue.

Leo flushed brick-red and his mouth screwed up sullenly. Robert gaped wonderingly at him.

"Shut yer mouth before it gets full o' flies," Leo snapped at him. "Where's this here playhouse?" he asked the girl.

"Upstairs. Watch yourself on the steps. Some of them are gone."

The narrow staircase was so dark the boys felt ahead with their hands and went on all fours. When Robert's hand plunged into nothingness as he groped for a missing step, he felt a cold chill blowing out as from some remote cavern underground, into the depths of which he might shortly go hurtling to his doom. There were three rooms upstairs, and each one had been swept clean of drifted leaves and fallen plaster. Spiders had filmed the corners of the ceilings, and mud wasps buzzed in and out of the broken windows and through the holes in the roof. These wasps rarely sting, but Robert winced each time one came near, its blue-black wings flashing iridescent hues. Rusty tubs, blasting powder kegs from the nearby mines, and wooden boxes, serving as furniture, were carefully spaced about the rooms.

"I even got a stove," said the girl. "I can cook on it. Made it out of an old one I found in the junk pile. I find lots of things there, some of them almost as good as new."

"Which junk pile you talkin' about?"

"The one on Melcher's place, just across Wild Horse Creek from the Sweet Springs."

"You ain't seen no junk yet. The junk pile down the other side of the Ground Hog mine's got that one skinned a country block."

"It has? Will you take me there some time?"

"Sure. Any time."

"It's not much fun playing house without a papa. It's lonesome, and it just doesn't seem real."

"I'll be the papa, eh? And Little Stranger can be our little boy."

"Wouldn't that be just fine and dandy? But I don't even know your name! Isn't that silly?"

"It's Leo Hurley. What's your'n?"

"Anna Leischer."

"Why, I've heard of you and yer father. He don't believe in God, and he come from Germany. The mail carrier brings him a letter from Germany every month regular. They say it's got money in it. Has it?"

"I think so. Papa never says, but he always buys things just after the letter comes. What makes people hate my papa so? Because he beats the Whore? He never beats me, and the Whore loves him just the same. He doesn't hurt her much."

"They hate him mostly because he talks ag'in God and religion, that's why! Is that woman you call the Whore your mother?"

"I don't know. She speaks German all the time, and papa always talks to me in English, always has since we came here ten years ago. He tried and tried to teach the Whore English, but it seems like she can't learn at all. She only knows a few simple words. Papa says he doesn't want to have anything around to remind him of Germany. Maybe that's why he hates the Whore sometimes, and talks so mean to her and even hits her. She cries most of the time, and she catches hold of me and kisses me with her great big slobbery mouth over and over, with a look in her eyes like a dying duck in a hailstorm. I feel sorry for her, but I don't love her. I don't want to believe she's my mother."

"You know what a whore is?" Leo smirked.

"Sure. A woman that goes to bed with a man for money. But *she* never gets any money, only what she eats and a few clothes. She does all the work as neat as can be, and she's a good cook. Sometimes she does sleep with papa, though, but not very often. She hasn't for over a year now that I know of."

Whore! It was a terrible yet beautiful word to Robert. The boys said Molly Neal was a whore, and her cottage in Green Valley was always eyed curiously by the small boys as they passed. They lay in the tall grass and weeds across the road from Molly's front door and pondered darkly about the sweet and awful mystery beyond it. After nightfall, the door opened frequently, light flooded out, and the silhouette of a man, half-crouched and hurrying, slipped inside. One day Molly beckoned to Robert.

"Will you go to Krausmyer's butcher shop and fetch me two-bits worth of sirloin steak?" she said. "I'll give you a nickel and a great big juicy kiss."

Robert's heart was still thumping furiously when he brought back the steak. Molly was standing at the gate, holding her brightly-flowered kimona around her, so loosely that Robert saw the swell of one breast and even the dark bud of it.

"Here's your nickel," she said, "and the kiss if you want it, too." She leaned forward, both breasts shaking free.

Robert wanted the kiss, but he felt as though he would smother. He grabbed the nickel and legged it away as fast as he could kelter, Molly's shrill laughing pursuing him as though it ran on feet. It was hard to think anything bad of Molly. She was so pretty, and smelled so sweet, not sour with sweat like Martha, his mother, who held that it was sinful for women to shave their armpits.

There were so many things that Robert guessed about. Leo would not tell him much. "Soon as you get some fuzz under yer belly, I'll tell ya," he'd say. Robert knew that Leo himself had only a little fuzz, but he was inordinately proud of what he did have.

Now Robert was learning things from the wild girl who had tormented poor Monty Cass. He liked her bold, unabashed way. She looked one straight in the eye, and never winked or shifted her glance as though she were afraid of being caught in a lie—of having someone read one on her face.

He could tell that Leo liked her, too.

"You must be purty strong," Leo said admiringly. "To horse all these heavy pieces from the junk pile and then up these steep steps."

"Some of the gypsy boys helped me. They're all gone now till next summer and it seems like somebody was dead when I pass by the camp. One named Ramon played with me all this summer. He sure was good looking and a good singer, and he sure could play a guitar."

"Oh, the gypsies!" Leo's voice froze. "Don't look like yer old man'd allow ya t' have no truck with them gypsies. They'd steal acorns from a blind sow, and won't work fer love 'r money."

"I've got nothing they would want to steal. And Ramon would work for love."

"What d' ye mean, fer love?"

"Well, he didn't ask any pay for helping. That's what I mean. What's it to you, anyhow? You're not my guardian."

"Nothin'! Nothin'! I know I ain't yer gardeen. This Ramon yer feller?"

"Well, I guess you might call him that. I never thought about it that way."

"Kin I be yer feller?"

"Well, I don't know about that. I'll have to know you better."

"That's easy. I'll be back t' morrer. And Little Stranger can stay at home fer oncet."

CHAPTER SIX

Leo and Robert knew they were poor, but it was only at intervals that the knowledge struck them keenly. When the sawmill closed down during a slack season, Terry worked for the neighboring farmers or sometimes on an extra section gang. He would not work in the drift mines. "I want room fer t' be jumpin' if the whole world tries t' settle on me back," he said. "And me legs ain't so supple as might be. Time was when I didn't mind the mine at all, at all, but I'm not so full o' ginger any more these late years."

Martha clung desperately to the remnants of her gentility. Each year the house had to be painted and the walls papered. She had declared that neither of the boys would ever go barefooted to school, but she had to give in on that, too. At first she had a little money of her own left, but the small pile soon melted away. Martha grew to blame Terry for all that had happened to her. The sap dried out of her body, leaving a residue of vinegar, and her face became as sharp as a beak, her chin pointing eternal reproach at Terry. Her mouth puckered like the bark that grows back around a skinned place on an apple tree.

Martha kept reminding Robert that he was to be a great poet, and he felt uncomfortable about it. Not that he did not love every ancient volume in his grandfather's library, not that he didn't want to be a poet. But he felt nervous about it, and in his heart was the fear that he would grow up to be a very commonplace sort of fellow, after all, and no poet worth listening to or reading about. Leo teased Robert about growing up to be a poet, and

Terry was ever a bit contemptuous of his younger son. Each evening, if the weather was not stormy or unusually cold, Terry and Leo took a walk to the edge of the town and back, and at times they walked farther afield, even down the road into Happy Hollow. Leo told Robert that it was dark as a stack of black cats in Happy Hollow after nightfall and there were suspicious crackling of twigs and luminous eyes glaring from the brush. A farmer of the neighborhood had killed a large black panther in his barn-lot a few years before, and Leo was sure that there were still panthers prowling in Happy Hollow after dark. All this made Robert feel apart, and lonely. He shrank from his mother's violent embraces, her high-flown melodramatic rhetoric, as she outlined his future:

"I shall live again my own wrecked life in you, my son," she told him solemnly. "All that I could have been, you must be for mother's sake."

Robert wanted to go walking with Terry and Leo, but he was never invited. His mother read to him from her favorite poets, and now and then embarrassed him by asking him to try his hand at a poem. "Just anything with beauty and joy in it; just anything that contains a message from God to man or from man to God."

In the evening after Leo and Robert had visited the house of The Hand, Terry and Leo set out for their walk. Each night it was the same. Terry would rise from his chair, stretch and yawn: "Well, Leo, me bye, how about steppin' off a few paces in the fresh air t' blow the stink off us?" Martha was glad to see them go; she livened perceptibly as soon as they slammed the front gate. Robert ran to the window and watched them as far as the street lights shone. They strode along briskly, side by side. Robert wondered what they talked about, and often asked Leo. "Oh, different things," was Leo's inevitable answer. And Robert would lie away in bed by Leo's side, feeling the warmth of his body next to his own, and peer wistfully at him, wondering about the secret understanding his father and half-brother shared.

Martha was reading aloud from *A Fireside Garland of*

Choice Literature, rolling her eyes rapturously at the especially florid passages, pausing for dramatic effect, and sighing thoughtfully betimes.

"I have seen a beautiful female treading the first stages of youth and entering joyfully into the pleasures of life," she read. "The glance of her eye was variable and sweet, and on her cheek trembled something like the first blush of the morning; her lips moved, and there was harmony; and when she floated in the dance, her light form, like the aspen, seemed to move with every breeze."

Martha folded her hands across her stomach, leaned back in her chair, and closed her eyes. She looks silly, Robert thought. Her Adam's Apple moved up and down now and then as she swallowed saliva, and at such times she made a clucking noise in her throat. Robert wished he might be along with Terry and Leo, even in the darkness of Happy Hollow, where the wild animals prowled in the brush.

"I returned," Martha resumed suddenly, a tremolo note in her voice, "but she was not in the dance. I sought her in the gay circle of her companions, but I found her not. Her eyes sparkled not there—the music of her voice was silent—she rejoiced on earth no more. I saw a train, sable and slow-paced, who bore sadly to an opened grave what once was animated and beautiful. They paused as they approached, and a voice broke the awful silence: 'Mingle ashes with ashes, dust with its original dust. To the earth, whence it was taken, consign we the body of our sister.' They covered her with the damp soil and the cold clods of the valley; and worms crowded into her silent abode. Yet one sad mourner lingered, to cast himself upon the grave, and as he wept he said, 'There is no beauty, or grace, or loveliness, that continueth in man; for this is the end of all his glory and perfection.'"

Martha's eyelids fluttered like an ecstatic camera shutter. "Oh, to write like that is to be next to God Himself. The great writer peoples his story and poem with characters almost as real as you and I, and, like God, he does with them as he lists. Do you think you could ever write as beautifully as Mrs. Sigourney, Robert?"

"I don't know. I wrote a poem in school last winter and the teacher said it was good, but I didn't want to show it to you because I thought it wasn't much to be proud of," Robert said. He had not intended to say anything about the poem, but he was really a little proud of it, and he now felt a vague pity for his mother and wanted to please her if he could.

"Oh, you did?" Martha almost squealed. "Why, you sly little rascal, you, not telling your mother. Where is the poem? Don't you be bashful, now. Maybe I can find some cookies in the kitchen and we'll have a little feast to celebrate the event. But first you must read the poem. You really must, now. Must mind your mother, you know!"

Robert had the poem hidden between the leaves of Palgrave's *Golden Treasury*, and after a little riffling of the leaves he found it and read it in a flat and sing-song monotone:

> "Across the frozen moorlands
> His icy breath doth blow.
> He cometh with the Winter,
> The Spirit of the Snow."

"Why it's beautiful. It's as good as Wordsworth; it really and truly is," Martha breathed. "But you should learn to say it with a little more expression, and use some appropriate gestures, like this."

She hopped about, gesticulating with her arms, and looking so absurdly gay that Robert was ashamed of her. She ran to the desk side of a "combination" bookcase she had not used for a long time, and searched rapidly through the pigeonholes. When she came back to her chair, she had a sheaf of manuscript in her hand.

"Mother used to write a little, too," she said shyly. "And this is one I started years ago and never finished. I had quite a number of my things printed, but when I could not see my stories in the places I had set as the goal of my heart, I grew discouraged. This story was to have been about a gruff old curmudgeon that had disowned his daughter because she had married beneath her. Years later, on the night the story opens, a stormy, snowy night, a mysterious sleigh drives up, and when the butler opens the door, there is a pretty golden-haired little girl on the stoop. This is his little grand-daughter, but the old grouch doesn't know it till he has fallen in love with the child's winsome ways. Then there is a reconciliation, and so on. Maybe when you get a little older, you'd like to take the plot and finish the story. I think it's a good idea, but I don't suppose mother will ever have time, or have the heart, to finish it or write another word of it. This is the way it starts:

> "The storm broke with the shriek of a thousand souls in torment. The venerable trees surrounding Featherstone Manse swayed and groaned as the demoniac winds sobbed through them, hurtling snow flakes hissing along the street, scratching like wild cats on the window panes, or piling high in the sheltered valleys of the roof.
> " 'Blast the weather!' fumed Percival Featherstone, Master of the Manse, stretching his long legs out before the warmth of the hickory log crackling on the hearth. 'And this d—d gout doesn't make it any more cheerful.'
> "A dark frown clouded his brow. He was thinking of raven-haired Isabella, his madcap daughter, and another night like this one when he bade her begone—out of his sight and life forever. From without, clearer and clearer on the frosty air, came the jingle of sleigh bells. . . ."

Robert thought his mother's story rather good, almost as interesting as *Jack Harkaway*. As she turned a page to begin anew, a soft but insistent knocking was heard at the front door.

"Well, well! That's strange. We almost *never* have company." Martha was flustered. "But it's not late yet, really. Just past dusk, really."

Robert followed her to the hall, and when the door opened, there stood Pastor Epperson, his hat in his hand, an ingratiating smile on his heavy, dark face. When he smiled, he looked very frank and pleasant. His teeth were regular and white, and his brown eyes eloquent as a spaniel's.

"Missus Hurley? Is *Mister Hurley* at home?"

"No, he isn't, but he'll be back soon." She was wondering whether it would be proper to invite the pastor in. Even though he was a Holy Roller, he was a man of God.

"I come to beg forgiveness. I just wanted to talk about my boy, Horace. It seems that your son, Leo. . . ."

"My *step-child*," Martha interrupted.

"Anyhow, I understand there has been some trouble between the boys. A fight or something of the kind. I know how boys are—working off their animal spirits in these tussles. I know Horace is no angel, and I only want to say now that I am trying my level best to direct him in the path of Christian duty. And I would like for you to pray for him, won't you?"

"Oh, I'm sure Leo was mostly to blame. I'll have to speak to him," Martha gushed. "And I *will* pray for both of the boys. I'm sure they need it."

"Yes, Sister Hurley! Ah, yes! How true, indeed. For does not the Word tell us: 'Dearly beloved, avenge not yourselves, but rather give place to wrath; for it is written, Vengeance is mine; I will repay, saith the Lord. . . . If thine enemy hunger, feed him; if he thirst, give him drink; for in so doing thou shalt heap coals of fire on his head.'"

"I'm ashamed I don't get to church as I used to," Martha said, her sentimental mood growing on her. "I don't know why it is. Mr. Hurley never goes."

"It's *so* easy to get careless, I know. But you ought to go *somewhere*, to have a church home. And let me say you are always welcome to our humble little chapel. You will hear people say we are crazy. Let them say it. We shall exalt the Lord by shouting His praises; and when He causes the gift of tongues to descend among us, we have proof that He is having His way with us. John the Baptist was called crazy, too, you know, by the unbelievers and unsaved of that day, and so was Jesus Christ, our Lord and Savior. The Word of God pointedly tells us: 'Yet if any man suffer as a Christian, let him not be ashamed, but let him glorify God on this behalf.'"

Martha's misdoings with Terry while he was still a boarder rankled on her conscience. Even though they *were* married the next Saturday, it was all the same in the sight of God. And she had been wanting to "get right with God" about it for a long time. Pastor Epperson's last words floated from him as soft and bright as bubbles on the air. Martha was impressed by his righteous manner, his fortitude and forgiving nature under persecution.

"Good evening, Missus Hurley. Now don't you forget that standing invitation to come and worship God with us."

He was gone, stepping almost daintily down the street, an aura of wistful pleading, humility, and strength withal, about him. His eyes roving from house to house and climbing modestly to upper-story windows, bathing with benign love all those who cursed him, persecuted and despitefully used him.

CHAPTER SEVEN

"Let's go down to the jungle and see who's there," said Terry. "Maybe some o' me old buddies 'll be driftin' this way one o' these days."

Terry and Leo frequently stopped at the jungle during their evening walks. Beneath a wooden railroad trestle spanning a small stream, the hoboes stopped for a boil-up and a mulligan, if the ingredients could be begged in the town or bought by pooling the cash resources of the group. On the trestle's timbers were carved the initials and trademarks of boes, and often arrows indicating the directions they were travelling, and the date. The ubiquitous A-No 1 had left his initials, and almost all the other well-known names of the hobo world of the day could be found by diligent search. Smoke-blackened lard cans were used for the boil-up, and no bona fide hobo would ever make off with any of these cans or damage them. On regular occasions, the railroad bulls descended on the camp, drove the hoboes into the brush by firing over their heads and at their feet, and then used the cooking utensils for targets.

Stepping down the ties, Terry and Leo could catch a whiff of the acrid scent of a bonfire fed by creosoted railroad ties, and when they drew nearer they could see the rose-colored smoke plumes and the flicker of the blaze. There was an eager anticipation about Terry that Leo could sense even in the dark. His father stepped briskly, and his shoulders, already humping, straightened a trifle. Leo, when the teacher was badgering him in school and he had been staring and staring at printed pages till a hollow roaring filled his head, thought bitterly of saying to hell with you, Dudley, and walking out of the room, catching a Red Ball for the Coast, and never coming back. He would do it some day, yet. He kind of hated to leave the old man. The old man didn't have any pud tied down to a measly one-horse burg like Green Valley.

Terry and Leo could hear a low buzz of conversation when they first came up to the trestle, but it died out as they slid down the cindered embankment and were revealed to about a dozen men and boys lying, sitting or standing about. The night was warm, and the fire was being used to cook a mulligan blubbering in a discarded wash boiler. One of the hoboes, a gaunt, heavily-whiskered chap, was stirring the stew with a wooden paddle.

"Evenin', gentlemen, evenin'," cried Terry, saluting with his hand. "How about sittin' down t' gas wi' ye a spell?"

Some of the boes muttered a greeting, but they all measured Terry and Leo suspiciously. Some of them could be seen hastily tying bundles for sudden flight in case the newcomers turned out to be John Laws or dicks. The dicks were always the more feared. Unless some crime had been committed in the town and the John Laws wanted to sweat a bo into a confession, an order to leave town was about the worst to expect. But many of the railroad dicks were extreme sadists who took a savage delight in "working out" on hoboes, whose complaints would never be considered seriously by the authorities.

"Rest aisy, gents," Terry reassured them. "It's no dick I am, and if I was I'd be that ashamed I'd not be showin' me mug amongst ye. An old timer, meself, but got to be a home guard, I guess, the balance o' me days. 'Tis an elegant smell that mulligan's got. Must be good stemmin', eh?"

"Not so good, Cap," the cook answered jovially. The taut atmosphere loosened. "I mooched the stem, and Dude there battered the privates. Most he got was a dimmer in cash at a time, and a few lousy vegetables. I made a gut plunge on butch fer a batch o' mulligan meat, but all I got was a soup bone that didn't have no great sight o' meat on it and would stink a dog offen a gut wagon besides."

One of the bums was picking boiled graybacks from the seams of his shirt, and another one—a middle-aged man with a broad, pasty face and bright, pouting lips—was talking in low tones to a boy beside him. The boy was whimpering, and his companion had his arm around his waist.

"I'm sick, Dude. Honest to God, I'm sick as a horse," sobbed the boy, turning toward the fire and away from Dude. The boy was not yet bearded, and, in tears, he appeared girlish.

"Why don't you lay off the punk, Dude?" growled the cook. All the boes bent hostile looks toward Dude, who loosened his hold on the boy.

"Why don't you mind your own business?" retorted Dude angrily, his voice rising to a shrill falsetto. "Who did you depend on for your scoff jack? And if I'd made a gut plunge on butch I'd have got more than a maggoty bone."

"Is that so, you wolf? You think I could breeze in there and order a t-bone like a swell? And got throwed out on my can. Naw, I told butch, please, sir, to gimme any kind o' meat he had for a mulligan, just anything, please sir—eye holes, nose holes, ear holes, bung holes, just so it's meat, please, sir. What more could a little red bull do? If you don't like the way I rustle 'em and the way I cook 'em up, Dude, you know what you kin do, and t' hell wi' ye!"

"I don't like this crowd any too well, anyways," said Dude. "Come on, honey, let's dust out of here."

"Let's stay, Dude," whined the boy. "Honest to God, Dude, I'm sick as I can be. I feel like my guts is comin' up between my teeth, and I don't believe I could drag my piles a foot." He retched a few times, and rubbed his forehead vigorously.

"I said for you to come on."

"You don't have to if you don't want to, punk," growled

the cook. "T' hell wi' that jocker. The sooner you ditch him, the better off you'll be."

"I said *come on*!" Dude repeated more emphatically, and the boy arose and followed him into the night.

"Hey, you gonna leave yer keister?" the cook called after Dude. Dude was a pitchman, and he had one of the small satchels which street merchants set upon legs to serve as a display stand. Dude came back and snatched the keister up; he had the boy by the hand now. As they left, he jerked the boy roughly and banged the keister against him.

"He knows how t' sling the crap to the rubes," said the cook, spitting thoughtfully in the fire, "and he's a handy bugger at rustlin' scoff, but the way he treats his prushun don't set wi' me."

Terry and Leo were sitting on a tie, leaning back against the timbers of the trestle and gazing into the fire. When the wind whipped the smoke around, they had to close their eyes. Terry began asking questions about places he had been and worked, and about old pardners. When he heard news from some old crony, he was speechless with delight, and would muse, "Well! Well! Well!" for a few moments before he asked about something or somebody else.

"How was the harvest this time?"

" 'Bout as usual. Rubes wantin' as much done as they kin fer as little pay as they kin possibly give."

Terry sat still a few minutes, scratching his ankle. Then he began to hum a tune, low at first, but gradually swelling.

"Sing it, Jack! Sing it! Don't be bashful," the cook urged.

"If ye'll all join in, then."

"I can't sing. I'm like the jackass that was invited to a party t' celebrate the landin' o' the ark. He says: 'Tell 'em I got no voice fer singin', no feet fer dancin', but long in the cool o' the evenin', when the tall lovin' begins, I'll be thah!' I can't sing, but I kin pat my foot."

"All right, buddy."

"O. K., Cap, let's hear ya start off with something."

"Drill, ye terriers, drill,
Drill, ye terriers, drill!
Oh, it's work all day,
And no sugar in yer tay,
A-workin' on the U. P. Railway."

"You tell 'em, Cap. I like the one they're a-singin' on the Coast. Same tune as that old church piece, *In the Sweet Bye and Bye*. Everybody knows that. Words goes like this: 'Long-haired preachers come out every night. . . .'"

He could not remember all the words, and sometimes hummed between the gaps in his memory.

"And the Starvation Army they play,
And they sing and they clap and they pray,
Till they get all your jack on the drum,
Then they'll tell you that you're just a bum.

"You will eat, bye and bye,
In that glorious land above the sky.
Work and pray, live on hay,
You'll eat pie in the sky when you die.
(THAT'S A LIE!)"

The last line was shouted so terrifically and savagely that Leo wondered why the men put so much anger in the jocose words. Almost every bo joined in the final shout, and eyes and teeth glinted in the firelight.

"Casey at the Bat," somebody demanded, and Terry knew that one. He was enjoying himself.

"Christmas at the Poorhouse," said the cook. "What about that one, Cap? Last time I heard it was at the Silver Dollar Bar in Denver."

This one was part of Terry's repertoire also:

" 'Twas Christmas in the poorhouse,
Happiest day of all the year,
And the paupers was contented
With their bellies full o' beer.

"The Master of the poorhouse
Strode through the dismal halls
Crying: 'Merry, Merry Christmas!'
But the paupers hollered: 'BALLS!'

"Then angry was the Master,
And he swore to them, by Jeez,
They'd get no Christmas pudding,
The lousy hunks o' cheese!

"Then spake a hard-faced pauper,
Springing up from where he sat:
'Ye kin take yer Christmas pudding, sir,
And go stick it up yer pratt!'"

Terry recited this with mock solemnity, and the more playful boes punctuated it with "boo-hoo" and wiping their eyes.

Here together for the first and probably the last time, Leo thought, looking around the camp fire. The bo who was picking the graybacks from the seams of his shirt scooted close to the fire, complaining that the boiled lice were almost invisible. "What's the odds?" asked the cook. "When you given 'em a good b'ilin', they ain't a gonna devil you much. It's that walkin' around and ticklin' wi' their toenails that sets my teeth on aidge." He stirred the mulligan briskly, and when the steam hit Leo's face he didn't relish the smell of it. Maybe never see one another again, thought Leo, feeling romantic and slightly melancholy. It would be dandy to be able to talk like these men about the yard bull in Fresno who kept a dog to chase boes because he was too fat himself to run over half a dozen steps. They could tell about the logging camps high in the blue cold mountains with their roaring streams and God what an appetite when the bull cook hollers, "Come and get it, or I'll throw it out!" and sleep under two blankets in that high, brisk air when maybe it's hot as the hubs of hell in the valleys and on the plains. They knew about the silver mines in the south so muggy inside a white man couldn't breathe even and the spicks worked like dogs for not enough to keep a louse alive; about the long stretches of track across the desert and the boes' terror when a trainman's lantern winks and bobs down the string of cars. Then it's try to dive in the lee of a reefer or swing through the little end door of an empty cattle car. One fellow was so scared, he said, that he busted a seal and landed right in a bunch of steers, and they cut his feet to ribbons but that was better than a tough shack making you hit the cinders a hundred miles from water or a house. You can find skeletons of boes ditched in the waterless, uninhabited desert by heartless shacks. Perhaps the shack followed him down the grab irons and stamped on his hands with hob-nailed shoes till he had to turn loose to suck at the pain in his broken fingers and fall, maybe beneath the whining flanges to be ground up like hamburger, or maybe to roll down the side of the roadbed, studded with pebbles like a plum pudding with currants, and a broken arm or leg to make you lie there till death came at last to put you out of your misery. Sometimes it wasn't so bad when the shacks stayed in the caboose and the engine's puffing a long way up the line wasn't so loud but that you could hear a coyote now and then and be glad you were riding high and safe on a running board under the grand old desert moon.

"Shack made a couple of us hit the cinders a right smart east of Rock Point, Wyoming," reminisced a bo. "God! No water! No nothing! Finally we thought, hell, might as well die a-tryin' to nail a red ball as to dry up and blow away out there and let the coyotes pick our bones. On the second day here comes a fast freight like a bat out o' hell. I nails a grab iron on the fly, but I couldn't get my foot on the sill step to save my soul from the devil. Wind blowed me out straight from the car like a flag in stiff wind. Goin' round a curve th'owed me ag'in the side, and I stuck a leg through the step and hung that way a hundred miles. Never seen what become of the other guy. Dark-complected kid headed home for Muncie and the old family pieboard. He wasn't on the train when it pulled into the division, I know that much."

I'll see the whole shootin' match when I get older, I'll ride every road in this country, thought Leo. I'll see it all; that's the way to learn things. Not in books. There's a lot you've got to *live* and books can't or won't tell you. The old man, he don't want me to be a-wandering away, but what did he do? Flew the coop when he was fifteen or before and been on his own ever since.

The cook was dishing out the mulligan in tin cans. Leo refused it with the excuse that he wasn't hungry, and Terry said he, too, had just put a big supper under his belt.

Terry was silent then with his hands clasped about one elevated knee. After a bit he began sucking on his pipe stem and making a horrible gurgling noise in it. He took his pipe from his mouth and aimed it at the fire, sighting down the stem as though it were a gun barrel. Some of the bums had stretched themselves out, composed for the night, flinging their arms across their eyes or turning their backs toward the flames.

Everyone started to a sitting or standing position when a loud scream was heard down the tracks. Another sounded near, and Dude's prushun stumbled into the circle of the firelight, his hands clapped to his face, blood gushing freely between his fingers.

"Oh! Oh! Jesus! He cut me! He killed me! I told him I was sick, but he kept on and kept on and wouldn't stop till I bit him. Then he got sore and slashed me with his razor. Ow, Christ A'mighty! Won't nobody do nothin'? I'm getting weak as Sally soup."

Terry caught the boy's wrists and tried to pull his hands away from his face. "Let's see, lad!" he commanded. "Let's see what the damned wolf done."

"Stand back, Cap," interposed the cook. "He's bleedin' like a stuck hog; he'll bloody ya all up. Now, you punk, take down them mitts from your pan or I aim t' kick yer butt from here to Casey and back ag'in."

The boy slowly lowered his hands, blood dripping from

his fingers. He wiped them on his shirt front, snuffling piteously. "I never thought he'd do that to *me*," he whimpered, shaking his head slowly and dolefully. Then he shuddered his head violently like a dog shaking water from its body and everybody jumped back to avoid being sprinkled with drops of blood.

"You ain't cut bad," said the cook. "I wouldn't name that much more 'n a pin scratch if it was on me. But it wouldn't do no harm t' have a croaker do some hemstitchin' or crochetin' on yer map t' save yer booteous countenance. Might save it from gangrene, and that's a God's fact. You got any money?"

"Not a red. I had two dollars I made pickin' apples but Dude he took it. He carried the money; and now he's gone." As he said the last words, their terrible meaning struck him for the first time with full force. "He's gone! Jesus Christ and the cows got out! Like as not I'll never see him again," he shouted despairingly.

"All the better fer you, you loony punk," growled the cook.

"But what'll I do? What in God's name will I do?" howled the boy.

"Awwssh! Ptui! Ptui! Ptui! Awwssh! Ptui!" spitting in disgust at the fire. "Go take a flyin' jump at a gallopin' goose fer all o' me. T' hell wi' ya and yer jocker, too."

The other men had been huddled into a knot, and now they suddenly sprang apart like an exploding bomb. Each started running and yelling.

"We'll run that jocker's ass ragged till it hangs so low it'll drag out his tracks!"

"We'll play fox and hounds with him. Maybe he won't be so handy pullin' a shive on anybody else!"

"We'll head that fluter down the line like the Cannon Ball with a wide-open throttle on a 40 percent down grade!"

The cook did not join in the hunt. He gave the boy a bandana to bind around his face, and Terry offered to take him to town to a doctor, and said he would foot the bill. Terry, Leo and the boy set out down the track toward the town, but the latter kept looking uneasily behind him, and when the bums hunting Dude cried out to one another, he paused.

"They oughtn't to hurt Dude," he said. "He wasn't hisself when he nicked me with that shive. I bit him too hard, and he lost his head. But he's as good to me as he can be when he's in a good humor."

"Fergit it!" said Terry roughly. "Come along wi' me, lad."

A series of cries told them that the boes had started Dude.

"They'll hurt him! Let me go back," yelled the prushun, and Terry was too late to catch him. At this moment Dude scrambled up the roadbed a few hundred feet away, running low on all fours. He waved his arms and beckoned to the boy.

"Come on, honey!" he hollered. "I didn't aim to hurt you thatta way. You know that Dude wouldn't hurt you if he stopped to think, don't you? It was mostly all in fun. I aimed to make a pass at you to throw a scare into you. Let's us pull our freight out o' here."

The boy was not long in reaching him. Together they made their way down the embankment and out of sight. The boes had given up the chase and ceased their excited baying. It was so still now that Leo and Terry could hear Dude and his prushun galloping across a pasture, their feet thudding like hoofbeats.

Terry and Leo walked along the track toward home. They had reached the city limits before Terry broke the silence.

" 'Tis a hell of a life, ayther way ye look at it. Ye take root in a town like this, and first thing ye know 'tis like a squirrel in a cage round and round and niver git nowheres. Ye don't know, me bye, how many times in the spring of an airly morning I ha' felt like throwin' my lunch pail far as I c'd and niver goin' back t' that hellhole of a mill . . . I . . ." His tone of passionate rebellion dropped, and he faltered. Leo realized shrewdly that his father had said more than he had intended when he began talking.

"But don't get it in yer topknot that the road's cake and pie. I cursed the day I left home many's the time and wished meself back, though 'twas another kind o' hell there. And what we seen t' night is only a wee part of all ye have t' endure and niver a word out o' yer chops. The more I think of it, the more I see it like this: They's two kinds o' people must be, and I'm of the kind that always gets the dirty end o' the stick, and the same you. I know ye hate the books and the school like poison, and the same did I. You take Bob, now, he'll be a prissy little clerk or something, God knows what, but his neck'll be chokin' wi' a white collar all his days. They's a slew of 'em about the mill, so nasty-nice they'd swab out their mouths if they happened t' let a 'fudge' slip out. A drop of their sweat would kill a rattlesnake."

"I don't want t' be no clerk. I ain't afraid o' work," Leo burst out. "I'm tired of old school and studyin' and studyin' when it ain't ever gonna do me a dime's worth o' good." He had been waiting for a chance like this. "Hoboin' wouldn't be no worse," he said slyly, casting a sidelong glance at Terry's face, the anxiety riding it visible as they neared the street lights.

"Ye little fool!" Terry stormed. "Some jocker'd be makin' ye eat out o' his hand afore a week. How'd ye like that?"

"I'd have something t' say about that. That boy's a fool. He ain't real bright, somehow. He ain't got all his marbles."

"Wait till ye 're five thousand miles from home, and not a bite fer yer belly nor place t' be layin' yer head. I been watchin' ye, me bye, and I know jist how ye feel. I need ye like everythin' t' lend me a helpin' hand if it be so ye kin. I spoke t' Mort Naylor, and he'll give ye a job tailin' a band saw. Not much pay, but there'll be a bit of a raise regular if ye take on proper as ye should."

Terry was so anxious now he halted and laid his hand on Leo's arm, searching for an answer. Leo felt the importance of his position. And what was best: No more school! Gee! No more school! This was all he could think for a while. But he didn't want to appear too eager. Nothing had been said about the money end of it. Some of the boys working at the mill were given spending money, while others had to turn over every cent to their parents.

" 'Tis discouragin'," gloomed Terry. "T' save me life, I can't make both ends meet any more."

Leo now felt sorry for his father, but he had not given up the idea of seeing the country. I'll see the whole shootin' match when I get older, he thought. When anybody mentions any little burg even as far away as California or New Hampshire, I'll say: I know that place like a book. Town is on the west side of the Frisco tracks. Just a beanery, grocery store, livery stable, and coupla other dinky joints.

"Well, I don't see why I couldn't work at the mill," Leo said. "I don't suppose you could give me a little spendin' money regular."

"Sure! Sure! Fifty cints a week, anyhow, right off the reel."

"Could I start in the morning?"

"And why not, I ask ye, me bucko?"

Terry stepped along more briskly now, and when they reached the drug store, he went inside to buy a nickel's worth of candy corn. They seldom tasted candy any more since Terry's wages had been cut. Terry and Leo ate all the candy before they reached home, relishing the secret they shared, and passing knowing looks between them after they had gone inside.

CHAPTER EIGHT

Martha was reading the Bible when Terry and Leo came in, and Robert was standing in front of the bookshelves, now pulling a volume down to look at the pictures, now burying his face between the leaves of one to catch the peculiar odor he said each book possessed. No two smelled alike. Robert could already read some of the books which gave Leo a headache just to look at them.

"Take one down and kiss it, why don't ya?" Leo jeered. He was awaiting Terry's announcement and anticipated Robert's envy. But the dear Little Stranger actually liked to go to school. All he knew was what the teacher told him. If he ever had to bum his way a mile some wolf would cabbage onto him and make him walk the chalk, all right. The fifty cents a week, though, would look as big as a wagon wheel. Robert's best trousers had two oblong patches on the seat, and the boys and girls teased him about the "eyes in the back of his—head." They always paused significantly before saying "head," giggling and nudging one another. They couldn't tell whether he was "a-comin' or a-gwine," they told him. Robert was ashamed of his flushed face then, almost as ashamed as he was of the patches.

Martha could sense something portentous hovering in the air. She closed the Bible on her forefinger as a bookmark, and her scrutiny of Terry was even more accusing than usual. She could not get Pastor Epperson and his orotund quotations from the Scriptures out of her head, and Terry's breaking in on her remorseful meditations had served to remind her more forcibly of her betrayal at his hands. That was the only blot on her soul, and she must be thinking of some way to wash it away, in tears and sackcloth and ashes, if need be. What's troubling him? she thought. Is it a guilty conscience at last? Leo was fidgeting around like a duck on a hot griddle.

"Fix Leo a lunch in the morning, too. He's goin' t' work at the mill wi' me," Terry said, as he sat down in Professor Darrell's favorite armchair. Martha often compared bitterly the contents of the two heads that had worn the plush on the head-rest shiny. How do I know what he was before I saw him? A hobo; that I know. Perhaps a murderer. Perhaps he had killed Leo's mother. And she was not at all sure Terry had a divorce from his first wife, though he insisted that he had. What did she know about him at all? Then she wondered if her scholarly father were not turning over in his grave, banging his patrician head against the coffin lid. If he only knew the indignity she had brought upon the Darrell name, which was traced for centuries in a massive buckram-bound volume on a shelf in the library. *History of the Darrell Family,* compiled by Herbert Waldo Darrell, Ph.D. There were some celebrated and proud names in that book.

In the dead of the night she would often awaken and sit up in bed to gaze earnestly at Terry as though he might be a stranger. Then she'd stiffen with distaste and scoot to the farthest edge of the bed.

Martha was not at all averse to Leo's quitting school and going to work in the mill. It was hard to keep both boys in school, and the extra money Leo earned would help to keep Robert going and provide for a little more clothing than he had been getting. Leo would never make anything of himself, anyhow.

"You hear that?" Leo asked Robert. The more he thought about going to work, the more excited he became. "I'll make six-bits a day right off the reel, tailin' a band saw. All you gotta do is stand behind the saw and ketch the pieces another feller shoves into it."

After they were in bed, Leo heard Robert sniffling.

"What ya cryin' fer, Little Stranger?" he asked. "I aim

t' give you a dime, or maybe fifteen cents, every week of the world t' spend all on yerself."

"I won't have *anybody* to play with, and all the kids at school make fun of me and pick on me if you ain't there to take up for me," Robert blubbered.

"You tell me which ones and I'll whale the sap out of 'em. You can go out to the ha'nted house and play with Anna Leischer."

"I'm afraid to go there without you."

"I'll go out on Sundays, and when we're off. They only work four days a week most of the time when business is slow. Well, I gotta get some rest. Gotta work t'morrer. I'm a laborin' man now." Leo flopped on his side and arranged the quilts around him.

Robert lay awake a long time thinking about the sawmill. He was not sure he'd like to work there, and he knew that he didn't want to quit school. He and Leo had never been inside the sawmill gates with their "Positively No Admittance. Apply at Office" sign, but they had climbed a tall maple tree and looked into the yard. Horse-drawn carts were moving here and there among the neat stacks of lumber, and workers were piling lumber and trundling bark-covered slabs in wheelbarrows. From the mill building came a steady drone, and intermittently the sharp wail of the saws. At times a log would prove too thick or too tough and the saw would slow down with many a deepening groan and rumbling bass note until it died, sounding like a phonograph record played on a machine that needs winding. Behind the mill a large pile of walnut logs reared like a young mountain. Now and then a derrick picked up one of the logs and thrust it into an upper window, where workers jockeyed it onto a carriage and dogged it down for the big saw. The boys sat engrossed till the quitting whistle blew and the workers came jostling out with their coats over their arms and dinner pails rattling against their legs.

I'll get me a pipe pretty soon, thought Leo, as he walked with Terry on the way to work. It warms your nose in cold weather and cools it in hot. Leo had been smoking surreptitiously for quite a while, and now he felt mature enough to flaunt his habit for all the world to see. He walked close to Terry and sniffed the smoke from his pipe. Getting a second hand smoke for nothing, thought Leo gaily, looking about him with interest. He seldom left the house so early. Only the mill workers were stirring. It would be hours before business houses would be open.

"Believe I'll get me a pipe," said Leo.

"Sure! And why not?" grunted Terry.

As they neared the mill, workers began calling Terry by name, exchanging morning greetings with him, and to each one Terry explained that Leo was his boy and was starting in that morning. The mill workers began to kid Leo and to give him jocose advice:

"Take it slow and easy; if you start in fast you can't last."

"Don't strain your milk."

"All you need is a weak mind and strong back."

"Don't forget to back up to the paymaster to get your check. I ain't had the nerve to look him in the face for six months."

"Listen, kid! Answer me this one: If a wood saw would saw wood, how much wood would a wood saw saw?"

"Which would you rather do or go fishin'?"

Leo felt better and more at his ease than ever as the group neared the gates. Others joined in the procession until, looking back, he saw men as far as his eye reached, most of the young ones shouting, laughing and joshing as they came. They jumped stiff-legged at one another, and punched one another lovingly and playfully with short jabs, losing their caps in the scuffles and shaking back their hair from their eyes. Leo thought he would enjoy this sort of combat after he became better acquainted.

The older ones shuffled along, sucking morosely at their pipes and spitting sadly into the wind. If they talked it was usually of the weather, which was going to be bad if the old men were authentic prophets. Leo noticed that almost every one of the older men had a finger or more missing and many hands were gone, dinner pails or jackets depending from the stumps.

The office was in a small frame building apart from the mill. A dozen men were clustered outside, pitching nickels at a line scratched in the cindered walk, while others sat flat on the ground, their backs resting against the building and their legs extending straight before them. Terry, with Leo in tow, pushed through the crowd and opened the door marked: "Superintendent."

"Here he is, Mr. Naylor," said Terry.

The heavy-jowled superintendent removed his glasses, blew on them loudly and moistily, then wiped them dry with a sheet of toilet paper torn from a roll on his desk. He looked keenly at Leo, who leaned against the door jamb to steady his quivering legs. Leo had a sick feeling in the pit of his stomach and he began to sweat from every pore.

"By God, Terry, he's puny! God! God A'mighty, man! Tell me the gospel now. How actual old is he?" the super cried.

"He's sixteen and over, may I niver slape on me wife's shirt tail ag'in if he ain't," returned Terry aggressively. "He's a mite light in the poop, that I'll own, but he's quick as a cat and strong as a bull. A little bull, anyhow. D'ye be expectin' John L. Sullivan fer six-bits a day?"

"Better turn out to be! Better prove to be! If I had knowed he was so spindly-shanked, I'd never hired him. Damn it, it's always this way when you hire a man sight unseen."

The three-minute warning whistle blew and Terry dashed off to his post. Leo felt injured at the super's slighting remarks about his size and probable utility as a hand. And he felt foolish, leaning against the wall, doing nothing, afraid to say anything, while the super rapidly leafed through sheaf after sheaf of typewritten papers, halting now and then to gaze intently at a sheet and to run his hand through his hair, causing it to stand erect in the manner pictured by a cartoonist as denoting terror. Leo ventured to clear his throat harshly. "Harrruump!"

Maybe I'm losing some money by not getting started on time, he thought.

It was nearing eight o'clock before the super sprang to his feet and started his swivel chair spinning like a merry-go-round. I'd like to have one of them things at home to make myself drunk with, thought Leo. He was thinking of a game that he often played with Robert: You spinned or turned rapidly until you walked unsteadily from dizziness and everything raced before your eyes in a mad and swinging blur. The boys called it "getting drunk." It would be much easier to sit in such a chair, propelling it with an occasional shove of one's foot.

"Come along, sleepin' Jesus," called the super, dashing for the door and shoving Leo through it into the hallway outside. "I ain't got all day to chaperon you around."

Inside the mill the whine of the saws, muffled and low in the office, climbed to a shrill screaming. The flashing disks were everywhere, catching and reflecting the light, and the fragrance of sawdust filled the dusty room, illuminated by wan bulbs that sent bands of light cutting through the whirling motes in the air. Leo had to jump to dodge hoodlum wagons, trucks with two large wheels in the center and a small one on each end, pushed by men with their heads down and their feet pressing hard against the floor. But the superintendent weaved through the trucks surely and swiftly.

He stopped beside a band saw. The operator, a concave-cheeked oldster wearing a skull cap, was tinkering with the machine.

"Here's your new disciple, Willie," roared the super. "He's too light for heavy work and too heavy for light work, and too damned lazy, by Christ, to do either. You want to initiate him good. Pour it to him hot and heavy; shove it in him to the red and make him like it or holler 'enough.'"

Willie nodded dourly, baring his tobacco-fouled fangs in a formal smile. Four fingers of one of Willie's hands were gone, and Leo soon discovered that Willie, when in deep thought, had a habit of placing his thumb, standing alone like the lone survivor of battlefield carnage, alongside his nose and resting his chin against the stub of his hand. In the weeks that followed he was to learn more of Willie's idiosyncrasies and ideas than he knew of his own father's, for he was forced to stand near Willie ten hours a day, tied as surely as though he had a chain riveted to his leg and locked to the machine. By a process of elimination, everything that Willie did or thought became of interest. He was the only living, moving object in a monotony as deadly as that of a prison cell.

Willie showed him what to do. Leo stood behind the saw and caught roughly-sawed gun-butts as Willie fed them into and past the whirring band. There were lines on the blocks to guide Willie in his sawing, and he leaned close to the band to see them. Leo wondered how he avoided getting his nose sawed off. Willie cautioned Leo not to let his fingers wander within a foot of the band. The noise of the saws made Leo drowsy, and it was not as much fun working as he thought it should be. It seemed a long time till noon, when he sought Terry and ate his lunch with him.

Terry was tending a row of the curing kilns. He had just opened one in which a number of walnut planks had been steam-cured for days. Steam billowed out in puffs and Terry was as wet with sweat and steam as if he had been ducked in a pond. He looks tired, Leo thought. So will I when I've had my nose to the grindstone as long as he has. Getting married sure puts a crimp in a working man. You can get plenty of good nooky if you know the ropes and not be tied to one piece all your life forever and ever; that's too long. He can say what he wants to, but a little bumming trip is more real education for a young man than he can get any other way.

The afternoon was better, and Leo began to feel lively as quitting time approached. For some reason he fell to thinking of Anna Leischer while he was planning how to spend his allowance. The two thoughts seemed to blend somehow, and he resolved to walk down to Happy Hollow and her playhouse if he wasn't too tired. Maybe he could take some gum drops or hoarhound sticks.

Then he began dozing and nodding at intervals, his head jerking forward as though it would snap off his neck. A sharp pain in his finger woke him fully. The saw had nicked him, and he was bleeding freely. Willie grimly halted the machine, cursed him dispassionately, told him where to find bandages and antiseptics, and fell to tinkering with the band. Willie was an old hand and knew how to simulate industry, working steadily away at nothing when there was nothing to do, to deceive the eyes of foremen or stool pigeons. The latter were harder to do anything with; one could never tell who they were.

CHAPTER NINE

"My gracious," Martha laughed, "that Leo is a sly rascal. The Epperson boy told his father about the playhouse Leo and that infidel girl have fixed up in the old Pollard place and Brother Epperson was saying something about it to me. Isn't that a caution? I'll have to tease him about that. Tell me all about it, so I can have him guessing how I found out. How long has Leo been going out there?"

"About a year. Since he started to work," Robert said.

"Fancy that, will you?"

Robert began to feel uneasy, for there was a badly-concealed tenseness in his mother's voice, and her mouth tightened now and then in spite of her efforts to keep it cracked in a grin.

"What about this loving? Was he hugging and kissing her out there like the Epperson boy said?"

Robert was sorry that he had admitted knowing anything about the playhouse. Everybody thought that Dogface was half-goofy anyhow. If I had only kept my wits about me, thought Robert, but she went at it in such a slick way, as though it was all in fun. He knew that he had unwittingly been helping to lay up trouble for Leo. It had all started when Dogface caught Robert and rubbed his face in a pile of cowdung until he told about the playhouse. Dogface had been attempting to follow the boys, but they always dodged him in the underbrush and among the hills in Happy Hollow. Robert could not stand having his face rubbed in the cowdung, and he told where the playhouse was, but he exacted from Dogface a promise that he would never say anything to anybody else about it or make an appearance at the house of The Hand. Fool that he was, he might have known that Dogface would never keep a promise.

"How about this loving? Did you see him loving her when you were out there?" Martha insisted, making no effort to appear casual.

"I didn't notice it."

"Oh, you didn't? Was he on top of her?"

"Ma'am?"

"Was he on top of her, I said."

"I don't know," Robert whimpered.

"Oh, you needn't try to story to me. I know all I need to know. That's what comes of a girl raised in a house where the word of God is never heard save in blasphemy and reviling. Mr. Leo will get the surprise of his sweet young life when he comes home from work tonight."

"Please don't tell him I said anything about it," Robert pleaded. It made him feel guilty to think of the many instances in which Leo had protected him and defended him, and of the 50 cents a week he gave him regularly out of his allowance of two dollars. Leo had been working over a year and was making ten dollars a week.

"Indeed and I will. If you don't want him to know his mean, nasty goings-on have been discovered, you're just as bad as he is. You can sin just as much in your mind as with your body, do you know that?"

Robert ran out of the house and away from Martha's steadily mounting rage against Leo and Anna. The sun was still high above the trees fringing the western sky. Robert's first thought was that Leo might thrash him. Then he remembered with shame that Leo had never struck him a blow worthy of the name. In fact, he could not, for the life of him, think of anything bad about Leo excepting his lordly air and his contempt for Robert's achievements at school, his ridicule of the verses Robert was always writing for school plays. It appeared that all the activities and attributes in which Robert excelled were considered as either useless or vicious by Leo.

Tortured by remorse, Robert ran on until he heard the

rattling of oak poles beneath his feet, and he realized that he was on the corduroy road in Happy Hollow. There was a caravan of gypsies in the camp, and as Robert loped past, fierce, lean dogs bounded from beneath the wagons and raced silently and ominously after him. He was terrified at the weird silence the dogs maintained. When they drew near, he could see their fangs gleaming beneath their curled lips and hear their low snarling. He looked about wildly for a weapon. A stout hickory cudgel, possibly discarded by a coal hauler who had been using it to gouge his recalcitrant horses, caught his eye. He stood his ground and struck out savagely at the foremost dog. It fell with a piteous yowl, regained its feet, and limped off on three legs, while the others turned tail and fled to the refuge of the wagons. Angry and gesticulating gypsies ran shouting toward him, and he sped on toward the haunted house, proud of himself and determined to tell Leo how he had routed the half-savage pack of gypsy dogs singlehanded. This was something that Leo could admire—something more important than making "E" in English.

He didn't know why he had come to the house of The Hand after he had arrived there. Nobody was about, and he had a creepy feeling that the house was haunted, indeed. Leo had bought some things to put in it—to brighten it up. Curtains for the windows, pictures for the walls, and other small articles that made the old house almost like a home, almost as though he might actually be Leo's and Anna's little boy. This was where Leo spent nearly every cent of the money Terry allowed him. Anna fried pork chops and wienies on the stove, and they ate real meals—better than the ones they had at home—tasted better, anyhow. Robert had seen Leo kissing Anna plenty of times, but never on top of her. He was telling the truth when he denied having seen that. He had never followed Leo and Anna into the "bedroom" part of the playhouse, and he couldn't figure out how Dogface had found out so much. Still, there were so many trees around, some of them rubbing their branches against the house and groaning like ghosts, indeed, when the wind was high and from a certain quarter. And there was the top of the porch, easily accessible to an agile climber, and plenty of cracks in the weatherboarding for the convenience of a peeping eye.

The more he sat thinking about it, about the good times the three had had together in the house of The Hand, about Leo and Anna—how jolly with him and good to him they were—all the more a realization of his meanness in telling Dogface about the playhouse in the first place weighed upon him. He winked with the first slow, hot tears, then cried unrestrainedly. He didn't know what to do in order to set right all the trouble he had brought on the two he loved better than any others, but he told himself that he should see Anna and let her know what had happened. But when he had traveled up the faint wagon road that bisected Butler Hollow and hesitated in the alder bushes at the edge of the small open space in which Kurt Leischer's cabin stood, he knew he could never face the old "infidel." "Infidel" was an awe-inspiring word in Green Valley, and everybody hated and feared the blasphemous German. All the good Catholics crossed themselves rapidly when they saw the tall, lean-faced atheist approaching. A bitter smile always twisted his lips, and his lower one stuck out aggressively beyond his thin upper.

There was nobody stirring about the two-room shack. Robert turned away. He felt that he could not bear to face Leo, for Leo believed that only the three knew anything about the playhouse, and he would have no doubt as to the identity of the traitor. In history he had been reading about Benedict Arnold—his fathomless degradation to which death would be preferable. Robert knew some of the bitter shame that must have galled Arnold's soul. If ever I get out of this, Robert thought fervently, I'll watch out that I don't put my foot in it again.

He slipped down the bank of the creek, honeycombed with muskrat holes. Everything he saw reminded him of Leo in some way. Here was the creek with its bright yellow sands piled into ridges by the high waters, and the small rills trickling between the water holes in dryer weather. In the water holes were the supple flashing minnows, darting into the refuge of brush tufted with leaves and mud, or under the rocks in which the water had patiently eroded holes by washing away gently at them for ten thousand years or more. The water had left a five pound catfish stranded one summer day, and the boys, wading through the water holes and leaving wet prints in the hot, dry sands between, came upon it. Robert dashed impulsively after it, and ran his hand under a rock to catch it when the fish fled to cover. The fish clamped down its horny mouth on his hand and skinned it badly. Robert felt giddy when he saw the blood. He sat down on the sand and bright spots floated before his eyes. It was Leo who leaped into the water and captured the fish. He told Robert that he could have escaped injury had he rammed his fist farther into the fish's body.

In the winter they trapped the muskrats who left the creek bank to forage in cornfields nearby, and the creek was interesting in winter, too. The pools were frozen solid at most times, but where the water flowed the ice was often white and there was a hollow space between it and the water. Under the clear ice of the pools the round white air bubbles from upstream floated or clung to the underside, white and shiny as silver dollars. Leo had a habit of pressing his foot above a stationary air bubble and causing it to break into smaller circles, moving under the ice to a new position. "Want change for this dollar?" Leo'd ask. "Here goes a quarter of it."

It was dusk before Robert reached the outskirts of Green Valley, and here and there in the sky a star popped out. The whim that he was a stranger here, that he had no place to go, possessed him. In his fancy he stalked the streets clothed in mystery and tragedy, like the Woman in Black who paid a visit to Green Valley each fall to peer sorrowfully into windows and to halt pedestrians for an intense scrutiny of their faces, then turning away with a bitter wail of disappointment. Robert dwelt so long on the idea that he was a lonely wraith that he became afraid of himself and the night, and started for home.

As he swung open the front gate, he heard the loud and angry voices of Terry and Martha inside the house. He stood irresolute, and the voices dwindled to an undertone of quarrelsome repartee. Robert sat down on the board sidewalk and suddenly his head began to pound and throb fiercely. He felt his brow, and it was hot; he fancied that it pulsed beneath his fingers. Maybe I'll take a fever and die, he thought, and then Leo will come and look at me in my coffin and forgive me all my trespasses. Since Martha had become a "saint" in the Holy Roller church, and had taken to quoting some scriptural passage about everything that came up, Robert found himself thinking in biblical metaphors. Martha had had the "power" three times in meetings at the church, and each time she had talked in the unknown tongue louder and longer, using more weird-sounding and jaw-breaking words than even Pastor Epperson had before. At Boone University she had been a brilliant student of Greek.

The front door slammed sharply, and before Robert could have made his getaway had he desired to leave the spot, Leo was at the front gate. He was shaking with great, throaty sobs.

"Leo!" Robert called timidly.

Leo walked on to the corner, where a street light was shining. Robert ran after him and caught his arm.

"Where you going, Leo?" Robert asked, trying to put in his voice the love and pity he was feeling for his half-brother.

Leo paused and turned his head.

"You dirty little snot," Leo said with low and intense resentment in his voice. "You got a nerve t' speak t' me after what you done. If I was you, I'd go and hide my head in a pile of cowshit ten feet deep and I'd never uncover it. I'd dive in it head first and let it smother me, that's what I'd do, you little fizzle-fart!"

"I'm sorry, bubber," Robert said, using a pet name he had had for Leo when he could not say "brother," and trying to convey somehow the shame and contrition he felt.

"A lot *that* helps! Who took up fer *you* with that no-account Dogface when he took the kitten away from you? Me and Anna tried our level best t' let you have as good a time as we did. Then you let that dirty Dogface know all about it. If you had t' be yeller-bellied about it, if you had t' squeal when he had you where the wool was tight, why in the name of God didn't you let us know that you'd told 'im? So's we coulda watched fer the sneak when he come snoopin' and peekin' around and I'd 'a' fixed him so's he'd 'a' cried ever' time he'd 'a' seen a winder 'r a knot hole afterwards."

"I didn't know he'd come out there. I never saw him out there," bawled Robert. "Honest to goodness, I didn't. And I was ashamed of myself for telling even before I got the cowdirt washed off my face."

"It's all the same, you little snot-nose. If I knew a secret like that, you could tear my tongue out by the roots and beat me in the face with it, you could burn out my eyes with red-hot irons, and I'd laugh in your face and say 'No, you got the wrong party if you think Leo Hurley will ever betray a friend.' That's the way I am."

He moved off down the street, as proud as an actor who has put a great deal of fervor in some dramatic lines and is anticipating the well-earned applause of the audience.

"Where you going, Leo?"

"None o' yer business, and I'm never comin' back. Take a good look at me, it'll be yer last, unlest. . . ."

"Unless what?"

"Unlest you tell what I told you about leavin'. If you do, I'll kill you some time when you're least expectin' it, even if I have t' dig my way up out o' hell. My mother was a Spaniard, and a Spaniard's nature is jus' like Indian nature, only a thousand times worse and crueler. They don't *never* fergit nobody that does 'em dirt, and they get him even if it takes a hundred years. See that you don't go shootin' off yer mouth about this. You got that straight in yer head?"

It was not the first time that Leo had threatened to leave home and to become a hobo, since, as he said, he knew all the tricks of the trade at first hand. Again he would bid Robert an eloquent farewell, darkly hinting that his minutes on earth were few, that the world was going to be sorry for the ill way it had used him when his mangled body was found on the railroad tracks. "All you got to do is to lay on the track, shut yer eyes, and the Kansas City Flyer 'll do the rest. It's all over quick and no more trouble ferever and ever."

Leo pressed on, and Robert did not attempt to follow him or to persuade him that he should not run away from home. "Don't humor him by running after him; he'll come back fast enough at meal time," Martha was wont to say when Leo would leave the house, shouting "Goodbye ferever!" as he slammed the door hard enough to shatter the glass. He *had* broken it one time, and Martha insisted upon deducting the price of a new one from his weekly allowance.

"He'll be back, and I'll be so good to him he'll forgive me," Robert thought comfortingly, as he opened the front door.

Terry and Martha did not quarrel often, but they were still at it. They were in the library, and Robert paused in the hall to listen.

"I have endured much," Martha said, "but I cannot and will not stand this. I wonder if this man who thought he could live without God is proud of his daughter now— a whore before she is a woman. 'The fool hath said in his heart, there is no God.' And as our Saviour said to the rich man: 'Thou fool, this night thy soul shall be required of thee, then whose shall those things be, which thou hast provided?' "

"I don't know about all them verses ye slip so aisy off yer tongue," Terry answered wearily. "I know that in me young days I'd 'a' done the same. Sure, 'tis not nachure if ye don't feel it, and when ye once get the idee in yer head ye can't rest day nor night till ye get it som'eres elset. Even the prastes must feel it, or the good Lord would not ha' fitted 'em out same as other men and all male bastes."

"You forget the holy bonds of matrimony. There is **a**

difference. God did not lose sight of anything or just leave things to chance, and if we obey His laws ——"

"Aye, I mind me 'twas the same way me old man talked. 'Twas one o' the raysons I tuk out afore I was fair dry behind the ears. 'Twas pray here and mass there and the old man damned careful to be on the safe side wi' the Almighty. Father Flynn says this and Father Flynn says that, and t'other, and the old man wurrkin' once in a great while but a-raisin' childer steady, and me old lady wi' a pot belly and tits like a haythen Hottentot—sure she could a-flung 'em over her shoulders and suckled a baby on her back—afore she was twenty-five. When she bellyached, the old man usta tell 'er: 'Och, 'tis you who should be a-complainin', when all ye had, me good woman, when I married ye, was yer arse and a prayer book.' 'Aye,' says the old lady, 'and if ye'd a-paid as much heed to one as t'other, ye'd have been Pope long since.' And so it was, with the old man a-mouthin' 'The Lord giveth and the Lord taketh away; bless ye the wurrks o' the Lord.' Aw, I don't know what t' make o' things. They's worse things nor what the childer done, that I know full well. And I'll not be the one t' be a-throwin' the first stone to'rds 'em fer what they got put in 'em by nature, or God, if ye will, and has t' be a-comin' out. No more should ye, if ye'll recall back ——"

"For my sins I have repaid ten-fold in tears and sacrifice," yelled Martha shrilly. "I know that sin has been taken away from me, and the desire for sin. 'Repent and be baptized every one of you in the name of Jesus Christ for the remission of sins and ye shall receive the gift of the Holy Ghost.'"

"The change o' life makes a lot o' difference in it fer a woman," growled Terry. "I'm goin' t' look fer Leo, and when I bring him back, ye'll not be houndin' him more. 'Tis an old man I am t' be a-takin' fut in hand and settin' out in the world anew, but it's not too late. Take heed o' that, madam!"

Before Robert could bound up the stairs, Terry was in the hall.

"Ye'll slape sound this night, I take it, after yer fine spyin' on yer brother. And now ye stand out here wi' yer ears cocked a fut wide. Little innocent fool, I hope ye learned something," Terry said coldly. His face was bleak, not even rage enlivening it, and the hump on his back looked as though it would never straighten up this time.

After Robert had been abed for three hours, lying awake, he realized with consternation that Leo had not been bluffing this time. He was actually gone. Robert was not used to sleeping by himself, and he was afraid. Martha insisted upon his reading the Bible, but he liked to pick his own passages, and he had chanced upon the one telling about Noah lying in his tent, soused to the gills, and how ashamed his sons were when they blundered into the tent and thus uncovered their father's nakedness. So ashamed that they backed into the tent, their eyes averted, and threw a rug or something over the old man for decency's sake. Robert knew how they felt, for he had unintentionally opened the kitchen door and had come upon Terry standing naked in a wash tub, sponging his hairy body. Terry was not embarrassed at all, but Robert felt that he had done something shameful and terrible. And now he felt that he had uncovered Leo's nakedness for Dogface and everybody else in Green Valley to stare at and wink at and nudge one another about. It had never seemed out of the way or wrong to Robert when Anna and Leo were making love in the house of The Hand, and he was finding it hard to understand the excitement the whole thing had caused. He wished that he could throw a blanket over Leo to shield him from Dogface and everybody else. He slept at last, and when he awakened in the morning he was still alone in the bed. He fell to crying again. He meant it when he said he wouldn't be back, Robert thought miserably. But he wasn't going to tell a word that Leo had said. He had done too much talking as it was.

CHAPTER TEN

After a week had passed without a word or a trace of Leo, Terry, too, became convinced that he would not return. Terry's attitude toward Martha and Robert became one of somber hostility. He went to his bed shortly after supper, and on holidays he spent the whole day away from home. Martha did not know where he went; she was busy with church work. The Holy Rollers met almost every night, and the conduct of Leo and Anna had been exhaustively analyzed according to the Gospels. Kurt Leischer was largely to blame, the chapter of Revelations disclosed. He called his housekeeper the Whore, and all this dovetailed with the theory elaborately worked out by Pastor Epperson after extensive labor with a concordance of the Holy Scriptures. Dogface had been a junior saint for six months, and it was because he thought it was his Christian duty, he said, that he had told his father all that he had seen going on between Leo and Anna. And Pastor Epperson knew it was his duty, albeit a painful one, to tell Martha about it.

Martha did not know that Terry had been going to Butler Hollow to see Leischer. Terry wanted to know if the infidel knew anything of Leo's whereabouts, but it turned out that Leischer had not known of his existence. Anna did not deny, when asked about Leo, that she knew him and had played with him in the haunted house. But she did not know where he was, she said; and, looking at her tear-filled eyes and her earnest, tragic face, Terry believed her. Leischer did not appear to be unfriendly, neither was he friendly. Each time Terry called, the Whore was washing dishes or sewing. She moved heavily about, her eyes downcast, and humility in her manner. Sometimes she raised her eyes for a fleeting second and looked at Leischer with the pathetic appeal of a dog who has been soundly beaten by a master it adores. If you could have melted half her fat off her, Terry thought, and turn back the clock thirty years, she would not be hard to look at. This was the coarse, oleaginous hull of what had been a rosy-cheeked, jolly German peasant girl.

Anna was often reading. One end of the room was filled with book shelves reaching to the low ceiling, and every shelf was crowded. Terry sat and smoked his pipe, feeling at ease, or as near at ease as he could with Leo gone. Leischer talked to him about the places Terry had seen, and said he had never been farther west than Green Valley, that he had lived in Germany when he was young and had come straight to Green Valley when he left there.

At times Terry thought sentimentally of how his own old father must have felt when he, himself, flew the coop so many years ago. He forgot that the old man had almost broken his arm with a barrel stave when Terry put it behind him to shield his backsides. And there were so many kids yapping in that shack from dawn till ten o'clock at night that the old lady must have felt more relief than anything else when they discovered that Terry was gone for keeps. He sometimes wondered how many more the old man had knocked out since he left.

Terry had visited the jungle almost every evening since Leo left, but he was discouraged when almost every bo swore that he had seen Leo and talked to him within the week, or even the same day. He had been right where Terry was standing not two hours ago, one bo told him. Terry asked about Leo casually, pretending that he had talked to him in this very jungle a few months ago, had taken an interest in him, and just wondered where he was and how he was faring. He said Leo had mentioned coming back through Green Valley some time. Leo was a great deal more handsome in his father's retrospection than he was in the flesh, and Terry was angry with himself sometimes when he gathered from the response of the boes that they took it that Leo was a pretty boy.

One day a bo replied to Terry's oft-repeated question: "Yeh, Dad, I seen a purty boy looked just like you say in the jungle outside Cinci. His jocker was waitin' fer 'im, hot as a hen layin' a goose egg, when I pulled in. Purty soon the punk blows in and he has mooched a lump. When the wolf untied the string around it and opened up the paper he squeaked: 'You little rat! Bring me back a bald-headed lump, will you? Robbin' the mail, eh? Where's the rest of it?' 'That's all I got,' sez the punk, and, bingo!—the jocker lays 'im out fer the count."

" 'Twasn't the one I have in mind," Terry cried loudly, springing to his feet.

"Oh, da'say not, Dad, da'say not!" agreed the bo hastily and soothingly. He had never witnessed the scene he described, but merely wished to be sociable and to tell Terry something that would interest him. The boes weary of talking to their own kind, and long to gas with rubes or home guards at times. And you can never tell whether one is going to take you home for a feed or not. If you talk agreeably, there is a chance. And it isn't hard for the versatile bo to invent stories to suit those willing to listen.

"It wasn't Leo," Terry kept saying to himself on the way home. But he wasn't a bit sure about it. His feet caught on the ties and his head sank lower than his shoulder blades.

After that he stayed away from the jungle.

Robert was unhappy at home, and in hot water most of the time. Since Martha had become such a fervent Holy Roller, she had renounced as too worldly her former ambition to make Robert a poet. She wanted him to get the Holy Ghost first of all, and then go forth into all the world and preach the Gospel to all living creatures. If he wrote, it must be to glorify God and his handiwork. Robert was still determined to be a poet or perhaps a novelist, but he could not conveniently avoid going to the Holy Roller church with Martha. Terry would never speak to him, and it embarrassed Robert to be alone with him.

It had been two months since Leo left home, and all this time his disappearance had been a godsend to Pastor Epperson. He had worked out no less than a dozen theories and opinions about the case, all of them well-documented by the scriptural proof. The church was packed at every meeting. The whole town was anxious to hear Dogface tell what he had seen in the house of The Hand, and this he did on several occasions. The saints groaned continuously and muttered "Praise Him!" or "Yes, Jesus!" as Dogface became more and more excited. At intervals, Pastor Epperson raised his hand in a majestic gesture of estoppel, and Dogface hushed as abruptly as a switched-off radio. This was done either because Dogface was getting out of bounds, or because Pastor Epperson wished to rivet an applicable moral with apt quotation from the Bible.

Martha had been after Robert to get up and testify, since younger boys and girls did so regularly. Robert was willing to admit that he loved Jesus in private, but he was not ready to get up and testify. He knew that half of the audience looked on either in amusement or contempt. Robert sat beside Martha, who, as yet, had taken no active part in the meeting beyond venting an occasional groan or a "Praise Him!" She nudged Robert as a ten-year-old girl arose, marched determinedly to the platform, and squared herself belligerently like a pugilist on guard and ready to take the offensive.

"I don't care who makes fun of me," piped the little girl. "I love my Jesus, and I tell everybody I meet—amen!—that I love my Jesus, bless His sweet name. Amen! Praise His holy name! He loved little children and He died on Calvary—Praise Him!—for me and for all little children, Hallelujah! And they can call me a Holy Roller if they want to, Amen! I just laugh at them—Bless Jesus!—I'm proud of bein' a Holy Roller, and I tell 'em they're not laughin' at me—Amen!—but they're laughin' at sweet Jesus—Praise Him!—and when they're roastin' and sizzlin' in hell and fire and brimstone and eternal torment—Amen!—and beggin' me for a drop of cool water to ease their scorched tongues, who'll be laughin' and makin' sport then?"

"Yes, Lord!" shouted the saints ecstatically, breaking into song:

> "Can't go to heaven on the dancing floor!
> *I'm gonna stay on the main line!*"
> "Amen!" "Blessed Jesus!" "Hallelujah!"
> "Can't go to heaven in a motor car!
> *I'm gonna stay on the main line!*"

Within the next few minutes, a good many of the saints sprang to their feet and began dancing, holding their arms above their heads and imploring the Lord to have His way with them. " 'Tis best to let Him have His way with thee," all of the singing voices agreed, some of them, however, carrying a mocking inflection. Dogface was sitting a few benches ahead of Robert. His eyes were closed, and he occasionally drew in his breath with a sucking sound, exhaling it with a "whoooeee!" ending with a staccato jerk of the head and body like an exaggerated hiccough.

When Dogface jumped to his feet and started dancing, he struck a lively gait from the beginning, but he did not attract as much attention as had formerly been his share. After a bit, he fell heavily to the floor, landing on his stomach, where he bobbed up and down unnoticed for a few moments. Some of the unbelievers, fools who came to scoff and never remained to pray save ironically, were snickering behind their palms at the way Dogface was doing, and pointing at him as he churned more rapidly.

Pastor Epperson was undecided as to the best course to pursue, for if he interfered with Dogface's oscillations this might be interpreted by the more orthodox saints as tampering with the will of the Lord. But the giggles swept the whole section of benches occupied by the unbelievers, and some of the saints were looking out of the corners of their eyes as they continued dancing. Pastor Epperson felt that the situation was getting unbearable, so he ventured to roll Dogface over on his back. But the giggles did not die nor did Dogface's gyrations cease. Pastor Epperson then laid hold of both Dogface's wrists and dragged his hands from his pockets, dropping them heavily on his stomach with a look that told him to leave them there. Dogface lay quiescent, a sleepy smile on his face.

As Pastor Epperson mounted the platform to deliver his sermon, he was thinking of the sensation he was going to cause by quoting chapter and verse to prove what should be done to Kurt Leischer.

"I used to get mad at 'em," the pastor said, with genuine tears in his eyes. "But, hallelujah! I don't any more. I pity 'em. God bless every scoffer. I pity every one of you poor ignorant folks out there that comes here to laugh and make sport. More can be done with love than hate any day in the week."

Pastor Epperson did not carry his Bible with him as he ranged back and forth across the platform, leaping upon the mourners' bench betimes. He had a reader stationed and posted in the audience, and when it became necessary to cinch a deduction or assertion with evidence from the Book, the pastor paused and called upon the reader. "And Jesus spake unto them saying—read!" At this, the reader arose and glibly rattled off the appropriate passage.

As Pastor Epperson gained momentum in his analysis of Leischer and what ailed him, Robert began to feel alarm. Leischer was inhabited by at least seven, and possibly more, devils, the pastor proved, and the way to get them out of the infidel was to take him down to the creek and to command the evil spirits, with proper ceremonies, to depart hence and go down into the water, and to plague the unfortunate man no longer. The pastor had never had any sort of luck in restoring eyesight or healing the lame by faith and prayer, and he was eager to try his hand at this new project, over which he had pondered for a long time and found absolutely fool-proof, for, as far as he could learn from searching the Scriptures, Leischer's part in the demonstration would be entirely passive. But to perform the healing feat, faith on the part of all concerned was a prerequisite.

Robert had suspected for some time that Leischer was hiding Leo in his house, though he had never been able to catch a sight of his half-brother about the place. On one of the first few occasions he had watched the cabin he had seen Anna walking in the yard, but he was afraid to say anything to her or to make his presence known. He hoped that she might come to the playhouse, and he waited there time and again. There was no indication that anybody had been in the place recently. The dust had settled so that he could write his name on every flat surface. He wrote: "I'm sorry, Leo. Come home and forgive me. Bob." The next time he came, falling plaster had obliterated the writing. The house was haunted in very truth now, and Robert could not bear to stay in it long.

One day he looked down into the well. The thought that Leo might be in there had weighted his mind, particularly at night as he lay alone in bed. He could see the white hand beckoning, the long fingers dripping and puckered, the pale wrist and arm descending into nothingness. Though he dreaded it and still half-believed in The Hand and its potency, he felt that he must have it over with or his mind would never be at rest. As he squinted down into the dark, he was terrified to see something resembling a head covered with greyish blue hair floating on the water. Obeying a mad impulse, he picked up a bit of rubble lying near the curb and shied it at the object. It burst with a soft "pouf" like the opened vent of a toy balloon as the stone hit it, and an overpowering and nauseous stench surged up and out of the well. It was a drowned rabbit that had chosen the wrong sanctuary from pursuing dogs.

Robert was sure that Kurt Leischer would not take kindly to the idea of allowing Pastor Epperson to exorcise the devils in his body, and he was afraid, too, that Leo might be in the infidel's cabin when the saints appeared to take Leischer down to the creek. The more he thought of the tragic possibilities of such an eventuality, the more uneasy Robert felt.

Before Pastor Epperson had finished his sermon, all the saints were positive that his plan would work, and there were cries that they should strike while the iron was hot and attend to Leischer that very night. The unbelievers were no less anxious, and joined their voices in the general hubbub. Robert sat fidgeting and sweating, his terror and misgiving growing every second. When a delegation of the saints set out to borrow some oil torches from the railroad round house, he edged unobtrusively off the bench and made his way to the door, past a group of juvenile saints who laid hold of him and tried to drag him back to the mourners' bench. He told them they had better let him go, since he had taken a big dose of castor oil that evening and could not stay in the room a minute longer.

Once outside, he struck a brisk dog-trot toward Happy Hollow; he knew where he was going, and was not in a panic this time. But as he plunged blindly along the corduroy road he remembered Leo's stories about the panthers in the brush. The tough oak and elm poles of the road had been worn smooth, and some of them were loose. Robert's feet made a terrific clatter, and more than once he stumped his toes and fell to his hands and knees, tearing his skin and barking his shins.

He was relieved to see a light in Leischer's window, and he set his course by it. His legs were lacerated by dewberry vines and his face lashed by the branches of trees he could not see in the dark. The moment his knuckles struck the door, he wondered why he had had the gall to come, but he could not turn back. The door opened wide and Leischer stood framed blackly in the flood of light from within.

"What do you want?" he asked.

"I want to see you, Mr. Leischer. Please let me come in," Robert panted. His breath caught in his throat with a sharp physical pain at each expansion and contraction of his heart. Behind Leischer, the shapeless bulk of the

Whore was planted. She wore a nightgown, and the kerosene lamp bracketed to the wall behind her silhouetted her body sharply.

"Come in, then," said Leischer, stepping aside.

"The Pentecostal people are coming to take you down to the creek and pray the devils out of you," Robert gasped, holding his side to ease the stitches in it. "They're coming tonight."

"So?" chuckled Leischer grimly, pinching his lower lip between thumb and forefinger. "I must thank these good people for their solicitude, but my devils I have with me a long time, and they are like members of the family."

"They say you're not yourself as long as the devils are in you, and they aim to take you whether you want to go or not. For your own good, they say. They say you'll be a changed man once the devils are out of you. They say the devils caused the trouble between Leo and Anna."

"Anna! Anna! Ah, yes!" cried Leischer, losing his cynical coolness and becoming animated with rage. "They need have no fear of my devils bothering Anna. Anna is gone from home a week now."

"Anna gone? Leo is gone, too. I thought maybe he had been here."

"No. I have never seen the lad. I don't know where she is gone. She said nothing; left no message. So it should be clear to the good saints that my devils can be of no concern to anybody save myself, and . . . and . . . this. . . ." He jerked his thumb toward the woman.

"I don't see why they have to cause Leo and Anna so much trouble," bellowed Robert.

"Trouble? Trouble! You know what causes trouble, my boy? Wait! I show you. I show you."

He stepped swiftly across the room and clutched the neck of the woman's nightgown. She stood passively, with a vacuous smile on her thick lips.

"There was a young man in Munich," said Leischer, "who was a lover of beauty and knowledge. A poet, he liked to call himself. Some people called him a genius. He was a young man, and—most of all—he was a fool. I tell you why. He gave up his friends, his profession, his family, his country even. For what? For this. . . ."

With a savage jerk he ripped the woman's nightgown down the front, and her flabby body, unhealthy and spongy looking as a toadstool in a dark cellar, emerged. Robert felt the same horror he always experienced when he ripped down the shucks of an ear of green corn to disclose a wrinkled white worm eating at the kernels and peppering the silks with its pellets of excrement. The woman stood docilely, her heavy freckled hands limp at the ends of her arms, not attempting to conceal herself. Her lolling breasts, corded with blue veins, the folds of her stomach, and the dark coarse growth beneath, the rubbery pallor of her flesh, like that of a fish's belly, were fixed on Robert's mind for a long time to come; and each time the thought of her recurred he experienced anew the sick distate that swept him when the garment was ripped from her.

"For this. For what a cow also possesses," Leischer continued, with more weariness than anger now. "Now it is all I have left; not even a daughter."

The woman calmly picked up her ripped nightgown, which had fallen around her feet, and walked into the other room. The skin of her hips was rough and red as an elbow. Then the creak of springs told that she was abed.

"You may go, my boy," said Leischer. "I shall assure the saints that I cannot consider parting with my devils."

But when Robert had opened the door and looked out into the black night, he hesitated. It had been bad enough in the excitement of coming here, but now he was tired and lame and his legs were badly skinned. He did not feel like running home, and he was too scared to walk slowly. He felt that he would begin running in spite of himself if he heard any noises in the brush.

"They'll be here after a while if they're coming," he said, "and if you don't mind, sir, I'll slip out and catch up with them when they leave. They won't know but what I've been with them all the time."

He was not a bit sure that the Holy Rollers wouldn't

take Leischer to the creek forcibly, but he decided to wait. Before an hour had passed the sound of faint singing could be heard. Leischer opened the door and the voices swelled:

> "The fight is on, O Christian soldiers,
> Face to face in stern array,
> With armor gleaming and banners streaming,
> The right and wrong engage today."

The smoky torches flared, and the saints huddled in a knot, a little skittish now that the objective was in plain sight. The unbelievers stood at a discreet distance behind, but with eyes fastened on the house, not wishing to miss anything that might develop.

Pastor Epperson stepped out of the mass and walked steadily and gravely toward the square of light in which Leischer stood.

"Kurt Leischer!" cried the pastor. "I come to you with a heart overflowing with love, and in the name of God, the Father Almighty, Creator of heaven and earth; and in the name of Jesus Christ his only son, our Lord, who was conceived by the Holy Ghost, born of the Virgin Mary, suffered under Pontius Pilate, was crucified, died, and was buried. The third day he arose from the dead, ascended into heaven, where he sitteth at the right hand of God, the Father Almighty; from thence he shall come to judge the quick and the dead. . . ."

Leischer stood listening politely, with his hand behind his ear.

"And if I by Beelzebub cast out devils, by whom do your children cast them out? Therefore they shall be your judges.

"But if I cast out devils by the Spirit of God, then the kingdom of God is come among you."

"My dear friends," Leischer said. "I don't want to see my devils driven from their warm and comfortable home in my bowels into the cold water. We have been together so many years now, and parting would be too much sorrow for either of us to stand. So, peace go with you, men of God. I serve another master. I am Faust! Do you hear that? Perhaps you have heard the name before. No? I sold my soul in Munich long ago."

He said this in a bantering tone, but at the terrifying words a low moan of horror burst out among the saints.

"That's not the man speaking, but the devils residing in his poor earthly tenement," called Epperson to his disciples. "Let us now with brotherly love and tenderness but with firmness proceed with this unfortunate wretch to yon creek."

Only a few were willing to come closer. Leischer reached slowly above the door and lifted down a shotgun resting on wooden brackets. As he raised the gun to a horizontal position, saints and unbelievers alike ran frantically in all directions save toward the house.

"Stop! Stop! Don't let the devils put murder in your heart," yelled Pastor Epperson over his shoulder.

The shotgun boomed, and echoes pealed back from the hills. Leischer pursed his lips and blew the smoke out of the barrel with a blast like that of a hunting horn. Howls of fright and excited inquiries could be heard for a moment, then only the cynical chuckles of Leischer.

"I was firing at the moon; no lower," he laughed. "You'll never catch them, my boy. I'll escort you out of the hollow."

"No, sir, you needn't," said Robert. He feared Leischer more than the dark and all it might conceal. He plunged into the night like a swimmer reluctantly diving into water he knows is cold and deep. The rear ranks of the invaders were not far away. Some of the unbelievers were laughing openly at the discomfiture of the saints. The saints themselves were convinced now that Leischer was indeed possessed by devils, but the job of ridding him of them was for divine rather than human hands.

Terry had given up the idea that Kurt Leischer knew anything about Leo, and he didn't see any reason for visiting him again. But a few weeks after the saints had been stampeded, Green Valley was electrified to hear that the Whore was dead—that she had killed herself with an overdose of laudanum. Leischer had come into town to tell the authorities that he had no money with which to pay her burial expenses. This surprised nobody, for the mail carrier had not delivered a letter from Germany for almost a year.

"I have no way of disposing of the body," Leischer told the mayor. "It is too heavy for me to lift, and I can no longer dig holes in the ground. Moreover, I believe there is a law against doing this without a permit. So I shall have to ask your assistance soon, since the carcass is beginning to stink."

Of course, nobody cared much whether the Whore lived or died, and those who believed that Leischer had poisoned her took only an academic interest in the affair. The problem of finding a place to bury her was of a great deal more moment. It did not seem proper to bury her in the woods, and no church congregation felt like allowing her to be planted among people who had led a righteous life and had kept the faith. Somebody happily remembered the Hunky graveyard at Squirrel Knob, where the diggings had played out fifteen years before. The colony of Hungarian miners was no longer there, and not a plank of the frame houses in which they had lived remained on the spot. Some of the boards were nailed to the sides of corn cribs as far as two counties away, others had fallen flat on the earth and crumbled into brown dust. But the graveyard was still there, and none of the Hunkies were left to protest about the Whore being buried there. They were an easy-going tribe anyhow, always playing accordians and dancing, drinking, and eating; plenty of the girls had been whores, and some of them were buried in the Squirrel Knob burying ground.

Terry decided to visit Leischer once more. He had heard that Anna was missing, too, and he felt sure that she had followed Leo. It turned out that Leischer did not know where Anna had gone, or at least he professed that he did not. Terry had imagined that Leischer might have been getting letters from Anna. No, Leischer said, he had been getting letters from nobody, nor did he want any. He sat listlessly in an armchair, the room in incredible disorder. Dishes with rotting food in them, and the tables fouled with mouse turds. Books were flung all over the floor, and from most of them all the leaves had been ripped. Leischer told Terry that he did not want to talk to anybody.

"I have been trying to cut my throat," he said, "but my pocket knife is too dull and my hand too unsteady." There was a small cut on his throat, but Terry thought it must have been nicked by a razor in shaving.

"Why don't ye try a razor?" said Terry contemptuously, as he stepped over the door sill.

Terry had walked a short distance from the cabin when Leischer shouted at him.

"See! This time I'll not fail! Success!" he screamed, swiftly and surely slashing his throat with a razor he held. He was gurgling triumphantly when Terry reached him.

Unbelievers to this day can give you a very logical explanation of the miracle of Kurt Leischer's grave. Grass will not grow on it. The unbelievers will tell you that the men filling the grave grew tired of worrying with the sticky clay that clung so tenaciously to their shovels, so they filled a good part of the hole with slag from the Squirrel Knob mine dump nearby, even though they had to walk a hundred feet to get it. It makes fine shoveling, but nothing will grow in it. The saints think differently, of course, and it is a fact that no sprig of anything green had ever rooted on the mound. The pine headboard at first bore the words: KURT LEISCHER, died 1915. Nobody knew when he was born, nor did they even know the Whore's name, whether she had another name or not. It would have seemed indelicate to put an obscene word on a grave, so her grave was marked: GERMAN WOMAN, died 1915.

There was such an obvious moral involved in these

deaths that Pastor Epperson could not let his opportunity pass by. He had practiced with a narrow paint brush for a long time and was quite adept. His handiwork could be found on ledges of rock and on barns flanking the highway for miles around Green Valley. "God Is Love," "Surely, I come quickly," "I am the root and the offspring of David and the bright and morning star," "Read Acts, 2:38," and others sprang out in bold and rather neat white letters in many places.

But Pastor Epperson's best job was at the graves. He used four colors and spent three days in producing a real work of art. On the Whore's headboard he wrote: "These shall hate the whore and shall make her desolate and naked and shall eat her flesh and burn her with fire." And on Leischer's: "But the fearful, and unbelieving, and the abominable, and murderers, and whoremongers, and sorcerers, and idolaters, and all liars shall have their part in the lake which burneth with fire and brimstone."

He did not use the old, knotted and splintery headboards already at the graves. He planed two very smooth oak ones that not only would last a long time but would provide a fine surface for the brush.

PART TWO: *THE GREEN DRAGON*

CHAPTER ONE

After he had changed trains at Blair and boarded the special to Probstville, Robert grew more alert to what was going on around him. He screwed around in the seat each time the coach door opened, trying to label every newcomer. Some were alumni bound for Homecoming Day at Boone University, others were students. There were also distinguished-looking men Robert knew to be members of the faculty. Farmers in cowhide boots clomped through the car, catching from seat to seat as the coach swayed. Robert was sensitive about his clothing, and he hoped that he looked like a student.

"How's everything at school?" asked the conductor as he punched Robert's ticket.

"Fine!" answered Robert. His happiness and excitement increased. It was a gray and nasty day; smoke from the engine whipped back along the windows. In the fields, flocks of crows rose up from corn shocks and the frozen furrows and flew away as the train approached.

"I beg your pardon," said a dark man with a Van Dyke beard, tapping Robert on the shoulder. "What is the name of the bird I see in such numbers in the fields?"

"Crows," stammered Robert. "Crows."

"*Crows!* Ah, yes! Thank you. Crows," said the dark man, moving down the aisle. There was a slight foreign accent on his tongue. He's a professor from some foreign country, thought Robert. There are famous scholars from all over the world at Boone. Robert's happiness at the conductor's mistaking him for a student gave way to disgust at himself for his awkward and embarrassed answer and the dark flush that came over his face when some stranger addressed him unexpectedly. He could always think of a suave reply after the event had passed. Students were reading from fat, stoutly bound text books, laughing, bantering, singing college songs. A quartette of alumni a few seats ahead drew together in a football huddle and began singing:

> "Yes, we'll e'er revere thee, love thee,
> As we brave life's stormy sea.
> Duty's ear shall ever hear thee,
> Dear old Varsity!"

As they heard the song, a good many of the men in the car joined in. Robert was proud now to think that his mother had written the song, and wondered if some of the alumni in the car might not be classmates of hers.

"If that song ain't a pain in the rectum!" he heard somebody say behind him. "Comrade Abraham, I'll even join you in singing *The Workers' Flag Is Deepest Red* if it'll drown out that ditty. Come on, Sol!"

"You surely are a great comedian, Al. You're a scream. You put stitches in everybody's sides when you're in your stride. The life of the party; Alan Vass, the boy terror of Traders' Alley, diving head first from an eighteen-foot ladder into a tank of solid concrete, playing the ukelele, eating raw liver and keeping perfect time! Ten cents, the tenth part of a dollah! . . ."

Robert turned around to see the two. Sol was a short, sturdy Jew, flashing his white and even teeth in a smile as Robert turned. He was dressed very shabbily, and his black curly hair clustered in tufts below his hat. He could never get the earnestness entirely out of his eyes, and he made almost everybody uncomfortable, though he tried desperately to make friends with all the people he knew or met.

The moment Robert saw Al he liked him, and he felt that Al was the sort of fellow whose acquaintance he should like to make. Al's face was not handsome, but it was an intellectual face, Robert thought. Alan Vass' nose was too long and his eyebrows were shaggy and black. His lower lip rolled out and the corners of his mouth turned down in a perpetual satiric quirk. He, too, wore his hair long, but it was not ragged and unkempt like Sol's. At the back it fell squarely upon the neck of his sweater with the big yellow B. U. across the chest. Alan was smoking a long-stemmed and expensive-looking pipe, his fingers wrapped around the bowl. He exhaled smoke rings with an air of philosophical detachment that Robert admired and envied.

"Wait! They're getting out of breath. I spoke too hastily, Comrade Abraham. What about those lowing hinds out there in the cow pastures? Aren't they sad specimens of capitalistic exploitation?"

"Keep it up if you get any good out of it," said Sol. He turned his head and stared out at the fields, now and then drawing closer to the pane in order to see something more clearly.

The singing had died down now; some of the alumni were joshing one another and passing flasks of hooch from seat to seat. Others among the visiting grads sat sternly erect and would not touch the liquor, nor even pass it. The news butcher came through the car crying: "Seegars, cigarettes, candy, latest magazines. . . ." He was a pimpled, sallow youth wearing thick-lensed glasses, and he wasn't having much luck. He paused by Robert's seat and plumped down beside him with a crafty and ingratiating smile on his face.

"Ain't no women back here, is they?" he asked, raising his glasses to his forehead, and peering up and down the length of the coach.

"No," said Robert. "Why?" He wondered what the fellow was driving at.

"I got some hot numbers here," said the news butcher, drawing a card from his inside coat pocket and shielding it so that only Robert could see. "You look like a sport. I sell a lot of these to the college boys that's quit believin' in the stork."

It was the first French postcard that Robert had ever seen, and he could not take his eyes off it, though he was ashamed to look at it too ardently.

"Right from Paris," continued the news butcher. "I take plenty risk handlin' 'em. Got a pack of ten I sell for a dollar. Really by rights oughta charge ten, but quick turnover, small profit, satisfied customers, that's me all over. Live and let live. Wha' d' ya say, sport?"

Robert knew that it would be absurd to spend a dollar for such things, and it would be wicked, too. But he could not bear to think of missing the chance of having ten of such pictures where his eyes could get their fill of them. Except for the unpleasant memory of the Whore, he had never seen a woman's naked body since he and Leo had lain on the hill and watched the gypsy women in Happy Hollow.

Holding his hand low, Robert passed the boy a dollar bill without saying a word. The news butcher slipped a sealed envelope into his hand.

"Don't open 'em till I'm out o' the coach, will ya, sport?" asked the boy. "Open 'em in the terlet if you can't stand the pressure. Might come in handy bein' in there, anyhow, eh?" He poked Robert in the ribs. "I'm layin' myself liable. It's a penitentiary act, and that's the God's truth."

He picked up his basket and walked rapidly out of the car. Robert waited for a while, the envelope resting like a living body inside his coat pocket, burning against his breast. Then he rose to his feet and made his way to the compartment stamped in flaking-off gold: MEN. He lurched from seat to seat, mortified that he could not walk as surely as the other passengers. He was not accustomed to riding on trains, and he was awkward at best.

As soon as he heard the lock of the toilet door click,

Robert was tearing at the envelope. The first card he drew out was *Leda and the Swan,* a dim reproduction of a painting. As he shuffled the cards rapidly, Robert saw *Venus Arising from the Waves, September Morn, Diana,* and *Adam and Eve Banished from the Garden of Eden.* He had seen some of these pictures in books in his grandfather's library, and some a great deal bolder. All the front views were impeded by leaves or convenient tresses, or the whole thing was so indefinite that Robert considered himself defrauded and outraged. No telling how many had been lured by that teaser the boy carried. Robert's first impulse was to raise a row with the slicker, but almost instantly he realized the futility of this. He'd know better next time. It wasn't the first time he'd taken the bait under, hook, line and sinker. He was looking sheepish when he returned to his seat. Alan Vass smiled quizzically in his direction, and Robert felt that he knew all about what had happened. Sol was still intently regarding the countryside as it slid by the coach windows.

If Robert had found in the envelope what he expected, the loss of the dollar—which he could hardly spare—would not have grieved him so. But along with the knowledge that he had been made a fool of came the thought that God had punished him for his carnal lusts. Every time he awoke in the night after dreaming of women and was repentant to find that he had sinned in his sleep, he asked God to take this terrible yearning away from him. That's unfair to God, though, he thought. Look how Jesus was tempted when Satan took him up on the mountain height and showed him the kingdoms of the earth. By resisting temptation we gain in grace. But Robert didn't know what to do about it when it happened in his sleep. He had never become a Holy Roller, although through all the ten years that had passed since Leo ran away from home Martha had begged Robert to let the Lord have His way with him. But Robert could never bring himself to the point of dancing and shouting. He just did not feel it within him, and he would never become a Holy Roller till he did.

What he wanted most was a college education. He wanted to get away from the sawmill and the men who worked in it; he wanted to explore the world his mother had once known and in which his grandfather had moved. He had worked after school in stores, delivered papers, carried out ashes, and mowed lawns in the summer and shoveled snow in the winter. He did everything he could to earn an honest dollar, or a quarter or dime or nickel, and in the year and a half since he had graduated from high school he had saved seven hundred dollars of his wages as a clerk at the sawmill. He didn't intend to enter the university until the next fall, but he was eager to see the place his mother had talked about so much, and he took advantage of the Homecoming Day excursion rates to spy out the land.

He was in a penitent and melancholy mood, and he flattened his nose against the cold window pane and wished the brakeman would come through the car calling: "Probstville! All out for Probstville!" He would be glad when the rest of the winter and the next spring and summer went their way, for then he would be out of the house that had never been the same since Leo ran away from home. Robert had heard a song or read a story somewhere with the name: *The House of Too Much Trouble.* When Martha and Terry were at outs, Robert would often murmur to himself over and over: "The house of too much trouble!" Martha was trying to get Terry to stop smoking and to attend the Holy Roller church, and he would do neither. He often said bitterly that he had nothing to work and slave for, anyhow, and that one fine morning she might wake up and find him gone and she'd never clap eyes on him again. Sometimes at night when he was dozing in the library, he'd spring to his feet when a knock sounded on the door and would run to see who it was. Terry would never acknowledge that he still expected Leo to come home some day, but Robert knew that he did. Terry never spoke to Robert unless he had to do so, and then only briefly and coldly, though he had never charged

Robert anything for his board when he was saving to go to the university.

Robert could not believe that Leo was dead. He had searched every inch of territory around Happy Hollow and had crept back into some of the old drift mines calling, "Leo! Leo!" He remembered that Leo had once said a man could live in one of the old mines if he wanted to hide from the police; it would be a good place for an outlaw den. At times when Robert felt strongly that the Lord would answer any sort of reasonable prayer he promised God that he'd spend the rest of his life preaching the gospel if He would only reveal where Leo was or what had become of him. And when the waters in the creeks were boiling yellow in the spring, he'd seal a note to Leo in a bottle, throw it into the current, and imagine it bobbing downstream into the Chariton, into the Missouri, into the broad Mississippi, the Father of Waters, and perhaps into the Gulf of Mexico and into the ocean, seeking Leo out wherever he might be, even in a foreign land.

While Robert re-created the past ten years of his life against the background of flying cornfields and pastures and farmhouses along the right of way, the alumni fell to singing again. Alan and Sol began talking. Robert's attention re-entered the coach, and his admiration of Alan increased when he saw that he was reading the *Atlantic Monthly*. Robert had seen every issue of the *Atlantic* from June, 1876, to February, 1906, in the library at home, and he wondered what it was like now. But Alan did not read the magazine long. He threw it down with a snort of contempt, and drew a green-backed one named the *American Mercury* from his hand bag.

"The *Atlantic Monthly* may have reached the change of life as far as I'm concerned," said Alan. "It's never lost its virginity, never been raped by the mad bull of modernism."

Sol did not answer him. He pressed close to the window again, watching the gray sky, the earth beneath, and the farmhouses with children standing in the yards and waving at the train.

The door at the opposite end of the coach flew open and the news butcher fled down the aisle shouting: "Charlie! Charlie! Hey, Charlie!" Behind the boy a stout man lunged from side to side, propelling himself along by pushing against the seats.

"Stop, you little thief!" yelled the fat man, his rosy face as angry as it could get. "Give me back my dollar, or I'll chase you clean into the engine and off the cowcatcher!"

The news butcher was pulling ahead, but when he reached the door he could not open it immediately, and his pursuer collared him.

"Give me my dollar! Fork it over!" ordered the fat man.

"I don't know what you mean, boss. I ain't got no dollar of yours," protested the news butcher, his glasses and his cap falling to the floor.

"Oh, you ain't, hey? Maybe this'll improve your memory!" He jabbed the cowering boy viciously in the face and the blood squirted. Robert saw a bright fleck land on his shirt front.

"Oh, Jesus!" howled the boy. "Somebody help me! He's killin' me! Charlie! Charlie! F' God's sakes!"

The fat man was husky and he had enough liquor under his belt to make him nasty.

"Maybe somebody wants to take it up," he sneered, looking up and down the coach. "Maybe somebody else wants some of it."

"I do," said Sol. He pushed past Alan and squared himself in the aisle.

"Why, you little snot!" bellowed the fat man. "You Goddamn sheeny! I'll sock you so hard it'll jar your grandfather Isaac in Jerusalem. I'll slue that hook nose around so's you can smell the back of your head."

"Come on, then."

Something about Sol's professional stance and his cool assurance told the fat man he had better let well enough alone. Sol was short, but he was well muscled and moved with easy grace.

"Don't go off half-cocked, young fellow," said the fat man, more quietly. "I maybe shouldn't 'a' hit him, but he did gyp me out of a dollar. You know yourself how crooked these fellers are. Have to be to get by."

"Sure!" said Sol, quickly. "Don't be so hard on him then if he's not entirely to blame."

"There's a Marxian moral involved here," said Alan. "Quote him Chapter Ten, Paragraph Eight, of the Revised Statutes of Marx, Sol, and you'll make a convert of him."

By this time the brakeman was in the car.

"Hey! What's going on here?" he asked.

The news butcher was sitting in a seat and stanching his nose. He had recovered his glasses and cap.

"I could 'a' handled him all right myself, Charlie," he said, "but I lost my glasses. Ain't worth a damn without my glasses. Can't see an inch ahead of my nose."

"I don't want no trouble, brakie," said the fat man, "but he knows damned well he gigged me out of a dollar. If he don't want to give it back now, I got my hands tied as far as takin' it out of his hide's concerned. But when the train pulls into Probstville, I know how to make it plenty hot for him, and don't you believe I don't."

"What about it, Benny?" asked the brakeman. "Don't you think the best thing to do is to give him the dollar?"

"Hell, take the dollar," said Benny, handing the fat man a bill. "I wouldn't go to no law suit nor mess with no John Law over a measly bone."

"You're wise, cocky," said the fat man, pocketing the dollar and moving out of the coach.

Robert could not feel much sympathy for the news butcher. It had never occurred to him that he might browbeat the boy into returning the dollar without revealing his own prurient interest in what the boy was professing to sell. The fact that the fat man had recovered his own dollar by bold action convinced Robert that he could have done the same. I'm as green as I look, he thought miserably.

Alan was kidding Sol.

"In this corner, ladieees and gents, Battling Solomon

Abraham, the Soviet terror. And in this corner, Kid Capitalism."

"Keep on! Keep on!" muttered Sol. "I wasn't going to see him smashing that spindly kid. Not a fat-bellied guy like that. Even if the kid did gyp him out of a dollar. . . ."

"He did," Alan said earnestly. "Those fellows are all crooks. You'll be in hell all your life, kid, if you try to straighten out the troubles of people that don't deserve it. The sooner you quit trying to take care of the world's grief and woe and attend to your own, the better off you'll be. I'm not worrying about people that are not worth worrying about."

"No use in going over all that again."

> "The troubles of our proud and angry dust
> Are from eternity and will not fail.
> Bear them we can and if we can we must.
> Shoulder the sky, my lad, and drink your ale."

Robert liked the way in which Alan quoted this, and when he thought that the train would be reaching Probstville within a short time and he might never get a chance to see Alan or talk to him after this meeting he felt as though he faced an imminent and final parting from an old friend.

"I wonder what time we get into Probstville," said Robert, turning his face squarely toward Alan.

Alan shot a quick and keen look at him, as though asking, "What's your game?" But Robert's face was guileless, and Alan smiled cordially.

"In a few minutes, I should think," Alan answered. "Look! There's the dome of Academy Hall."

He pointed to a bulbous dome roofed with gray slate and surmounted by a glittering gold ball visible through the window. Robert felt a queer fluttering and smothering sensation in his breast now that he was actually nearing the place he had pictured to himself so often, and which had been described to him by his mother time and again before she became such an ardent saint. "The wisdom of man is but foolishness in the sight of God," she often told Robert when he spoke of the university. "If your education will help you to win the world for Jesus Christ, then it will be a blessing. Always remember that, and never open a book or go to a class without first kneeling at the throne of God in prayer to ask Him to help you to go into all the world and preach His gospel so that they who believe in Him may not perish but have life everlasting."

"I've never been there, but my grandfather, Professor Marcus Anthony Darrell, was a professor at Boone University for years and years," said Robert.

"You don't say!" Alan was hardly interested. "Why, we use Darrell's *First Principles of Narration* in Composition and Rhetoric class. You're not starting at the second semester, are you?"

"No. I want to come down next fall. Just came down on the excursion to look around."

"If you don't know anybody there, go over to the room with Sol and me, and we'll show you around a bit. Won't we, Sol, old bolshevik?"

"Sure," said Sol. Robert liked Sol's looks when he showed his large white teeth and his eyes sparkled with animation.

"Sol's a bolshevik. Got his pockets full of bombs," went on Alan. "Say! This is Sol Abraham, my room-mate, and I'm Alan Vass. We're both from St. Luke, that big wicked city on the Mississippi."

"Glad to know you, fellows. Mine is Bob Hurley, and I hope to be a freshman next fall."

The three shook hands solemnly.

"What was that verse you quoted a while ago about 'shoulder the sky, my lad, and drink your ale?'" Robert asked. "I like that a lot."

"Housman. I like Housman, too. Davidson is great stuff. Ever read Davidson?"

"No, never did, but often wanted to." Robert was ashamed of his ignorance of all the modern literary currents. The library at Green Valley was a very poor one, and he could not afford to buy books or magazines.

Alan groped in his bag and brought out some volumes bound in limp leather. "Quite a conglomeration," he said. "Strindberg, O'Neill, Cabell, Schopenhauer, Rabelais, Voltaire, Thomas Paine."

He spread the books out on the seat and felt in the bag again. He drew out a very handsomely bound book with the title *The Heart's Desire*, by Gareth Shallore.

"Here's something Sol and I feel a personal interest in, I guess," Alan said. "It's by a fellow named Gareth Shallore, the editor of *Caliban*. He's written about a dozen books. He hangs out with the rest of us down in Traders' Alley at the Green Dragon, a bohemian joint where all the painters, poets, writers and damned souls of St. Luke congregate. This book of his is taken from Omar. That is, I mean, the title is. You know the verse that goes something like this:

> 'Ah, love, could you and I with fate conspire,
> To grasp this sorry scheme of things entire,
> Would we not shatter it to bits, and then
> Remold it nearer to the heart's desire?' "

"Shallore's real name is Abner Harris," Sol told Robert, smiling a little wryly. "If he wasn't worth plenty of coin, his verse would be called lousy. He's able to pay to have his poems printed, and he can put 'em out in million-dollar shape. Abner Harris wasn't a fancy enough handle for him after he felt the call of the Muse, he said. He felt as though he *must* write poetry, beauty burned so madly in his breast."

"Horsecollar!" scoffed Alan. "You're just jealous because he won't run any of your revolutionary 'Arise, ye prisoners of starvation' crap in *Caliban*."

Robert was looking at the book, "issued from the Caliban Press at the sign of the Green Dragon, St. Luke, MCMXXIV, in a first limited edition of five hundred copies, each signed and numbered." On the fly leaf was the inscription: "For my dear friend and fellow-disciple of the Muse, Alan Vass, whose feet are sturdily trudging up the rugged slopes of Parnassus. Gareth Shallore."

It was as pretty a book as Robert had ever seen, and the verse was good, too, he thought. Some of it was as good as Kipling or Robert W. Service.

"Do you write poetry, too?" he asked Alan. He was glad that he had become acquainted with such an interesting and clever fellow.

"A little. Haven't done anything yet that I think is worth a damn, but Gareth is always after me to do something for *Caliban*. Let's see. Here's the last issue."

Caliban was a handsome magazine, and the illustrations were gay and sophisticated, printed on excellent paper. Robert could not understand some of the verse. It lacked punctuation, and even the words were scrambled and misspelled, making the poems look like some of the hideous scrambles found in the *Green Valley Sentinel* after Andy Wallis, the compositor, had been feeling high from a few slugs of hooch. Near the back of the magazine Robert saw a poem by Alan Vass: *Crucifixion*, which ran:

> "Oh, Christ, the ribald soldiers casting dice,
> The rabid rabble's obscene revelry,
> All this was bitter, but I hold it naught
> Beside the pain that strikes when shifty lies
> Must meet the eager question in young eyes.
>
> Oh, Christ, the rugged road to Calvary
> Was hard. I, too, must pay my price."

"Did you write this?" Robert asked. He was surely glad that he had decided to speak to Vass, and it seemed to him that the Green Dragon must be an interesting place where one could meet the sort of people worth knowing.

"Oh, that!" said Alan with assumed diffidence. "Ain't that the ungodliest crap? I wrote it for a joke, and Gareth nabbed it for *Caliban*. I threatened to sue him if that ever got into print."

"Like hell!" said Sol Abraham. "He groaned and sweated over that for two weeks. He couldn't work in 'putrid,' 'Gargantuan,' 'asinine' and 'buttocks,' but he'll put 'em in the next one or die the death of a dog."

Robert could see that Vass was sore about Sol's remarks, and he tried to smooth it over by saying nobody knew, he guessed, how much work went into the simplest poem that took only a moment to read. Nobody but a poet could understand. He had written a few verses himself, none of them good enough to publish, but the judges in a high school contest had been foolish enough to award him first prize, an Eversharp pencil, for a poem about the Unknown Soldier.

"Have you got it with you?" asked Alan Vass.

"Oh, no! I'm too ashamed of it to pack it around. I hope nobody ever sees it again."

"It couldn't be any rottener than some of Sol's revolutionary doggerel. Talk about putrid stuff! It stinks on ice. . . ."

CHAPTER TWO

The train was pulling into Probtsville. It slowed down, alarm bells clanging at the crossings, and aged watchmen creeping from their shanties to hold out perfunctorily a red flag. This gave Vass an opportunity to get a rise out of Sol. He pointed to the lowered safety gates and at the watchmen and their flags. "Look, Comrade Abraham," he said, "the barricades in the street, and the red flag waving. . . . Workers of the world, unite! You have nothing to lose but your chains; you have a world to win. . . ."

The train passed by the rear yards of hovels, dismal with rotting trash and gray washings flapping on the clothes lines. Then the more prosperous section of squat bungalows and paved streets with young trees not large enough for shade, then straight for the business section, with the university buildings rearing beyond.

As the train shuddered to a stop, Vass picked up his calfskin bag and Sol drew from under the seat a papier-mâché old-fashioned suit case. It looked so shabby and out of date that he had been hiding it there.

"Come along, Hurley, if you want to," said Vass. "We'll show you the campus."

The red-capped baggage-smashers were crying: "Take yo' bag, suh? Lion Hotel, suh! Bus leavin' right now." It had turned colder, and when he saw that almost everybody else had an overcoat, Robert wished that he had worn his old one, even though the plush collar was shiny and the mouths of the pockets greasy and soiled. In spite of all he could do, his lower lip began trembling with excitement and cold. He caught it in his teeth, but thought that this would appear silly, too. Down the street, to the left, he could see the tops of the university buildings above the trees, with Academy Hall high over all. Sol Abraham had no overcoat, but he had a heavy short mackinaw jacket warmer than Robert's thin coat. Just the same, Robert would have been ashamed to wear it. It looked out of place; it didn't look like the kind of clothes a college student should wear.

The streets were wide and arched with trees. Squirrels were running about, and nobody bothered them. If this was in Green Valley, thought Robert, some of the sawmill hands would get out their shotguns and go hunting right on the streets. Then they came to the business section with bookstores and haberdasheries displaying smart-looking collegiate clothing in the windows. The bookstores were bright with the jackets of new novels and books of verse, and Robert would have liked to stop for a while, but Vass and Abraham hurried along, past the Varsity Theatre, the Varsity Grille, the Varsity Cleaning and Pressing Parlor, the Y. M. C. A. and onto the campus. The concrete paths wound among the ivy-covered buildings and were bordered by neatly trimmed privet hedges. When Robert saw the name "Darrell Hall" across the façade of a building, his eyes began to water in the absurd way they had when he was overwrought or overjoyed about something, and his knees felt wabbly.

The dormitory room of Sol and Alan was comically small, but it was strewn with books and papers and the walls were decorated with pennants. After Sol and Alan had taken off their outer clothing, Alan opened a bureau drawer and pulled out a bottle of colorless hooch.

"How about a snort?" he said. "It's aged in the woods and bottled in the barn. It's all right. I always uncork the bottle, shut the doors, and leave the bottle set for an hour or so. If it doesn't peel the varnish off the furniture, it's harmless for man or beast."

Robert had never drunk any liquor before, but he didn't want to appear a sissy. He had heard that a sudden swallow would always make an inexperienced drinker sputter and cough, so he sipped very slowly and cautiously and managed very well. He liked the warm feeling that crept through him. Sol took a small drink, and Alan made the bottle gurgle several times before he lowered it.

Alan had a number of magazines Robert had never heard about. Some of them were poorly printed, full of typographical errors, and thin, but others were fat, embellished with cuts, and set in artistic type faces. Robert picked up one named *Joybells*.

"That's the prize!" snickered Alan. "Published by a virgin school teacher at Orris. Look what she says in the *Just Between Us Folks* column: 'Which of our gallant riders of the noble steed, Pegasus, has a birthday next month? If you do, send in a quarter and your name will be published here. Maybe you'll get a shower of birthday greetings from your fellow poets and poetesses, and, who knows, some disciple of the Muse may be inspired to indite an original poem in honor of the occasion.' Talk about putrid crap! It stinks on ice! Well, there's a reason for all this. If the poor girl had been seduced twenty years ago, *Joybells* wouldn't be with us now. Here's *Spectre*. Pretty decent stuff on the whole, not bad at all. Here's a story by Danny Maupin. Daniel Stark Maupin, you know. You've heard of or read his *God Rest You, Merry Gentlemen*, haven't you?"

"I've heard of it, but I've never had a chance to read it," lied Robert, who was becoming more and more aware that he was completely ignorant as to what was important in contemporary literature. Daniel Stark Maupin must be rather important, and he had never even heard of him.

"Here it is. Damned good stuff. Danny was in Paris for a year, and knew all the Latin Quarter bunch there." Vass opened the book so that Robert would be sure to see the autograph: "For my friend and fellow lecher, Alan Vass, the Casanova of Traders' Alley, the Don Juan of the Green Dragon. Daniel Stark Maupin."

"Oh, you know him well," Robert said.

"Why, sure! Known him for years, since grade-school days. Little half-pint runt, like an owl, has to wear blue glasses and can't see a foot ahead of him when the sun's shining. But when the shades of evening gather, when that evening sun goes down, if you'll pardon the poetry, he wakes up and gets out amongst 'em. Can drink more liquor and stay on his feet than any other man in the Mississippi Valley. If you're ever in St. Luke, be sure to come down to the Green Dragon. I'll give you a knockdown to all the local literati and so on. . . ."

"I surely will. It's pretty dull in Green Valley, you know. Only mill hands and coal miners and farmers and woodchoppers. I'll be glad when it's fall and I can leave that burg. For good and all, I hope."

"Ever see this?"

It was an anthology: *The Year's Sheaf, 1924,* edited by Shelley Hale. Somehow, Robert knew that Alan Vass would have a poem in it, and so he did.

"A lot of pretty putrid stuff finds its way in there," said Alan apologetically. "Hale is pretty well respected, though. His anthology always pulls some good reviews."

"This looks like a fine collection," Robert said. "I wish I was good enough to get in it."

"I've got a couple of extra copies. I'll give you that if you'd like it."

"Oh, say! That's too much of a good thing. . . ."

"Don't be too thankful," said Sol. "He's got plenty of 'em. He had to buy ten copies in order to get his poem in. Might as well unload 'em on you as anybody. And its gets good reviews because a lot of newspaper reviewers fondly imagine they can write good poetry, and you'll find most of them in *The Year's Sheaf.*"

"Listen to the dog in the manger," said Alan. "Try to get some of your 'comrades, make haste to the barricades' crap in it, and see how fast it comes back."

"Yeh, because that wouldn't be 'art' to some of the fat rich dames and pansies that have plenty of rhino and are generous with it. And because I haven't got twenty bucks for ten copies, and wouldn't buy 'em if I did."

"There isn't much sale for poetry of a serious kind," Alan said. "And plenty of successful authors print their own stuff, or pay to have it printed. Upton Sinclair does, and so does Bernard Shaw, they say. I heard that Robert Frost paid to have his first book printed. Nothing wrong about buying a few copies to support the venture. It's a co-operative press."

Robert was proud of the anthology, and he felt that Sol must be a rather churlish sort of fellow, probably jealous of Alan's superior talent.

"If we're going to show Hurley around, we'd better do it," said Sol. "He'll want to see the parade, of course."

"No hurry," said Alan. "Sol's a great little guy," he told Robert, "but he mistakes fever for poetical fervor, and heat for eloquence. I'm for heat in its right place, but to serve as a good subject for poetry, heat must be below the waist."

Robert thought this was a rather clever thing to say. When they reached Academy Hall, alumni and students were grouped about, craning their necks toward the dome. Most of the older grads were talking angrily about the report that the university authorities were going to raze the dome as unsafe. A crack, zig-zagging like a lightning bolt, ran down one side of the dome. A young man, sleek and groomed like a bond salesman, pointed his cane toward the crack.

"But that's a menace to life and limb, Pater. The whole thing will come crumbling down about the ears of some of the art students some day. I remember how that dome used to creak and groan even when a little breeze sprung up, and even old Jennings, who tried to teach us Art Appreciation, deaf as a post, took alarm and dismissed the class early on several occasions. Not only that, but the bally thing is an architectural monstrosity. Looks like some of those onion-shaped protuberances that make the skyline of Moscow hideous." The young man had been a Rhodes scholar, and affected Oxford accent and mannerisms.

"Poppycock!" fumed the old man, his blue-veined red cheeks puffing out like those of Boreas exhaling on ancient maps. "That crack was there away before *your* time, young fellow, me lad. To raze that tower, with the sacred memories of years clinging around it like a hallowed shroud, would be an act of vandalism, pure and simple. Repair the tower, aye! Restore it to its pristine magnificence. I'll be the first to sign a check to help to do that. That golden sphere atop the dome has glittered in the suns and amid the storms and tempests of many, many years; the heart of many a son and daughter of old Boone, journeying from afar to stand once more in her classic halls, has leaped to see that the old tower stands serene and unchanged by the tooth of time. My campaign to restore, not raze, the tower is gaining headway. I have this day in the name of the Boone Alumni Association sent a cablegram to President Allison in Vienna, demanding that this despicable act of vandalism be nipped in the bud. . . ."

"Oh, I say, Pater! Had no idea you felt so strongly about it," said the young man, half seriously.

Sol and Alan were smiling at the absurd burst of oratory, but to Robert it was all very impressive. He felt a keen personal interest in the old man's campaign, and hoped that it might be successful in forestalling the proposed razing of the dome. Robert's heart warmed as they walked from building to building. "My brow seems tightening with the doctor's cap, and I walk gowned," he murmured happily to himself, cocking his head upward as they passed beneath the arch erected as a memorial to Boone students who died "that this nation, under God, shall have a new birth of freedom, and that government of the people, by the people and for the people shall not perish from the earth," according to the inscription.

"Well, that's about all," Vass said when they had seen the new stadium.

"Maybe he'd like to see the university farm, and the herds of cattle," Sol said.

"Not everybody's as goofy about farming as you are, kid," said Vass. "And it's a long way out there, and the parade's about ready to begin."

Robert cared nothing about the farm, and he could see

plenty of cattle in Green Valley. He preferred the company of Alan Vass to that of Sol Abraham, anyhow.

"Well, I promised mother I'd look up some places she used to know," he stammered. "And the train leaves at two."

"I believe I'll walk on out there, then," said Sol. "See you in the fall or before, Hurley. Glad to have met you. See you later, Lord Tennyson," he said to Alan.

"Same to you," said Robert. "See you in September; maybe before. But I'm not rich enough to make a trip down here every week or so. If you ever get to Green Valley, look me up."

"Sol's a great little Yid," said Alan as he and Robert walked toward the campus. "Christ! He's had a hell of a time. His old man's a plasterer, and doesn't work half the time. House full of kids, and all that. No wonder Sol's bitter and wants to turn the whole system topsy-turvy. Jesus! I feel sorry for the little guy. He's white as they make 'em, and a pal for true. He'd go through hell and high water for me. His clothes are always impossible and he never has a date. And living in the city all his life has made him crazy about the farm and growing things and all that. He'd give his right arm to be a farmer. But who ever heard of a Jew farming? Thinks he's a poet, too. If he was writing for dung, he wouldn't get a smell. He doesn't know how to tell poetry from propaganda, and those two elements are like oil and water. You can't mix 'em and do any sort of a decent job."

By the time they reached the campus the parade had started. First came the prancing drum major, mincing along with feminine movements of his hips and handling the baton with deft grace.

"Look at that Goddamn fairy, Ralph Gibson," said Alan. "Look at the way he shakes it up. He's tried to make every freshie on the campus. Bunch of 'em took him out and knocked a couple of teeth down his throat, and you know what they claim? That the next night he came right back to the house where they roomed, and stood across the street and waved at 'em and hollered: 'Yoo hoo, boys!

I'm afraid of you, but I'm not mad at you!' He makes a good drum major, though. He's got the motion. Got an Elgin movement for true."

The snare drums gave a long roll and the brasses burst forth. The singing voices of the graduates immediately behind the band rose in an effort to rise above the music:

> "Yes, we'll e'er revere thee, love thee,
> As we brave life's stormy sea.
> Duty's ear shall ever hear thee,
> Dear old Varsity."

Robert was afraid that Alan would sneer again about Martha's song, and, since going about the university, Robert had begun to feel a great renewal of tenderness for his mother. She had once had a part in all this, and an honorable and distinguished part, too. He thought sadly of her ambition to be a writer and how it had come to naught, of her present fanatical behavior.

It seemed that only the older graduates sang Martha's song seriously. The students bellowed it with about as much seriousness as the unbelievers sang the Holy Roller songs in Pastor Epperson's church in Green Valley.

"Here come the engineers," said Vass. "They're always scrapping the lawyers. Kidnapped the belle of the lawyer's ball last fall and took her clear to Orris and kept her all night.

"What did they do to her?" asked Robert, with lively interest.

"Oh, nothing. Just held her prisoner till the ball was over."

The engineers came by singing:

> "Saint Patrick was an engineer, he was, he was!
> Saint Patrick was an engineer, he was, he was!
> For he invented the monkey wrench
> That screwed the lawyers to the bench. . . ."

> "The engineers
> Have long ears

And live in caves and ditches.
They whack their socks against the rocks,
Those hard-boiled leather britches."

"They have different words for 'socks' and 'leather britches' when there ain't too many faculty members around," Alan said. "Well, it's about over. I guess you'll be wanting to look up the places your mother asked you to."

"Yes. I've surely enjoyed myself today."

"So long. See you soon, I hope. Say! Why don't you write me a letter now and then and tell me what's going on in Green Valley. About some of the rustics, the woodchoppers, and so on, there. I'm trying to whip a novel into shape, and Danny Maupin has promised to speak for me to his publishers. I'm not going to hurry with it, but if you know any good characters or run across any good dramatic situations or can remember any, let me hear about 'em."

"I will. I'd like to hear from you, though I'm not much of a letter writer, I guess."

Most of the houses and places Martha had asked Robert to look for were no longer to be seen. There was a filling station on the corner where she had roomed, and the church she had attended had been razed to make a place for the Varsity Theatre.

There were only a few people on the train going back to Blair. The coach seemed like a tomb and the trainmen silent-footed mourners tiptoeing among the dead. The news butcher hurried through the coach when he recognized Robert, and he did not return. Robert opened one of the books that Vass had pressed upon him as a loan, to be returned next fall, *The Age of Reason,* and found it so interesting that he was surprised when he heard the brakeman bawling: "Blair!"

CHAPTER THREE

During the remainder of the winter and through the spring and summer Robert received many letters from Vass, and wrote many in return. Robert had bought a second-hand typewriter, and was trying his hand at verse. He had not sent any of it out, but he knew it was better than some of the tripe he had seen in *Joybells* and *The Muse's Throne*. But, he decided, he might as well aim high to begin with and try to turn out something good enough for *Caliban* or *Spectre*.

In one of his first letters Alan Vass wrote:

"Dear Hurley: I am not surprised that you were shocked at *The Age of Reason*, for religion is one of the most pernicious and insidious foes of science and knowledge. Did you know that the church has fought every forward movement of history? You ask me what the atheist has to offer in place of religion. If I were to cut away a cancer that was eating your flesh off your body, would you ask me to put something in place of it? Or would you be content with getting rid of it?

"You say that man has to believe something. That's baloney, too. The less you take life seriously, the better off you'll be. And don't try to learn too much.

> 'For, sweet, to feel is better than to know,
> And wisdom is a childless heritage.
> One pulse of passion, youth's first fiery glow,
> Are worth the hoarded proverbs of the sage.'

"I'm a bum quoter from memory, but that's Wilde, or something like Wilde, and it's true as the gospel is supposed to be. Read Schopenhauer. He says we are never happy, really; we merely get a respite from being unhappy now and then, and pain is the prevailing motif of existence. We are like silly lambs gamboling beneath the watchful eyes of the butcher. Pain is, I really believe, the object of existence. Why isn't a tooth just a bone without a jumping nerve in it to raise the devil with a fellow? And women have their flanks torn open in giving birth, when the Almighty, if he exists and gives a damn about what happens to his children, could just as well have equipped their bellies with a flap to unbutton at the proper time. . . .

"Sol just came in from the farm, wet as a dog. He's been helping milk out there, and he likes it! They pay him a little, too. He has to work around at odd jobs betimes, and then has to cram like hell to make his grades.

"And now may the grace of our Lord and Saviour, Jesus Christ, etc.,
Alan."

And at another time:

"Dear Robert: You're damned right I am interested in hearing about Monty Cass and Kurt Leischer, too. They'd both make swell stories, but, after all, Cass was more or less a nut. He was just as absurd as people who make a fetich out of Christ, or Marx, as Sol does. 'God is a lie, hope is a whore, and a flea has more for his labor than a man.' Hope you read *The Shadow Eater*, by de Casseres. But to return to Leischer. He's the kind of man that sticks above the herd like a mountain peak, because he refused to live a lie or to give in an inch to Christian hypocrites. We all do more or less. I mean give in. I don't want to make a martyr of myself; I haven't any yen for martyrdom. But I can admire guts when I see them. Monty Cass died because he believed in some union leaders who were just as corrupt as capitalists, and as avaricious, by Christ. The have-nots are just envious of the haves, and that's a fact. I'm going to write a novel about Leischer and call it *The Unvanquished*. And whenever my time comes, I hope

I'll have the guts to step resolutely into the dark just as he did, without any whining or begging for mercy. Tell me more about him. Shakespeare says: 'Cowards die many deaths before their time; the valiant never taste of death but once,' and it's true. When you come here in the fall, you'll have to help me get that novel started. Danny Maupin has a great pull with Noel and Lassiter, and—who knows?—we might put you across, too.

"Sol will get his tail canned out of Boone yet. He's always making cracks in history and sociology classes, and the instructors hate his guts.

"Well, as Saint Calvin puts it, have faith in Massachusetts, have faith in Mother, in the Home, our firesides and the virtue of our women, and in

> Yr Obt Svt,
> Alan."

Before the summer had gone its way, Robert was doubtful about a lot of things he had always believed in. Alan Vass mailed him books and magazines and wrote him long letters. It seemed that Alan had an answer to all the feeble arguments that Robert put forth.

"Dear Bob," Alan wrote. "You say there must be some kind of plan or 'urge' behind a universe as orderly as the one we live in. Maybe there is, but forget the picture of good old Jehovah sitting on his gold throne with stars twinkling in his long white beard and the sun for a lamp. And I think the 'urge' is the kind that impels cats to fight and yowl at night and the studes here to go down by the abandoned ice house for a rendezvous with some of the beauteous Negro maidens. One fellow here likes 'em so well that he won't look at a white girl unless she wears long black stockings.

"The reason the Holy Rollers didn't hurt Leischer was because he was too brave for them. He was a lion roaring at jackals, and they tucked their tails and slunk away. Christians are like a wolf pack. They'll attack only in numbers and only when their adversaries are at a tremendous disadvantage. Did you ever read Shelley's *Queen Mab?* Goes something like this in one place:

"I was an infant when my mother went
To see an atheist burned.
She took me there.
The dark-robed priests were met about the pile;
The multitude was gazing silently.
And as the culprit passed with dauntless mien
Tempered disdain in his unaltering eye,
Mixed with a quiet smile, shone calmly forth.
The thirsty flames crept round his manly limbs,
His resolute eyes were scorched to blindness soon.
His death pang rent my heart. The insensate mob
Uttered a cry of triumph, and I wept. . . .
'Weep not, child,' cried my mother, 'for that man
Has said there is no God!'

"Probably misquoted as usual, but what the hell. It's a true picture of what the Christians would do today if they dared.

"Now, as to this poem you sent. I don't want to be ultra-critical, but Jesus X. Keerist, it's not so good. That last stanza:

'Oh, gypsy hearts like mine can never rest,
And, though my feet to distant shores may roam,
My heart must always wander toward the west
And to the humble cottage she calls home.'

"This shows you know how to put words together, but don't turn the sentiment on full force. Gareth Shallore is sentimental as an old maid, too, but he's a damned good poet, and such a swell and generous guy that you can forgive a lot of it. Any writer that is hard up can always depend on old Gareth for an X or even a XX. He's rich, but he's a Socialist, and is always paying some striker or radical out of the hoosegow. A wonderful chap in every respect. The Green Dragon could never pay the rent if it wasn't for Gareth, and *Caliban* never has enough subscribers to pay the printer. Gareth makes up the balance out of the old sock. . . .

"A hell of a stiff criticism showing one's faults is better than a lot of soft soap. Danny Maupin made me sore as a boil when he ripped the stuffing out of some of my stuff. But I thank him for it now. Don't get discouraged about the poem. Why don't you write one about Leischer? There's a good subject for you. If it pans out in satisfactory shape, I'll send it to Shallore and ask him to run it in *Caliban*. It's hard to make *Caliban*, though. Lots of the big-pay writers would give their right eyes to get into *Caliban*.

"And if you think your stuff is punk, you should see some specimens of Sol's 'revolutionary' dithyrambs.

Auf wiedersehen,
Alan."

Robert did not think his poem was so punk, and he was disappointed that Alan did not like it better. He had had a notion that Alan might send it to *Caliban* and get it printed. He knew that "pull" had a great deal to do with literary success. Robert was encouraged to think that Alan was of the opinion that a good poem might be written about Leischer. When he thought of the present amount of his disbelief in religion and other things he had accepted before he met Alan, Robert was a bit horrified. The seeds of doubt and skepticism had thrust radicles into his mind and were growing vigorously. At first he was afraid to say anything about books in his letters to Alan, but as he grew more familiar with Alan's tastes and prejudices, he learned to frame his letters accordingly, and then he was gratified when Alan praised his discriminating taste and developing awareness. A little nettled now at the criticism of his poem, Robert wrote Alan to ask him why he admired Christ so much if he felt such a bitter contempt for his church, and reminded him that Alan's poem "Crucifixion" in *Caliban* dealt with Christ in a sympathetic way.

"Christ was all right," Alan answered. "Christ was a

good scout. You know, he was always hobnobbing with whores and the down-and-outs and defending them. You should read Upton Sinclair's *They Call Me Carpenter*. If Christ were to return to earth today, he'd be thrown out of the church built in his name so fast it'd make his head swim."

As the hot days of summer were passing and there was a whiff of crisp breath of fall in the air of the early mornings, Alan's letters kept coming from St. Luke, telling about the high old times in the Green Dragon, and what Gareth Shallore or Danny Maupin had said about this or that. It made Robert feel good to know that he had found a friend who could be of some help to him in winning a literary reputation. He felt that it would mean a great deal if he could only get a poem in *Caliban*, for other editors would surely notice the poem and perhaps ask him to send some of his work to their magazines. Or, at least, they would read the poem and remember the name of Robert Browning Hurley the next time they saw it.

CHAPTER FOUR

Robert had everything packed and ready for his trip to Probstville, and he and Martha were spending the last night together in the library. Terry had gone to bed early, and he apparently did not care where his son went or what he did. He would not speak to Robert if he could avoid it, and when he looked at him it was with a level cold scrutiny that always reminded Robert of the night Leo left home.

"You think mother's old-fashioned, don't you, son?" asked Martha, drawing her chair close to Robert and laying her hand on his knee. "You'll find people at Boone who don't believe in God any more. It's a fad that smart alecs have started. But you'll always do the clean, manly thing and never be ashamed to confess your love for God and your allegiance to Him. Mother wants to read you a passage from an essay by Dr. Pusey about the temptations thrown in the way of intellectuals."

She ran her finger along the backs of the books in one of the cases and took out *A Fireside Garland of Choice Literature*. She read:

"Every gift of God has its own special temptations, and intellect has temptations more like those of Satan than of mankind. Others forget God, ignore God, steal away from Him, rob Him of their hearts, and give them to the world. But they do not come face to face with Him. The temptation of intellect is to measure itself against God, to criticize God, to dispute His being, to dethrone Him in His creation, to set up His laws against Himself, to question His providence, to doubt His wisdom, to pull to pieces His revelation, to mend it for Him, to make conditions with Him on what terms it will acknowledge Him, to require Him to abdicate His absolute sovereignty, to set up an idol in His room; to re-create their Creator instead of being 're-created by Him in Christ Jesus.' And yet withal they often mean, poor things, nothing less. They have got loose from the old beliefs in God; they have lost all knowledge of things supernatural, nay, even of their own external existence. Yet some of them have gifts which might be used to the great glory of God if they would but cease to measure by their own created intelligence the mind of the uncreated, which conceived theirs, and of which theirs is but a little spark. These, and especially at the universities where intellect has often not yet taken its side—either to be willingly beneath God or to be against Him—would be a special subject of prayer that they might find their wisdom in the uncreated wisdom and their knowledge from the Omnipotent."

Robert sat listening to Martha, trying to look solemn and attentive, but he could not help reflecting sadly that the stultifying effects of fanatical religion were here demonstrated. Martha had ceased to take any pride in the house her father had left her; she worried no longer about the condition of the shingles or the cracks in the weatherboarding. The wooden pilings beneath the center of the house had sunk or decayed and scrub water always ran toward the wall nearest the middle of the building. Of the fence around the yard nothing remained save the two-by-fours to which the pickets had been nailed. The pickets had fallen off or had been jerked off by mischievous boys or Halloween pranksters long ago, or more than likely Terry and Martha had yanked a good many of them off for kindling wood. The place was looking so seedy all around that nobody could be proud of it any more, and Robert would be glad to get away from it. In the library the books were going to pieces; every time one was opened carelessly the binding cracked and leaves fell out. The worms and insects were playing havoc with many of the volumes. Martha was looking ahead to her future in heaven and didn't care much how the house looked or how she looked, and Terry was living in the past when he was a roistering young buck, drinking and whoring, and when he had had Leo with him for what now seemed to him a precious little while.

Dr. Pusey's treatise seemed utterly banal to Robert, but he looked as piously impressed as he could while Martha was reading it. He did not see any reason why he should precipitate a storm by running counter to any of Martha's notions as long as he was in her presence. He knew that he could never believe in orthodox religion again since his eyes had been opened by Alan Vass, but he had a vague idea that he could hide his disbelief from Martha as long as she lived. Martha walked across the room to her desk, and came back holding an envelope sealed with wax. She was smiling wistfully and sniffling and gulping so that her red Adam's apple moved up and down. Robert felt sorry for her, but he could not help thinking she looked silly.

"There's something in this envelope mother wants you to read one month after you get to the university," she said. The envelope was addressed: "To my dearly beloved son, Robert Browning Hurley, hoping that these words will help him to conduct himself in a manner befitting the grandson of Professor Marcus Anthony Darrell." "I know that you'll follow this counsel," Martha said, "and I shall never worry about you."

"I'll read it, and I'll go by it," Robert said, kissing her on the forehead. "Don't you worry about me. I'm going to make something of myself."

Robert heard Terry opening the front door, and it occurred to him that he should make some sort of gesture of farewell, whether Terry regarded it kindly or not.

"I guess you'll be gone when I get up, dad," he said as he stepped into the hall. "And I just want to say good-bye and good luck and take care of yourself." His smile was as forced as one in a toothpaste ad, but Terry was tremendously moved. He had always wanted to be closer to his younger son, but he had never known how to manage it. The men at the sawmill complained that Robert was stuck-up, and Terry could never forget the unadmirable part he had played in the events that led to Leo's running away from home. But now that Robert was leaving home, Terry could not forget that he—no less than Leo—was his son.

"Good-bye! Good-bye! Good-bye, me boy!" said Terry heartily, grasping both of Robert's hands. "And ye'll be lettin' the old man know how ye navigate, eh?"

There were tears in Terry's eyes, and before Robert could stop himself he was winking and sobbing and had thrown his arms about his father.

"I'll never quit being sorry for the dirty way I did Leo, dad," Robert said. "You don't know how much I've worried about that and laid awake and wished I could go in his place and let him come back. I don't believe Leo's dead, dad, and if he's on this earth I'm going to hunt and hunt till I find him and beg him to come back to us."

"I wish I could think the bye's not dead," said Terry. "Wi' so many old shafts open around the woods, and the bye runnin' heartbroke through the woods. Aye! Maybe we'll niver know. Ye did a dirty trick, 'twould not be I would be after sayin' ye didn't, but that's past and gone, and the water that flows under the bridge niver comes back. Jist you try t' be a man and when ye git yer fine edjication, don't think ye know it all. Ye should know that the men at the mill they think ye're a snob and ye think ye're better than common wurrkers. Maybe ye jist didn't notice yer uppity ways; maybe yer mind was on yer books. I hope ye'll niver see the day ye be ashamed that yer father wurrked wi' his hands."

"Why, I want to be friendly with everybody," said Robert. "I just guess my mind's been too much on my books." But he did not intend to seek companions among such men as worked at the sawmill. He was thinking about the talented crowd at the Green Dragon, of jolly nocturnal bull sessions in the dorms with keen-minded studes parrying thrusts, matching wits, disposing of the profound questions of sex and literature, and of that ultimate glorious day when the chairman would say to a distinguished audience: "And now, without further ado, I want to introduce to you a man who needs no introduction, a man whose name and work is known wherever good literature is known and discriminating readers are found. I take the greatest of pleasure in introducing that celebrated poet, Robert Browning Hurley."

But he was feeling soft and sentimental, and now believed that he must have nourished a great deal of latent affection for his father all these years. He promised to write to Terry regularly, and he did so for three weeks after he had enrolled at Boone. After that he found it difficult to spare the time.

CHAPTER FIVE

"Is everybody here? Don't let any of the worthy candidates escape," said Hotstuff Blake. "Step out here in the moonlight, worthy candidates, so we can look you over."

A group of twelve freshmen came out of the shadow of the abandoned ice house and into the moonlight. Hotstuff peered into each face. "Where's Bauer? Lost his nerve, I guess. Well, too bad for him. Foorrrd Maarrch! Right Faace!"

The column of freshmen passed into the ice house. There were dim flambeaux burning in the cold-storage room, and the light could not be seen from the railroad tracks outside. The inquisitor and the degree team were dressed in black tights with white markings to represent the bones of a skeleton. The first question asked by the inquisitor of the Ancient and Mystic Brotherhood of Barbarians was: "Did you bring any precious stones with you?" "No," answered the candidate. At this, the inquisitor cried in a terrifying voice, "He doesn't need 'em any more! Bring the corn knife!" Two members of the Barbarians' degree team ran forward, brandishing huge corn knives, and dragged the struggling candidate off to the sanhedrin, an inner chamber, from which agonized howls sounded. The howls were actually emitted by a member of the degree team, but the other candidates believed the worst and shivered in fright.

Robert was nervous and anxious to have the ordeal over. He answered that he did have precious stones with him, whereupon the inquisitor demanded that he produce them. An investigating committee was appointed to look over the precious stones, and before long Robert was blindfolded and kneeling to kiss the hand of the King of the Barbarians, and to swear loyalty to the Barbarian cause, to harass the orthodox fraternity men at every opportunity, and to carry terror and woe into their frat houses, and in every possible way to make life a burden for them. Robert's hands were tied behind him as he leaned forward and touched his lips to soft flesh. I know that's no hand, he thought. The blindfold was suddenly untied, and Robert saw one of the Barbarians, who had been bending before him, slowly stand erect and begin to pull his lowered trousers up.

"Let the worthy candidate be instructed in the sacred rites of Venus," said the inquisitor. "Proceed."

This was what Robert had been dreading. He had heard about this part of the ritual, but he had scarcely believed it. Each candidate for membership in the Ancient and Mystic Brotherhood of Barbarians was required to get first-hand information about the sacred rites of Venus from Truckhorse Devereaux, an immense Negress who had become too fat to make much money as a prostitute. She was an insatiable nymphomaniac, and called herself Fifi. Everybody else called her Truckhorse. She said that she was of creole blood, had been born in New Orleans, and one side of her family boasted noble French ancestry. She had seen the day, she often bragged, when she was younger and had her figure, that the most prominent business and professional men of New Orleans had been glad to give her twenty-five dollars and often more a night. She was always overjoyed when the Barbarians rounded up a new batch of candidates, and not for the money alone. Some Barbarian with a grotesque turn of mind had inaugurated this part of the ritual years before and it had persisted.

The sanhedrin had been fitted out as near in oriental splendor as the Barbarians could manage. There was a bed made of two sawhorses with planks across them and an ancient bedspring and mattress piled on. But the Barbarians always rustled around and found gaudy draperies for the couch, even though they might be painted on paper. Truckhorse weighed more than two hundred and fifty pounds, and as Robert saw her lying nude and glistening with sweat he felt the same sick horror at the pit of his stomach that struck him when Kurt Leischer ripped the nightgown from the Whore's body. He had heard Truckhorse moaning in ecstasy as he stood outside the door of the sanhedrin waiting his turn. He was pushed inside, but he braced his feet and halted just at the threshold.

"Oh, sweet papa! Sweet jellyroll! Tell me how long do I have to wait; can I have it now or must I hesitate?" groaned Truckhorse, wriggling till the rusty springs squeaked.

"Come on, worthy candidate. You've got to show your right to the title of a true Barbarian," urged the inquisitor.

Robert knew that he could not go any farther with this. He had heard that the sanhedrin's walls were full of holes for the peeping eyes of the full-fledged members. He could not stand it even if nobody was looking.

"To hell with Truckhorse! To hell with the Barbarians!" shouted Robert, darting past the inquisitor, who was so astonished he could not move or speak for an instant. Then he yelled: "Stop him! Coldcock him there, you guys! Don't let him get by with it!"

Robert was insane with fright. As the Barbarians ran to stop him, he struck out at them with all his might. He felt a man go down before his fists. He felt blows on his body, he staggered against a wall and saw stars blossoming and floating away, but he never stopped, and in a few seconds he was outside, racing down the tracks toward the station and up the steps leading to the viaduct that spanned the railroad yards. He was safe for the time; the Barbarians would not follow him onto the main streets, but they could and would make life miserable for him on the campus. It was the first time Robert had ever struck anyone in anger since he was a child, and it pleased him to know that he was strong and active when he needed to be. He made up his mind to pay more attention to gym, and to take boxing lessons. Perhaps he'd try out for football.

Alan Vass was a Barbarian, and it was he who persuaded Robert to join. Alan said he did not approve of some of the Barbarians' horseplay, but they were the only organized group against the poisonous fraternities, and hence should be encouraged. After Robert's flight from the ice house, the Barbarians did plague him for a while. He would be walking around the campus and would notice everybody pointing to him and snickering. Somebody would tell him about the placard pinned to his coat tail. "Male virgin from Green Valley" it would read, or "Mr. Fifi (Truckhorse) Devereaux." He found threatening notes in his books and in his room. He did not room in a dormitory, but as there were several other students in the house, he did not feel mystified at the appearance of the notes. After a time these manifestations ceased, and only the ordinary indignities inflicted upon freshmen were his lot.

The walks were plastered with handbills addressing the freshmen as: "Consumptive, cockeyed cowards, elephant-eared Ethiopians, slimy, seditious, scoundrelly snakes." Freshmen must not walk on the campus grass, they were obliged to salute courteously when passing a sophomore, and they were not to be caught abroad on the campus after nightfall.

Robert had forgotten all about the sealed envelope Martha had given him until near the end of the first semester when he ran across it in a bureau drawer. He tore it open and read:

"My dearly beloved son: You are now a student at an institution of learning to which your grandfather, now in heaven, lent distinction for many years. Your mother, the writer of this epistle, in her humble way achieved some fleeting honors while enrolled as a student. If she accomplished but little, if her accomplishment at last came to naught, she at least did nothing to debase the honorable name of Darrell. May you, my only son, be as careful, so that the Darrell escutcheon may remain unsmirched. Your mother, through her wider experience and more mature judgment, has been able to formulate certain rules of desirable conduct, or rather to enumerate things it would be well to avoid. She thinks you will find it to your advantage to consider them prayerfully. Viz.:

A Score of Impolite Things

(1) Loud and boisterous laughter.
(2) Reading when others are talking.
(3) Reading aloud in company without being asked.
(4) Talking when others are reading.
(5) Spitting about the house, smoking or chewing.
(6) Cutting finger nails in company.
(7) Leaving a church before public worship is closed.
(8) Whispering or laughing in a house of God.
(9) Gazing rudely at strangers.
(10) Leaving a stranger without a seat.
(11) A want of respect and reverence for seniors.
(12) Correcting persons older than yourself, especially parents.
(13) Receiving a present without an expression of gratitude.
(14) Making yourself the hero of your own story.
(15) Laughing at the mistakes of others.
(16) Making a joke of others in company.
(17) Commencing talking before others have finished speaking.
(18) Answering questions that have been put to others.
(19) Commencing to eat as soon as you get to the table.
(20) Not listening to what one is saying in company—unless you desire to show open con-

tempt for the speaker. A well-bred person will not make an observation whilst another of the company is addressing himself to it."

Robert's first great disappointment at the university was to find that most of the instructors were pompous fellows with single-track minds. At least this was the evaluation placed upon them by Alan Vass, and as his acquaintance with Alan ripened, Robert grew more and more convinced that he was usually right.

Professor Barcus, who taught the Shakespeare and Elizabethan Drama course, came in sleepily to his desk. He yawned and patted his mouth beneath his small blond mustache, apparently finding it difficult to keep open his dark eyes with the wrinkled pouches beneath them. He recited the most orotund and impassioned lines with scrupulous attention to emphasis and metrical effects but utterly without spirit or fire.

Miss Wilson, who taught the Cicero's Orations class, was twittery and long-necked, reminding Robert of Martha before she became so religious. Miss Wilson brought flowers to class, sniffed them noisily during recitation, and gave splendid grades to everybody, whether they were earned or not.

Before the first semester had passed, Robert lost most of his reverence for Boone University. He could see now that the venerable buildings were in a bad state of repair, windows were broken out, and the classrooms were swept by cold draughts. And the instructors had stopped reading at the same time his grandfather had, it seemed. As Alan said, W. D. Howells and Mark Twain were interesting young upstarts to Dr. Reynolds.

It was in Dr. Reynolds' Modern American Literature class that Robert first saw Nell Ravenel. She was as lithe as a movie vampire and wore dresses that accentuated her hemispherical breasts and slim hips. Her brow was high and bulged slightly, and her heavy black hair fell back from her upturned face as she listened to Dr. Reynolds' dull and perfunctory lectures. Her lips parted in an appearance of wistful eagerness, but Robert learned later that she found difficulty in keeping her mouth closed over her somewhat large but evenly spaced teeth. She must be a good hand at shorthand, Robert thought, as her long fingers flew across the pages of her notebook.

Robert liked Alan more than any man he had ever known, but he was a little afraid of the girls Alan associated with—ultra-modernistic girls who began talking about sexual problems and trying to analyze the sexual significance of their dreams, impulses and behavior. Whenever the talk shifted to this quarter, even in a bunch of males, Robert felt uneasy, for he had never had any sexual life.

It was not long before Robert began saying hello to Nell, and then he began walking with her on the campus. He soon found out that she wrote verse, too, and that she lived in St. Luke. She had never heard of Gareth Shallore or the Green Dragon, and this seemed inexplicable to Robert. Nell had had verse published in several poetry magazines, among them *Joybells* and *The Muse's Throne*. She noticed that Robert smiled at the mention of these two magazines, and quickly added that she was somewhat ashamed now of having her stuff printed in such lousy publications. She did not know where to send her poetry, that was the trouble. Robert promised to borrow some better ones from Alan Vass for her. "That's the trouble," said Nell. "I can't keep track of all the places. The writers' magazines don't publish the addresses of many of them, and they are born and then die so fast it makes your head swim. Oh, I guess I'm no Sara Teasdale anyhow."

Robert and Nell became more intimate as time passed, but there was never any foolishness between them—no kissing or mooning. They were like two boy chums. One of their favorite walks was down the railroad track past the ice house, past the cemetery high on its hill, and into the open country beyond. They liked to balance themselves on the rails, clasping hands. Nell liked to walk in the rain, to let the rain beat her heavy hair and on her pale rapt face as she gazed at the sky and recited verse. She liked Willa Cather's *Grandmither, Think Not That I Forget* for a stormy day, and she said it very effectively:

> "Grandmither, gie me your clay-cold hands
> That lie upon your breast,
> For mine do beat the dark all night
> And never find me rest.
>
> Grandmither, gie me your clay-cold heart
> That has forgot to ache
> For mine be fire within my breast.
> And yet it may not break."

Robert thought as he looked at her face: "The apparitions of these faces in the crowd—White petals on a wet, black bough." He had read this in one of the anthologies Alan Vass lent him. There was none of Alan's work in this particular anthology, and he said it was because he did not have a pull with the editor. It took pull in the literary game.

Robert was not very fond of walking in the rain. He thought that Nell must have a poetic temperament for true; not many normal girls would be so crazy as to walk in the rain, getting their clothing soggy, their hair drenched, and their makeup washed off and streaked.

"Oh, I guess people think I'm cuckoo," Nell said one night as they trudged back toward town watching the sunset gilding the clouds and firing the sphere above Academy Hall. "The folks at home will be talking to me and all the time I'm thinking of a poem and don't hear a word they say. Some lines struck me so hard right on the street in St. Luke one day I thought, O for a pencil! My kingdom for a pencil! but I didn't have any, and I ran up to a man and gasped, 'Please, sir! Have you a pencil you'll lend me a moment?' He looked at me as though he'd like to call the booby hatch, but he gave me the pencil and I scribbled down my lines in a magazine I was carrying."

CHAPTER SIX

It would have been hard for either Robert or Nell to tell just when their friendship changed to a more enduring affection, but they came to realize that they were more than just amiable companions to one another. Nell said that she was a pagan at heart, and she could give herself for love only. When she loved, she loved with her whole being and she would never be ashamed of her love. "I want to squeeze life like an orange," she said. "I want to come to grips with it, to hold it in my hands, hold it close and to taste to the bitter dregs its vileness, to enjoy to the fullest its ecstasies." Robert thought that this sounded as though Nell would be a great poetess, and it occurred to him that he and she might be like Robert and Elizabeth Browning. Nell told Robert that of course he was the first, and he would be the last, too, for she was a one-man woman. Robert was a little frightened at the serious way she had of looking at things. He told her it was his first time, too, but she didn't know whether to believe him. She wanted to be able to believe him always, she said. She cupped his face in her palms and looked intensely into his eyes and begged him to tell her everything he had ever experienced in his sexual life. She told him that she knew men were naturally polygamous creatures, and she'd never care what was past and gone just so he was true to her and would tell her frankly how many there had been before her, and just how and when it happened. At last she believed him and said they really belonged to one another and would be inseparable through all the eternities of time.

Nell told Robert that she found it easier to write verse

since she had yielded her virginity. Life had a deeper meaning for her. Nature, the sky, the stars and the moon, other people, everything took on new significance to which she had been blind before. She had written quite a few poems since her first intimacy with Robert, and one of them had been accepted by *Caliban*. It would be published in the next issue. This made Robert a little jealous, and he at once set to work on the poem about Leischer. Alan had asked him to write it long ago, but every time he tried to start it something came up and he felt impelled to postpone it. But now he worked earnestly at it, and after two weeks he decided that it should pass muster. He had called the poem *The Atheist*. He was a little doubtful about the dog in it. Leischer had never had a dog, and he wouldn't have been kind to it if he had one, but to make his point he didn't seem how he could leave the dog out. The poem read:

"The bitter years had not subdued his pride,
 Even in death it flaunted from his face,
 And when the rustics learned that he had died,
 They all flocked in to see the haunted place.

 His well-thumbed books they eyed with awe-struck fear,
 For everyone among them knew too well
 These books had damned the man upon the bier
 And sent him on his pilgrimage to hell.

 Only his dog looked on with mournful stare—
 No other mind to grief or pity ran.
 He could remember naught but love and care.
 He could not know that God had cursed the man."

"Ummmh!" said Alan, pinching his chin between his thumb and forefinger. "Not bad! Not bad at all. Your stuff is improving; you're coming right along. Don't exactly like that sentimental dog stuff, but what the hell. Off it goes to Shallore with my strong recommendation."

Robert was sure that the poem would be printed now. He had managed to acquire a rather thorough knowledge of all the modern poets, and this helped him to avoid the more obvious *clichés*. He had given up the boxing lessons he began shortly after his flight from the Barbarians' initiation, and he no longer cared about football. He was certain that he wanted to be a poet more than anything else, even though he had to live in a garret with only a taper for light.

"Did you hear about Sol Abraham?" asked Alan. Robert had almost forgotten about Sol, and had seen him only a few times since he came to Boone.

"No. What about him?"

"He's had to quit school. His old man died. They were about to starve to death anyhow. That's the hell of having a house full of kids. I'm glad I'm the only son and heir, the only child, as far as that goes, and I don't think there'll be any more little strangers. The old man was too cut up when mother died."

"That's too bad about Sol. I guess he struggled hard trying to get an education."

"He did for a fact. And I think I was the only real friend he had on the campus. You had to know him like I did, live with him, to get next to him. The poor little bugger tried his damnedest to make people like him; always going out to the country to talk to farmers about their crops and how they were making it and all that. They always looked at him like they thought he was just there to snoop around and probably come back to rob the house and murder all of them. The farmers around here don't have any use for Jews; call 'em white niggers, or niggers turned inside out. I never felt more sorry for anybody in my life than I did for Sol one day when he and I went out toward Avalon to get botanical specimens. That was soon after we came back to school in the fall. We stopped at a farmhouse for a drink of water, and the old rube with spinach on his chin drew us one with an old oaken bucket for all the world like the song out of the spring, cold as ice. Sol stood there grinning like a damned monkey and thanking the old gent for the good drink, asking him how old the well was, how his crops were, what kind of a change in government the farmers needed most. He was about to spout some of his bolshevik stuff, and in another minute he'd have been dishing out one of those pamphlets he always carries. I knew how the farmer would take it. They're mostly all Ku Kluxers out there, and Sol being a Jew and talking against the government would be just too bad for him. So I tried to hurry the little fart away; got him around the corner, and stop he *would* right there to look over some ducks in a pen. Then I heard a woman ask: 'Who was that, Wes?' and the farmer says, 'A white boy and a damned Christ-killer kike asking all sorts o' silly questions. He ain't up to no good, and you can bet yer bottom dollar on that. I don't see why they don't run them white niggers out of the country. This one wasn't much lighter than a nigger, nohow.' Christ! I felt like going right back there and pasting the big-mouthed yokel one. Sol heard the whole thing, and he looked like he shriveled up inside. I couldn't liven him up any way or anyhow all the rest of the day."

"It's too bad he had to quit school. Well, let me know what Shallore says."

Within a week Alan stopped Robert in Academy Hall and told him Shallore was going to run the poem in *Caliban*. Now I'm getting somewhere, thought Robert. Alan had told him about Lionel Edwards, who had a story in *Caliban* reprinted in an annual anthology of best short stories, where it attracted the attention of a book publisher, and the first thing Lionel knew he had a contract for a novel.

Nell's poem appeared in the December *Caliban* just before the holidays. Robert thought it was a musical thing, but he couldn't get much meaning out of it. The first stanza read:

"There shall be April in wan winter lands
Beyond the utmost waters of the world;
The creeping grass shall clothe the barren sands,
A thousand hills bear crocuses unfurled."

Robert thought he could not bear to leave Nell during

the holidays, but she laughed with tears in her eyes and told him it would be only a little while and she'd be thinking of him every minute. But it was a dull time he spent in the old house with Martha and Terry. Terry wanted to be friendly, but he didn't know what to say to Robert or how to entertain him. He knew nothing of books or intellectual pursuits and Robert knew nothing else. So he was glad when the second semester began and he returned to Boone.

Robert began to worry about the rate at which he was spending money. After his intimacy with Nell began he bought better clothing, and there were other expenses he had not had before. Nell liked concerts and shows, and some of the more refined eating places where string music could be heard. She said a gypsy put his whole soul into playing a harp. Robert had spent two hundred dollars before the first semester was ended, and he did not consider that he had been extravagant, or at least not very extravagant. But Alan told him he could get both of them a job during vacation with a highway engineer who was a friend of his.

Before the second semester was half through, Robert was thoroughly tired of the wearisome routine at Boone. Only the presence of Alan and Nell kept him on. He had to endure the compulsory military drill; he told himself that his instructors were stupid and rooted in the past.

When the poem about Leischer came out in *Caliban*, Robert expected some letters about it, but none came. Still, he knew that plenty of prominent poets, editors, and critics had seen the poem, and surely some of them must have liked it.

When he thought of leaving Nell for three months, Robert was alarmed at the prospect of doing without her that long and asked her to marry him, even though both of them were only kids. Nell told him they were never to marry; their love was too precious and too deep for that. "I mean it," she said. "A love like ours is too great to need marriage to cage it. We both want our separate careers; we don't need to be tied together by law. When love is caged it beats its glorious wings to bits against the cruel, confining bars. But we want to let ours soar forever free in the cool blue heights high above the petty miasmic swamps of little lives that need a ring and a book and a minister of the gospel to tell them when they may love."

She told him the summer would be long, but she'd write to him every day and he must finish some poems during vacation. He didn't see how he could write much if he had to work. It wasn't much fun lamming down a heavy maul on stakes or dragging a surveyor's chain through cornfields and bramble patches.

The summer's work with the road crew was over early in August, and Alan accepted Robert's perfunctory invitation to spend the rest of the time before school started with the Hurley family in Green Valley. Robert had not expected Alan to accept, for they were working nearer to St. Luke than to Green Valley. Now Robert was disturbed to think of the coming meeting between Martha and Alan. Alan could never keep his tongue still when religion was mentioned, and Robert had never told him of Martha's fanaticism, for he was ashamed of it. He had never anticipated a crisis such as the one he now feared, and he hesitated to ask Alan to pipe down on his atheism while in the house. Alan let it be known that he never gave quarter to a foe when it came to arguing on the difference between superstition and science.

Nothing happened for a few days after their arrival. Alan and Robert were busy exploring in Happy Hollow. They visited Leischer's grave and the site of the House of The Hand, which had burned down. Robert tried his best to keep Alan away from the Holy Roller church, but the shouting grew so loud one night that Alan insisted upon going down there. Worse, he went inside and sat down well past the middle of the room. He grinned and guffawed and talked behind his palm to Robert, who smiled wanly at times. The fat's in the fire! The fat's in the fire! Robert kept saying to himself. He saw Martha glowering at them from the front benches reserved for saints. Pastor Epperson, a little rheumatic but still able to leap upon the benches, found an opportunity to speak about the colleges that were turning out fools who called themselves atheists. "There's no fool worse than an educated fool," shouted Pastor Epperson, looking right at Robert and Alan. Then he walked down the aisle and thrust his forefinger under Alan's nose.

"If the shoe fits you, young man, wear it," he said.

"Thanks. You take care of God and leave me alone," said Alan, coloring.

"You think it's a mark of intelligence to cut up and skylark in the house of the Lord, I suppose. I hear you're a college student. Is mocking the Lord and making sport of his humble servants one of the things you learn in school?"

"I don't know what you're spouting about. I don't recognize any such being as you're talking about. I'm an atheist," said Alan angrily.

Robert knew that the crisis was here. He would have to stick by Alan and show him that he was not afraid of threats of hell or could not be intimidated by his mother or the pastor. Robert intended to begin work on a novel in the fall, and Alan had promised to help him with it. Robert would rather die than return to Green Valley to stay—to live among sawmill hands and woodchoppers. The university was a stifling place, but it was better than the dry rot of Green Valley. Alan had been hinting that he might not return to Boone, that he might go to work in St. Luke. He wasn't learning anything worth while, he said. Robert knew that Alan was the only one among his acquaintances who could help him along the literary road, and he did not intend to lose contact with him if he could help it.

"The best thing you can do, young man," said Pastor Epperson, with dignity, "is to remove your obnoxious presence from this temple of God. You pollute the atmosphere you occupy."

Alan arose and left the room, Robert following him without hesitation. He was sure that Martha would have something to say about the incident, and he was actually relieved to think that this was an opportunity to let Martha know just what he thought while he had Alan to help him. Robert and Alan walked about for a while, talking about their plans for the future, about the novel Alan was writing and the novel Robert was going to write. Robert was sure that Martha would be waiting in the library when they came in, and so she was.

"Young man," she called to Alan. "I am afraid that it is my painful duty to inform you that you are no longer welcome in this house. Since you were my son's guest, I tried to show you every courtesy our poor circumstances permit, but you have abused that hospitality. So I must ask you to leave these premises at once."

"Very well, madam. Naturally, I'll leave at once."

"Wait!" said Robert. "I've got something to say." I mustn't back down now! I can't back down now! he told himself. "Alan is my guest, as you say. I hope I have some privileges in this house. If he goes, I go. Is that plain?" He was proud of himself for making this resolute stand.

"My son!" cried Martha. "Are you mad?"

"No, I'm just getting my eyes opened, and Alan helped to open them."

"My son! You are dearer to me than life itself, but my Redeemer is dearer than all. If you leave this roof in the company of yon atheist, you go never to return! Never darken my door again if you do! Mark my words!"

"All right," shouted Robert. "You're the judge."

"Don't, don't!" begged Alan. "Jesus! This is serious. Don't let me break up the family, Bob. Let me go alone. You understand, eh? Everything will be all right."

"You mean by that that your foul intimacy with my son will be renewed elsewhere. I must exact a promise from him that he will never speak to you again."

"You see," Robert said. "It's come to a showdown. Now, I've been trying to avoid this, mother—trying to spare you, but I tell you I've had my eyes opened. I'm an agnostic; I'm not what you'd call an atheist. The atheist absolutely denies the existence of a supreme being, while the agnostic neither affirms nor denies. I honestly say I do not know. But atheists have as much right to their beliefs as Christians do. Since I have never seen any conclusive evidence of a supreme being, I cannot believe in one ——"

"No evidence? No evidence? The air you breathe, the sun that warms you, the sun around which the planets wheel in the heavens illumined by His blessed handiwork! The billions upon billions of stars and countless universes stretching away to infinity beyond the imagination of puny finite minds. Bah! You ask for proof! —"

"That's no proof. Why —"

"Go! Go! Before my heart bursts in my body!" howled Martha, her face purpling and foam gushing from her mouth. She fell writhing and her tongue protruded.

"Get your old man," shouted Alan. "I'll get a doctor."

Terry had slept through it all in his upstairs bedroom. Robert bounded in and shook his shoulder violently. "Dad! Dad! Mother's taken awfully bad! Terrible! Alan's gone for the doctor. Do you understand what I'm saying?"

"Eh? What?" Terry grunted, rolling to the side of the bed and automatically groping for his shoes before his eyes opened.

They stumbled downstairs, and Robert fetched a glass of water. But Martha's teeth were clenched, and the water dribbled down her quivering chin and onto her dress. She was muttering: "Go! Go! No blasphemers in this house! No longer my son! No longer my son!" Alan arrived with the doctor, who said that Martha's fit would not be fatal, but it was dangerous, and she must be kept quiet, with nothing to disturb her mind.

Robert called Terry into the hall and told him how it

was. That it would be better for him to go. But he'd let Terry know where he was and just what he was doing all the time. He was going to look for Leo, too.

"What a house!" mourned Terry, wagging his head. "Aw, I don't know what t' make o' things. I don't know where t' be a-turnin' in me old days. If ye must go, ye must; and that's that. But I'll be a-shakin' o' yer hand, me bye, and a-sayin' good luck and don't forget the old man."

Robert could never forget the balance of that summer. Any place Robert and Alan took a notion to see, they saw, for the freight trains were running and the shacks indulgent to college boys. It was only the crummy boes that the bulls harassed. The boys decided that they could learn more from life itself than they could out of books, and they'd not go back to Boone. Alan knew where both of them could get fairly decent jobs in the office of a steel mill, and there would be the Green Dragon and its crowd at night, and everyday contact with such fellows as Danny Maupin and Gareth Shallore.

Nell Ravenel was downhearted when she found out that Robert was not coming back to Boone, and she told him to remember that they belonged to each other and that nothing could part them but death. Robert's conscience was twinging a little, but he reflected that she had been as willing as he, and when he landed a good job or got to making any sort of money with his writing, he could send for her. Alan told him that Danny Maupin didn't make much off his artistic stuff, but he wrote detectives, westerns and so on for the pulps, under an assumed name, of course. It was as easy as falling off a log and it paid.

Nell wrote him that since he had been away she realized what losing him forever would mean, and she was so stirred emotionally about it that she had written a poem which had been accepted by *Spectre*. She sent him a copy:

> "He passed me proudly on the street today;
> Without a word, he looked the other way.
>
> They say that there must dawn a dismal hour

When the great sun shall burn to ash and die
And haggard moons shall hurtle through the sky.

The stubborn pine upon the icy hill
Must know at last that love lies cold and still."

CHAPTER SEVEN

"Here they come," said Sam Miller, whose Green Dragon and *Caliban* name was Jacques D'Autremont, rushing in from the street. "Alan's got three in tow. I know one of 'em. Mrs. Stephen Spencer Hensley. Got diamonds as big as oranges. You see her in the society section every Sunday. To your posts!"

Everybody dashed about, touching matches to candles stuck in the necks of bottles. The electric lights were switched off. The room was furnished with rough pine table and benches, but the walls were decorated with paintings, poems scribbled in the handwriting of the authors, and grotesque plaques of women with agony stamped on their features and long pendant breasts sprouting nipples as long as an ordinary finger. Smocks and berets were hastily put on, and the room was settling into order when Alan opened the door, not wide enough to enter at first. Seeing that the atmosphere was all right, he stepped back and allowed three women to come in. The poets and artists were sitting at the tables, some of them reciting, others engaged in brilliant conversations which had served before. They smiled cynically, crushing cigarettes with carefully gauged nervous gestures on the table.

"Oh! Lovely! I didn't know there was such a place in all St. Luke," breathed the fat lady, folding her hands across her breasts. "A picturesque bit of Greenwich Village—or the Latin Quarter!"

"Yes," said Alan soberly, leading them to one of the tables. "It is a profound irony of fate that such an artists' rendezvous should exist in what was once a busy mart of trade. This was the commercial section before the railroads cut in so heavily on the river traffic; now business has moved from the levee, and these old buildings on this street are occupied by dreamers and poets, whom business men all despise and ridicule. Traders' Alley, once a busy hive of commercial activity, became a sad and desolate spot, occupied by cobwebs and the dust of the years silently forming in velvet layers. Then some young people who felt out of place in the prosaic life of St. Luke went seeking over the city for a place to meet, to work, to commune with one another, to feel that fellowship that the artistic temperament demands. This place could be had for a reasonable rent; it is away from the vulgar prying eyes of Philistines. We like it. We hope you find it interesting, Mrs. Hensley."

"Oh, it's divine!" she said. "Isn't it, girls?" The other women agreed, but without enthusiasm. They sat stolidly and somewhat frigidly, complacent as cows, and it became apparent to Alan that he was not making much headway with them. He turned his attention to Mrs. Hensley.

He sat down at the table and leaned his folded arms upon it. Then he managed a bit of a whimsical, rueful smile, his wistful eyes winking to make Mrs. Hensley believe there were tears.

"Art," he said with mild bitterness. "Art! How many of the Babbitts, the money-grubbers know what art is? I don't know myself. Yes, I do know. But how can I put it in words? It's the dust on a butterfly's wing, the petals of a wild mountain rose. It's up there riding high on a star (flinging his right arm toward the ceiling). I reach out. It seemed to be right before me. I try to grasp it (clutching the air). I try to analyze it. I think I have it in my hand. I open my hand (spreading his hands palms upward on the table) but when I think I have it, *it's gone!* . . . *It's gone!* . . . Oh! . . . Oh! . . ." (His voice breaking with sobs as he lowers his face on his arms, his shoulders shaking).

"Oh, I shouldn't talk like this. I forget myself," Alan said, raising his head and hoping his face looked haggard and ascetic. "Oh, nobody understands! The people here *try* to understand. The vulgar world can never understand. But I keep it here (tapping his breast with a gentle smile). It's there forever and a day. . . ."

Mrs. Henley had been listening wide-eyed. She leaned across the table till Alan could see the valley between her breasts and apast it to the first folds of her stomach. She patted Alan's hands, and smiled reassuringly through her tears.

"*I* understand," she gulped. Alan squeezed her plump ringed fingers gratefully, and rubbed his eyes, assuming what he hoped she would take to be bewilderment at life's strangeness and unconcern.

"Good hunting! Good hunting!" shouted Jacques D'Autremont when Alan came back from showing the women to their car. "What luck?"

"Gimmee a can of that beer," said Alan. "I'm hoarse as an auctioneer after that spiel. Say, you guys don't know how to use *finesse*. If you rush them, they shy away like a shrinking gazelle. It'll take five or six sessions before she finally blows her lump, but she'll come across with plenty when she does."

"Did you lamp them breastworks? Oi! Oi!" said John Davis (Hjalmar Steffansson).

"Boy! O boy!"

"How'd you like to lay behind them and shoot?"

Several of the boys began waving their cans of homebrew and singing:

"Do her tits hang high?
Do her tits swing low?
Can she tie 'em in a knot?
Can she tie 'em in a bow?
Can she fling 'em 'cross her shoulder
Like a European soldier?
 DOOO HERRRR TITS SWIIINNNG LOOOOW?"

This was one of the thousand and one nights at the Green Dragon for Robert. He had been disturbed many times at Alan's "horsing the fat gals" as he called it. But Alan answered: "What the hell? They *want* to spend it, and they *will* spend it. You wouldn't begrudge the poor gals a little shivery thrill now and then. Most of their husbands are too preoccupied with business or their stenographers, and it's risky fooling with chauffeurs and icemen. It's got to come out of them or they'll go nutty. Read Freud. Read Kraft-Ebbing, you dope." He said they had to pay the rent on the building, and there was a fund for those fellows who were out of work and had to live somehow. Many a sumptuous "gala" had been financed by the generosity of romantic patrons of the arts.

Robert sat at a table with Danny Maupin. Danny was a short, slender chap with shaggy red hair and an absurdly childish face. He wore thick-lensed glasses, and when he took them off to wipe them, as he often did, his eyes were revealed as small and squinting, the whites flecked with clots of red. The last few months Danny had been in a funk. He sat reared back on his tail bone, low in his seat, his feet extended stiffly before him. He belched continually, and a spasm of pain contorted his face at each burp. He kept drinking until he had to feel his way out of the place, but he never appeared to get high. His hands had taken to trembling and his chin quivered like that of a child who had been scolded. When Danny put his hand up to quiet his chin, both shook, and he swore unheatedly to himself. Robert did not know what to make of Danny. If I had two novels published, and a third under contract, I'd be happy as a lark, he thought. I guess I should be satisfied at making *Caliban* and *Spectre* so often, but it seems as though I've been going around in circles and getting nowhere the last few years.

Some of the fellows had girls with them in the Green Dragon, but Nell had never taken to the bohemian life as Robert thought she would. She preferred the theaters or the movies. Robert was afraid that she might become a Philistine yet, though she had been brave in defying her folks and leaving home and coming to live with him in their studio above the Green Dragon. And she still refused to marry, saying that true love was stifled by fetters imposed by law. Her folks had cavorted and raved, and even threatened to complain to the authorities that she was living in adultery with Robert, but they had never brought themselves to do it. He had no doubt that she loved him sincerely, for she had given up her college course the next year after Robert had come to St. Luke. She never wrote verse any more, and she often interfered with Robert's writing. If he wanted to sit up, she'd tease him until he was ready to go to bed with her.

Robert believed that Nell would have been willing to marry him long ago had it not been that she hated to see the prophecies of her parents fulfilled. They had predicted that she would have to conform to the rules of society or pay the penalty of a wrecked life and broken heart. She would find that in order to hold any man a woman had to have some sort of deed and title to him, with appropriate penalties if he defaulted. So Nell held stubbornly to her first position about marriage. She had ceased to be much of a pagan in other respects.

When Danny Maupin left comparatively sober, Robert arose, too, and walked outside into the cool air. His stomach was rolling uneasily and the sour twang of homebrew yeast was on his tongue. He rounded a corner and walked down hill toward the levee. There were some Negroes sitting on bridge timbers near the water's edge, laughing and talking, the music of their voices flowing as smooth as the water. Robert drew near, catching his toes now and then on the rough cobblestones. They'll think I'm a drunk from the Green Dragon, he thought.

"Good evening, boys," he said, and sat down.

"Evenin'! Evenin'!" But the talking and laughing ceased; there was uneasiness and tension. Robert wished that he might walk up to the Negroes and be accepted into their conversation as a matter of course. He rose and made his way down the river fifty feet to sit down again. Tonight he was sick of the Green Dragon. He was sick of the dull days in the office adding up payrolls, and getting sick of the nights of hysterical gayety when clerks and students gathered in the Green Dragon to pretend they were gifted with something that set them apart from workaday folks. Another Negro, one of heavy build, had joined the group beside the water.

"Fatfolks, how's your conduck?" said one of the Negroes to the newcomer.

"Obnoxious, Sunbeam; obnoxious, son!"

"Say, Fatfolks, y' wanta watch out. They's lookin' fo' you."

"Who that lookin' fo' me?"

"The buzzards! Kyah! Kyah! Kyah!"

"Damned if you don't get sillier ever' day, Sunbeam. What you need is a whoppin' dose o' that Lenin speerit. That gonna make you feel like a fightin' cock on a frosty mornin'. Ain't it the trut'. Yasuh! Make you love ever'body oney them as needs to be hated, and move all that malicy poison outen yo' bosom."

"You know what ol' Shagnasty Powell done said? His ol' lady she done jine that Lenin party, that Commun*e*ist party. You know what he done said? He says afore my ol' lady done jine that Lenin party she so damned cranky and cantankerous *nobody* couldn't sleep wit' 'er. Now, sence she get that Lenin speerit, *anybody* kin sleep wit' 'er. Kyah! Kyah! Kyah! Got to share ever'thin' eekil. Kyah! Kyah! Kyah! Kyah!"

"Big mouth, empty head. Talk, talk, talky, talk, but don't say nothin'. Talk on, big boy, but don't come cryin' 'round me when them big bosses lick all the 'lasses offen yo' bread, then call you black nigger."

Robert saw Alan staggering down the levee singing: "Pale Hands I Loved Beside the Shalimar." Every time that Alan managed to get good and soused, he searched all along the river front for a Negro to adopt as his man Friday. He wanted a Negro who would be both a servant and companion, bound to him by both obedience and love. Alan had it in his head that he might find one he could educate and train. Seeing the group of Negroes, he decided to try his luck here.

"Hail, brother! Hail, noble son of Ham!" he said to

Fatfolks. "Let me kneel to tie the laces of your shoes as a gesture of humility."

"My shoes is tied, brothah. No use botherin'. I shake yo' hand comrade style if yo' want to."

"All men are born free and equal. In ancient Egypt the whites were slaves of the Negroes."

"Nobody ought t' be slaves. Ever'body ought t' have comrade speerit."

"You like white nooky, don't you? You colored boys go wild about that."

"What's yo' game, brothah? Let's hear what's on yo' weary min'."

"I believe you're just as good as I am, and if you like white nooky I'll see that you get it. That's the kind of a man I am."

"I ain't studyin' my min' 'bout nothin' like that."

"What are you studying about?"

"I jus' talkin' t' these boys 'bout that Lenin speerit when yo' come up. I got that on my min' here o' late. Seems lak las' thing I remember when I go t' sleep, fust thing when my eyes pops open."

"I'll be damned! The hell you cackle! You remind me of poor little Sol Abraham. You know that little runt? If you do, tell him to come around to the Green Dragon again. Tell him his old pal, Alan Vass, is yearning to get in his hair."

"Sho', I know Comrade Abraham. He comes to the forum most ever' Sattiday night. Whyn't you come out there some Sattiday night? Would hurt you nor nobody t' git some o' that Lenin speerit. All comrades out thah! All brothahs. That's whut I been tellin' these boys. 1145½ Western Boulevard, upstairs. Workers' Center, that's the place. Workers' Center, 1145½ Western Boulevard. We got all kinds o' good books out thah; clear them capitalis' cobwebs outen yo' brain, and when we kin rustle enough dough, we have a little supper, or feed, or somethin'."

"Well, I don't have much time. Maybe some time. But you tell Sol anyhow. And I'd like a heart-to-heart talk with you. I need a friend. I need a pal and a slave combined. I need a man Friday."

"I got a job fo' Friday, brothah, but thank you kindly."

Alan began roaring with laughter and made his way up the river bank toward the Green Dragon.

"Who that?" asked Sunbeam.

"Some o' that Green Dragon bunch. Clerks and counter hoppers all day; make-b'lieve artists and sich at night. I heerd Comrade Abraham, fella he asked about, talkin' 'bout 'em. Talk like crazy in the head t' me."

"Ain't it the trut'?"

"Shet my mout' wide open!"

"Burn my clo'es!"

"Yes, Lawd. Nutty as a pet coon. Kyah! Kyah! Kyah!"

When Alan first came to the Green Dragon he did not care about the indifference or scorn of the outside world, for Alan said that prosaic grubbers knew nothing of the divine madness of poets and dreamers. "Harlots and hunted have pleasures of their own to give which the vulgar world can never understand," he quoted. And Robert for a long time believed that he was being supremely courageous by flinging defiance at the mob. Now he was hurt somehow when he heard the ridicule of these Negro workers, just as he had been hurt when his appearance injected tension into the atmosphere. Hearing of Sol Abraham reminded him again of the earnest little fellow he had first seen on the train to Probstville, and of whom he had often thought casually, never with sufficient interest to seek him. 1145½ Western Boulevard. 1145½ Western Boulevard. Robert repeated the address to himself as he walked toward the Green Dragon and when he reached the radius of a street light he set down the address in a notebook he carried. The notebook came in handy when he wanted to jot down ideas for poems or stories, but he had not used it much of late.

As he pushed open the Green Dragon door, Robert saw Alan and Gareth Shallore arguing. Shallore had not been in the room when Alan brought his prospective angels in, and, had he been, Alan would have been a great deal more subdued. Shallore paid the printing bills for *Caliban* and could be depended upon for a check to pay the rent in a pinch. Most of the habitués of the Green Dragon did not dare to wear their hair as long as Shallore's. They had to become clerks or otherwise mingle with Philistines during the day. But Shallore could afford idleness and eccentricity. He affected Windsor ties and even berets on the street.

One of the most frequent arguments between Alan and Shallore had to do with the question: Which is the more effective as a social force, hate or love? Shallore, who was a Christian Socialist, pleaded for love; Alan, a self-styled anarchist, defended hate. At one time Robert had enjoyed this clash of wits, but it had begun to seem a little silly to him.

"If I were fire, I'd burn this world away;
If I were water, I'd soon let it drown!"

quoted Alan, gulping homebrew from a tin can. Shallore ran his slender fingers through his long hair and answered:

"Let me be written in the Book of Love.
I care not how you write me in that Book Above.
Erase my name, or write it as you will,
So I be written in the Book of Love."

SHALLORE: Look how far Jesus advanced his social beliefs by preaching love.
ALAN: Yeh, but see how his followers practice love. Where would all the revolutions come from if we depended on love? Where would the French be if they had tried to stop the Germans with kisses instead of bullets?
SHALLORE: Two wrongs don't make a right.

Robert sought the door. The loft above the Green Dragon had been partitioned into studio apartments rented by the bohemians, and one of these Robert and Nell occupied. She was undressing when he came in, and clasped her clothing about her to hide her nakedness, uttering a soft "Ooh!"

"You can't tell when somebody'll come barging in here," she said, slowly lowering her clothes to reveal herself. She enjoyed seeing his eyes brighten at the sight of her body, which she knew was a good body. Nobody would ever throw her out of a bed. She had posed nude for some of the amateur artists who hung out at the Green Dragon, and, while Robert tried to be broad-minded, he knew how Green Dragon hangers-on who couldn't tell which end of a brush to grasp sometimes kidded art-struck girls into posing nude, and then boasted about the feat. "Women are born exhibitionists," Alan said. "You can tell that every time you ride on a street car. See how they place themselves in a convenient position and then roll sidelong eyes to see how many are enjoying the glimpse of the Promised Land. It's just born in them; they can't help it, poor dears, and God knows I don't *want* them to help it as long as my eyes hold out."

"I saw a keen picture tonight," said Nell. "Oh, marvelous! Al Jolson in *The Singing Fool*. I don't care how hard-boiled you pretend to be, I'll bet you couldn't see it without crying. I saw dignified-looking old men sniffing and crying like women. In the part where Al's boy has died and he has to go on with the show though his heart is breaking for he's a trouper and the show comes first and he thinks he can't make it and then sees a vision of his little dead Sonny Boy, and sings just marvelously:

> "Climb upon my knee, Sonny Boy.
> Though you're only three, Sonny Boy,
> You've no way of knowing,
> I've no way of showing
> What you mean to me, Sonny Boy."

She was getting into bed. Robert undressed, and took hold of the light cord. "Want this any more?"

"No!" As the room darkened, he could hear and sense her expectant stirring. She flexed her limbs and stretched like a kitten.

"Life doesn't mean much to a woman after all unless

she has given birth to a child, does it?" Nell asked. "Somehow her life doesn't seem complete. It's cramped."

Robert didn't like to hear her talking this way, for the prospect of having children dependent upon him filled him with dread. A woman doesn't have a soul, Alan told him; she has only a womb. Robert mumbled ambiguously, and in a moment she was caressing him as she always did. She could never keep her hands off him when he first came to bed.

After she had expended her passion, Nell fell asleep as tranquil as a child. Robert lay watching the window, through which a light gleamed momentarily now and then. Here he was in bed, and in the morning he'd arise, bathe and shave, eat some toast and drink some coffee, then board a street car and ride to the McAdams Steel Co. There he'd pore over payrolls, pound a typewriter a bit, eat lunch, pore over payrolls in the afternoon and perhaps pound a typewriter again, come home, eat, go down to the Green Dragon and listen to the same old talk down there, then upstairs and to bed, where he would give Nell the attention she demanded each night. He remembered the first time with Nell and the first time he had seen one of his poems in *Caliban*. He had become so accustomed to both now that he recalled wistfully his initial zest that familiarity had dulled.

He was convinced now that he would never see Leo again, even though his half-brother might be alive. And he'd be a man, dull-eyed and banal, not like the boy who played with Anna Leischer and Robert in the House of The Hand. Yet Robert was weary of clever people who tried to make every phrase scintillate—who searched books and magazines for the ideas and words of others to retail as their own.

CHAPTER EIGHT

It was near the end of October, after the stock market crash, when Robert mounted the narrow dark steps ascending to the Workers' Center at 1145½ Western Boulevard. Upstairs there was a long dingy room, bare save for a table and a scarred piano at the far end, a bookcase and a table piled high with pamphlets and magazines at one side. There were folding chairs stacked against the walls; a single bulb burned over the table and a girl was seated there counting money, mostly nickels and pennies, and writing with a pencil in a notebook.

"I beg your pardon," Robert said. "I wonder where I might find Sol Abraham."

The girl looked him over keenly before answering, then her face hardened.

"I don't know any such fellow," she said.

"Fatfolks told me I'd find him here," Robert said, remembering the name of the Negro whom he had heard on the levee.

"Oh, Fatfolks! Well, you might stick around. Would you know him if you'd see him?"

"Yes, I'm sure that I would."

Robert unfolded one of the chairs and sat down. The girl resumed her counting and writing, and he picked up one of the pamphlets. There was nothing in it to interest him. It was about the cost of living, and strikes, the reduction of wages and other things that were of no vital concern to him. He walked around the walls, looking at the pictures. There were portraits of Lenin, Marx, and Debs, and a framed motto: "Workers of the world, unite! You have nothing to lose but your chains. You have a world to win." And there were pictures of the Communards of Paris defending the barricades and of a demonstration of workers in Moscow's Red Square.

Then he walked restlessly to the window and watched the passers-by on the opposite side of the street. Shoppers with brown parcels of food or clothing or meat for the Sunday dinner. A neon sign first spelled out the words Y NOT EAT and then flashed it all at once, and in the restaurant Robert could see a man sticking a toothpick in his mouth and talking to the cashier, who was smiling at the customer as he took up his change from the little mat bristling with rubber spines.

Robert twisted his head about each time he heard somebody enter the room, but Sol did not show up. The girl had left off her writing and was talking to a group of those who had arrived.

"Go get the coffee," she said to a Negro, handing him some money, "and take it down to Joe's restaurant. We have to have it out at Taylor and Beems by ten o'clock."

Robert was not sure he was looking at Sol Abraham when he first appeared. He was thinner, and he came in slowly and heavily. When Robert came up, Sol apparently did not recognize him.

"Hello, Abraham!" said Robert. "You don't know me, do you?"

"No, I believe not."

"Hurley. Bob Hurley. I met you on the train going to Probstville."

"Oh, yes! I remember now. What are you doing, and where have you been?"

"Working for the McAdams Steel Co. Payroll clerk. I see Alan Vass every night at the Green Dragon."

"Oh, yes. The Green Dragon." Sol's manner seemed a bit cool.

"I heard a colored fellow mention you and the address, and so I thought I'd come out to say hello." Now that he was here, Robert wondered uneasily just why he had come.

"Well, glad to have you here. I don't know how much of a crowd we'll have; just the regular forum. No outside speakers tonight."

"I can't stay long." Robert had somehow expected Sol Abraham to revitalize him just as the ancient wrestler was renewed by contact with the earth. He felt a little foolish now, and the place seemed dull. Sol moved through the room, speaking to each one, and sat down at the table. The girl who had been counting the money followed him. Robert uncertainly moved toward the front.

"This is Comrade Sally Vinson," said Sol. "Bob Hurley. I knew him during my short college career. Maybe you never heard I was a college fellow, did you?"

"I thought he was a dick. He looks like one. Well fed," said Sally, shaking hands firmly. She was a solid, muscular girl with plain, strong features; and Robert thought of some of the pictures he had seen of Russian peasant girls laughing as they were bringing in the sheaves of an abundant harvest. He had heard the name before; seen it often in the newspapers. This was the girl known as the "Red Firebrand"; she at various times had been before the police judge and received a lecture on good citizenship because of picketing or speaking at protest meetings.

"The cops have been a little solicitous about me since I've been around the Taylor and Beems plant where they're on strike. They're out solid, but I don't know how long they'll stay. The company is about whipped; but there's always danger of a sell-out. Cochran, the union's business agent, is sorer at the Reds than the police even. We're going to take some coffee out to the pickets tonight. Do you want to go along?"

"I'd like to."

Robert was relieved when the meeting was over, though the others appeared to enjoy it. Fatfolks came in and brought along with him a skinny, light-colored Negro who proved to be the Sunbeam of the river bank. Sunbeam closed his eyes and grinned widely and sleepily before he began to say anything, stroking his chin as he talked. Often he broke into explosive cackles at his own jokes.

"Heah I am, brothah Fatfolks," he said. "Let that Lenin speerit commence t' wuk, 'cause I ain't got long t' mess around heah! Turn it on and let nature take its course, brothah."

"Lissen, Sunbeam. Cain't make no first-class haid outen a punkin in five minutes. You foller me, boy, you gonna get that Lenin speerit till it won't let loose—till it won't quit, and that's a fack."

"Bettah not jim me up! Bettah not mess me up! Boy, I'll tune yo' haid wit' one o' them foldin' cheers same as a man would be a violin!"

Sol Abraham gave a short talk on Marxism, and, since Robert knew nothing of Marx, he was glad when this was over, but the discussion that followed was no more interesting. At half past nine, the meeting adjourned and Robert trailed six others down the street to Joe's Day and Nite Lunch Room.

"Coffee! Coffee! Where's that monstrous can o' coffee, Joe?" asked Fatfolks.

"Coffee?" Joe, a walrus-mustached Greek, elevated his spread palms, arched his eyebrows, and shrugged. "Coffee? I donno from nottink 'bout no can o' coffee. Nobody say. Who say?"

"What?" Fatfolks shouted. "Eustace Harvey never brought no coffee here and tol' you t' make it fer us? Boy, I bet I make that scoundrel cry ever' time he see a drop o' coffee! Aw, you lyin' like a dog, Joe!" as he saw a grin spreading over Joe's face.

"Sure! Sure! You take 'im fast; all okay when you get 'im there. Only five blocks. Hot like hell now. You shake ol' brown, get 'im there okay. Come on!"

With the can of coffee the men hurried down the street past the lighted shops and into the dark canyons of the factory district. Five pickets stepped out from the shadow of a wall and halted them.

"Hey! Where you goin'? What d' ye want?"

"We got hot coffee for the pickets. From the Workers' Center. Drink up, boys, while it's hot," said Sol.

"Oh, the Workers' Center. Thanks!" One of the pickets took the cup Sol handed him.

"Here comes Cochran," said another of the pickets. "I guess he thinks there's trouble; he thinks they're tryin' t' run in a bunch o' scalies."

Cochran's headlights spotlighted the coffee can and those who had fetched it. The car's brakes squealed, and there was the stink of burning rubber. Cochran, an angular fellow with a receding chin and bulging forehead, tumbled out. But his voice was metallic and hard as a brass gong.

"What kind of a party is this?" he said. Behind him a burly chap with a flat nose and cauliflower ears edged his legs out of the car. He stood with hands resting on his hip pockets.

"Coffee from the Workers' Center," said Sol. His companions shifted about awkwardly, and Robert knew that trouble was in the air. He sauntered casually a few steps in the direction of the squares of lights marking the shops. It was dark down by the factory and there was a queer smell of tar, paint, and iron rust.

"Hold on, brother," Cochran called after Robert. "Don't go off in the heat of the day without your blanket. Just stay put, will you? I want all of you to get an earful of what I'm goin' to spill."

He strode over to the can and suddenly kicked it. The coffee flooded out and steamed on the ground. Fatfolks sprang at the can and righted it.

"That's what we think of coffee from Reds and foreign agitators," Cochran snarled sourly. "This is an American strike, and it's gonna stay that way. We don't want none o' *your* help and we don't want none o' your java. See the point? Then go and set on it!"

"Hey! We paid money fo' that coffee. That good coffee, and these men could use that coffee right handy. You think you cuttin' a fat hog in the ass, don't you?" said Fatfolks, stiffening like an angry mastiff. "Anybody want what little coffee's left?"

"Hey, listen, Sambo! Another thing. We don't want no

lip from shines. Get that? This is a white man's strike, too. We ain't takin' no dictation from niggers, neither."

"You ain't no man. You ain't no piece of a man. You wanta start trouble and then lay it on me. I know you want trouble. I ain't gonna let you cause no trouble, but I ain't skeered o' you nor none o' yo' kin'."

"That was a plug-ugly with him," said Sol disconsolately as he and Fatfolks swung the empty can between them on the way back. "He had a gat on him and itching for trouble. That's what you have to contend with. The gangsters have muscled in on a lot of the unions and the rank and file don't have much to say about how things are run. We'll get out a thousand leaflets calling for a mass meeting Tuesday night and distribute them. That way we'll reach the rank and file."

Robert had promised to come back to the Workers' Center Tuesday night. So here I am, he thought as he climbed the stairs, which seemed darker than before. I'm a little late; the meeting must be started. He was surprised to find the upper hallway so dark, and when he groped his way inside he saw that the room was dimly lighted by candles. Sol Abraham, Sally Vinson and Fatfolks were sitting at the table on which were guttering the candles in pools of their own wax.

"Here comes somebody," cried Sol Abraham, his voice booming with a hollow sound. "Oh, it's Hurley."

"Where's the meeting?" asked Robert. "Where's the lights? Are you going back to the primitive?"

"Oh, the light company turned off the juice. Seems as though they insist upon payment of bills, and we didn't have the dough, so. . . ."

"Where's the mass meeting?"

"Everybody's late. That's the trouble with meetings of this kind. You set the date at seven, and they get here at nine. They'll be coming. We should have a good turn-out. We got the leaflets around in fine shape and practically all of them were read. I think they were taken to heart, too."

An hour passed, and only five people had shown up.

Three of these were regulars. Sol began to pace the floor nervously and asked Fatfolks whether this or that person had not promised to be on hand.

"Sho' did," said Fatfolks earnestly at the mention of each name. "Promised fair and square t' be on hand."

After eight o'clock Sol ran down the stairs every five minutes to peer up and down the street.

"It's cloudy," he said. "Maybe the weather keeps them away."

At nine everybody knew there would be no mass meeting, even Sol had to give in, and he said just before he blew out the candles:

"I hope the few comrades here won't be disheartened by our poor showing. We'll just have to try and try again, that's all. Perhaps you remember the story in our school books about the persistent spider that tried time and again to swing its web, and finally succeeded. Not many lessons we can take from our school textbooks of noble kings and holy wars, but we want to look back to the dark days in Russia under the czar. Some day we're going to fill the streets just as the Russian workers jam Red Square." He snapped his finger against the poster of a Soviet demonstration tacked on the wall. "So don't get discouraged. Everybody work all the harder, and come back next Saturday and bring two or three with you."

Poor little man, thought Robert, he's fighting against indifference on one hand and greed on the other. He's fighting a losing fight, but he can't see it or won't see it. Like Monty Cass. He'll beat his brains out trying to butt a breach in a stone wall before he ever jars loose a grain of plaster. At one time during his talk, Sol threw his arms wide in a horizontal gesture, the candle outlining his shadow in the semblance of a cross. "These Christs that die upon the barricades," Robert thought of the verses, "God knows that I am with them in some things." He's crucifying himself on a cross of indifference and greed. You can't help sympathizing with him, but, when you see a man drowning, it's no use to jump in with him and drown, too.

In the streets the silver mist had thickened. Robert buttoned his coat collar and rambled aimlessly to the higher ground above the factory section; below him the city twinkled toward the dark river rolling to the Gulf. The headlights of motor cars streaked the wet asphalt, and the street lamps flooded it with pools of flame. The trolley cars spitting blue overhead and flanges whining on the curves. "I love thee, infamous city," Robert whispered, "I'm not going back to the old Green Dragon bunch. I've got to fight it alone, proud and desolate. I'm going to get a definite amount of writing done each day. Serious stuff, and I'll ask Danny Maupin to look it over. I guess I'll always be a bit lonely and apart. If I could only get away from that damned office and put my whole time and my whole soul to writing. Novels. You couldn't keep a flea alive writing poetry."

A raw wind surged up with the city's effluvium: the muddy, acrid tang of the river; the fetor of the streets. Robert sniffed rapturously, and slow, pensive moisture oozed from his eyes.

> "With heart at rest I climbed the citadel's
> Steep height, and saw the city as from a tower:
> Hospitals, brothels, prisons and such hells
> Where evil comes up softly like a flower."

Baudelaire! Villon! The mad and the brave. They lived furiously while they did live and died without a whimper. Poor little Sol! What was the phrase? "Miniature overalled Dantons, screaming like mad French eagles."

His head was high and bared to the mist as he descended the street toward the city's heart and past it to the riverfront and the Green Dragon and above it his bed and, in the bed, Nell. He hummed an old ballad as he went:

> "Western wind, when wilt thou blow
> That the small rain down can rain?
> Christ! If my love were in my arms
> And I in my bed again."

CHAPTER NINE

For a month Robert cast about for a plot for his novel. Alan had made several false starts on a novel about Kurt Leischer to be named *The Unvanquished,* but try as he might Robert could not get very enthusiastic about Leischer as a heroic figure. While he was still scribbling tentative outlines and tearing them up, there came a telegram for Robert from Terry. Martha was dying, had been operated on for gallstones, and if Robert wished to see her alive he must hurry. She had sent word that she forgave him fully and freely for all the anguish and pain he had brought into her life, and if she passed away before he arrived it was her hope and prayer that they would meet in heaven, never to part. The telegram must have cost Terry five dollars; and it was probably the first he had ever had occasion to send.

Robert and Terry rose in unison from the davenport in the hospital waiting-room as a white-clad nun came in, her feet stealthily rasping along the concrete floor.
"And how is she?" Terry asked.
"The doctor is with her now. He'll come down soon." She sat down at a table and engaged herself with some letters and bills. Why don't I feel any sorrow? thought Robert. What's the matter with me? I'm thinking about the most absurd and unimportant things. She'll die, of course. He stepped into the shadowy hall; passed niches occupied by statues of the saints with candles flickering below them. The sunshine was hard and bright and the air brittle. Across the yard, desolate with frost-wilted grasses and plants, an artificial grotto of rough stone had

been built, and toward this he sauntered. The shrine was dusty and ticklegrass and fallen leaves had drifted there. "Just count the Chevrolets!" admonished a yellowing newspaper, transfixed by rain and wind against a wall. Back inside the hospital, he stared at the walls of the waiting room, kalsomined a mustard yellow. The words of one framed motto in verse chased one another around and around in his head. The verse had to do with a fellow who had been no great shakes during his life, a little rough and wild, but one of his daughters had taken the veil, and that would certainly erase a good many items from the debit side of the ledger when he had to face St. Peter:

> "When my days on earth are over
> And my earthly work is done,
> I'll just say to St. Peter:
> 'I'm the daddy of a nun.' "

The nun sat cool and pale, now and then turning her face to the window to squint at the rising sun. I wonder if it's true that nuns are shaved bald; if they shave all over as they say they do, thought Robert. He remembered the lurid tales of the roistering monks and nuns of the old days, the pamphlets telling of the tiny skeletons planted in monastery graveyards, the Capuchins with their grottoes built of human skulls and bones. *Love Letters of a Portuguese Nun,* a little blue book given him by Alan. What does she think? Robert thought. John Davidson's *Ballad of a Nun.* "Her body seemed to burn the wind."

A shapeless woman wearing house slippers slap-slapped into the room.

"Here you are!" she cried. "Thought we was goin' up on the roof this mornin' fer a private sunrise prayer meetin'. I was there and I prayed. But where was you? I prayed fer you, but you don't deserve it."

"I forgot all about it," smiled the nun, her white teeth cold as icicles in her mouth. "I had my mind on these bills. Bills! Bills! Sister Agatha does nothing but worry about them now."

"You throw out the crumbs fer the birds?"

"Yes. Look." They both drew near the window. "Most of our birds have left us. They're going to the sunny south for the winter. Aren't they the lucky things; and they don't have to worry about their bills, do they? Those little sparrows will have a picnic now; they'll get it all. Won't we miss all our little feathered friends, though?"

"We will that. I'll miss them chatterin' martins. They woke me up ever' mornin' with their chitaree, to-wit, churr. That birdhouse on the tall pole looks like a weddin' cake, don't it?"

"It does, doesn't it? It's the birds' wedding cake." For an instant the nun's marble face was tinted with a warm, wistful smile like the sun's pink, then froze into composure and resignation. Wonder if she misses love? Is she sexless, or has she ever known love? thought Robert.

The doctor had come in unseen. He shook his head and smirked mirthlessly, rasping phlegm in his throat. "Good-morning, gentlemen."

"How is she?"

"No matter how long we have them with us, we're never ready to give them up. I remember when my own old mother died at the ripe old age of 85."

"Then she's dead?"

"Not yet, but soon. Come quickly, but she will not know you again on this earth."

"Martha Olivia Hurley was the only child of Professor Marcus Anthony Darrell and Mrs. Sarah May Darrell (*née* Bascomb). She was born August 18th, 1874, near Probstville, Missouri, attended the public schools of Probstville, and matriculated at Boone University, from which she graduated with signal honors. Sarah May Darrell passed away on the ninth of June 1885, and in the fall of 1896 Marcus Anthony Darrell and his daughter, Martha Olivia, moved to Green Valley, where the former followed his beloved spouse into the Great Beyond on the seventh of July, 1897. Martha Olivia Darrell entered into the bonds of holy matrimony with Terence Hurley in the year 1904, and to this union one son, Robert Browning

Hurley, was born one year later. Sister Hurley gave her heart to God at a tender age and lived a devoted and consecrated Christian life ever since. She united with the Pentecostal Church of the Nazarene in Green Valley several years ago, and was always a tireless worker in the Lord's vineyard, taking a prominent part in all church activities until her health failed her. She died affirming her faith in her Redeemer, in the church triumphant and the resurrection of the body, and expressing the hope that she would meet all her loved ones and friends in that land where the saints of God meet in life everlasting to part no more."

Pastor Epperson, his long hair peppered with gray, signaled to a girl sitting at the folding organ. She began pumping her feet vigorously and the organ whined, soughed, and yelped, then burst into a peal. A quartette of female saints rose noiselessly from beside the bier and sang dolorously:

> "My heavenly home is bright and fair;
> Nor pain nor death can enter there.
> Its glittering towers the sun outshine.
> That heavenly mansion shall be mine.
> While here a stranger far from home;
> I'm going home no more to roam."

In his sermon Pastor Epperson found a chance now and then to mention atheists, and nobody doubted that he was preaching directly to Robert, who had been chased away from home because of his friendship with an atheist.

"What happens to the atheist when his hour strikes?" cried Pastor Epperson. "That great infidel, Robert Ingersoll, when the death pallor began to dampen his brow, confessed that he had been wrong and advised his children to repent and be saved. I am thinking now of a story, a true story in every respect, set forth in that admirable compilation, *Moral Tales and Sketches*. In a great city a society of infidels were in the practice of meeting together on Sabbath mornings to ridicule religion and to encourage each other in all manner of wickedness. At length they proceeded so far as to meet, by previous agreement, to burn their Bibles. They had lately initiated into their awful mysteries a young man who had been brought up under great religious advantages and seemed to promise well; but on that occasion he proceeded the length of his companions, threw his Bible into the flames and promised with them never to go into a place of religious worship again. He was soon afterward taken ill. He was visited by a serious man, who found him in the agonies of a distressed mind. He spoke to him of his past ways. The poor creature said: 'It all did well enough while in health, and while I could keep off the thoughts of death.' But when the Redeemer was mentioned to him, he hastily exclaimed: 'What's the use of talking to *me* about mercy?' When urged to look to Christ, he said: 'I tell you it's no use now! I tell you 'tis too late . . . 'tis too late! Once I could pray, but now I can't.' He frequently repeated: 'I cannot pray—I will not pray!' He shortly afterward expired, uttering some of the most dreadful imprecations against some of his companions in iniquity who came to see him, and now and then saying: 'My Bible! Oh, my Bible!'

"My friends, let that awful message sink deep into your hearts. Man is of but few days and full of trouble. I saw in my humble little chapel a young man being led astray by a scoffer. What will this young man think when he sees the fearful flames of hell bellowing up out of the gulf of eternal torment in that last dread hour? I am a plain-spoken man. I say with all love and compassion for this erring young man, who is within the sound of my voice, that I hope he repents and is saved so that he may join his sainted mother in heaven. Shall we pray?"

As Pastor Epperson bowed his head, Robert flushed at all the glances directed at him. He wasn't going to let him get by with it. He jumped to his feet; everybody stiffened with astonishment.

"I'd like to have a little word," Robert said. "Of course, everybody knows who this poor narrow-minded man means. I know it is useless to argue with a fanatic. They retreat to the Bible, advance it as infallible proof, and by taking different passages in the Bible, one can prove anything." He halted to try to bring back to mind some of the contents of *100 Contradictions of the Bible*, a little blue book Alan had given him, but he could not recall one that he felt sure of quoting accurately. When his voice stopped, he was conscious in the silence of heavy breathing, of open mouths.

> "The fight is mine, and swim or sink
> My own war I am captain of.
> No holy fire of Pentecost
> Can force on me a saviour's love.
> I want no Jesus Christ to think
> That he could ever die for me. . . ."

Giovanitti's poem did not sound so thunderous as when he had first heard Alan delivering it; Robert knew his voice was a bit shaky and reedy.

"Voltaire said: 'I wholly disapprove of what you say . . . and will defend to the death your right to say it!' That is how I feel. The Christian has a right to his belief, and so has the atheist, or the agnostic. I'm not an atheist at all. I'm an agnostic. There's this difference. . . ."

"My dear young friend," said Pastor Epperson sweetly. "May God bless you. I love every hair on your head. But let me say this. If there is any difference between the various sects of godless people, those who deny God's sovereignty, it is like the difference told of in the story of the Indian medicine man who had two matchless remedies, one of which sold for a dollar a bottle, the other for two. 'Just what,' inquired an inquisitive customer, 'is the exact difference between your hicockalorum tonic and your locockahirum tonic? To me they taste identical; and the effect on my constitution and that of my friends who have taken it appears to be the same.' 'There is a marked difference,' replied the wily Indian medicine man. 'It is true that both remedies are made from the bark of the wampus tree and the process of manufacture is the same, but the hicockalorum tonic is made from bark shaved *up* the tree, while the locockahirum is made from bark shaved *down* the tree.'"

There was a small titter, but the people remembered the coffin among them and hushed abruptly. Oh, what's the use? thought Robert. You offer them logic, you offer them science, and they pay more attention to a rotten joke. He threw up his hands in token of resignation, and the organ wailed again. The undertaker stepped into the room, rubbing his moist fat palms together. "All those who wish to take a last view of the remains, please pass quietly this way and outside the house."

Robert pushed his way out of the room, shoving aside knees, stepping on toes, returning glare for glare. He was not feeling much grief at Martha's death, and he had it in his mind to horrify the saints as they had never been horrified before. He stood in the door and shouted one of Alan's favorite quotations: "God is a lie, hope is a whore, and a flea has more for his labor than a man!"

But it was with a definite melancholy that he entered the yard and stood for a while looking at his old home. Now some of the windows were broken and had been patched with cardboard. The floors had not been swept for weeks. Robert could not forget the night when Martha had read the beginning of her unfinished story. This was the night when Pastor Epperson had come calling to talk about the trouble between Leo and Dogface over the kitten, and Martha had never been the same woman since. Her fanaticism had grown steadily till it possessed her whole being and mind. Before she gave in to it completely she had tried hard to keep the house as orderly as when Professor Darrell lived in it. Now as Robert opened the front door he noticed that the large wooden sphere that had topped the newel post at the foot of the stairs was gone, and the rusty bolt that had held it in place stuck up. The sphere used to come in handy to stop the descent of Robert and Leo as they slid down the bannisters. The stair carpet, once a bright green, had faded and was worn to ambiguous gray tatters.

Terry knew how to cook only mulligan stew, and the

stale odor of onions had invaded all the rooms and clung even to the books in the library. The books were looking all the more sad and dusty, and the stove was reddening with rust.

Terry came in and began taking off his black suit, worn for the second time in all the years he had owned it. When Robert saw the awkward lump in which Terry had knotted his tie, he regretted that he had not helped his father to dress. But what did it matter in Green Valley? Pastor Epperson looked no better.

"I ain't much of a cook," said Terry. "Seems like I lost the hang of it these last years, not bein' obliged t' do it fer meself."

He led the way to the kitchen, and rattled the pans in the cupboard, drawing one out. He looked at it closely; sniffed it.

"Looks all right; smells all right," he said. "I sometimes can't tell which 's been used afore. Aw, it don't matter whin 'tis only meself that be eatin' out of it. But today there's comp'ny."

The disorder which had swept over the whole house was accentuated in the kitchen. Terry had dirtied two sets of dishes without being put to the necessity of washing any, but he would soon run out. The tables and shelves were piled with empty cans, jaggedly stabbed open; with rotting onion and potato peelings; and with waxed bread wrappers wadded into balls. The desolation affected Robert keenly, and he was eager to get away from it and back to St. Luke. He had been thinking about the novel he was going to write, and it now seemed reasonably clear to him what it would be about. But he could not trust himself, for many times before he had imagined himself sure of what he wanted to say, only to find his mind incapable of putting the idea on paper in coherent order.

"You're going to stay on here alone?" he asked Terry.

"Sure." Terry stopped jabbing with a screw driver at a can of beans.

"Well, you mustn't try to cook for yourself, and you

must let me know every week how you are, so I won't worry."

"I will that whin I git strung out a bit. Poor woman! She was nate as a pin afore this madness tuk 'er, and with it all she had many endearin' ways if a body could overlook that she was touched in the head. But I'll be stayin' here, all right, 'cause I've lost me cravin' fer wanderin'. At times whin yer poor mither would fair drive me daffy wi' her preachin', I'd take down t' the railroad tracks, havin' it in mind t' jump a freight and clear out. But whin the ingine would come a-snortin' and a-bellerin' like a bull on the rampage and the cars, lookin' monstrous high and big, flash by me eyes so much faster, it seemed like, than in me younger days, me knees fair trimbled, me belly got sick and shivery, and me joints seemed stiff-like till me laigs felt like them of a man on stilts. Ye've waited too late, Terry, I told meself; and back I'd go wi' me tail betune me laigs like a shape-killin' dog t' take another tongue-lashin'.

"It was hard, too, t' see her dyin' and then holdin' out t' the last agin goin' t' the doctor. The saints kept tryin' t' pray her ailment away till the house was nothin' but yelps and groans and howls day in and day out, from sunrise t' sunset and from sunset till daybreak agin. She died in mortal fear, poor soul, and she said her faith was not strong enough or the prayers of the good saints would have cured 'er."

Robert was on the train and half way to St. Luke before he happened to think that Terry might be short of money. And nothing had been said about it. He must remember to mention it in a letter.

CHAPTER TEN

A rather slight, dark fellow. He said he'd be back Thursday," said Nell.

"What did he want? What did he say?" asked Robert.

"He wanted to see you, and said you would be glad to see him. He kept grinning as though he might be holding back some good joke."

"That was Leo," said Robert, and he was more sure of this than he had ever been of anything else before.

"Your brother? Surely not. How would he find you? And if he was, why didn't he say so?"

"He wouldn't. That was Leo, as sure as you're alive."

Thursday evening came and as soon as he opened the door to a knock Robert knew positively that his intuition had been correct. It was Leo, sure enough. A little heavier, but the same face—and the same manner.

"Hello, Bob," said Leo. "How's the little stranger?"

Robert had often visualized such a meeting, and had planned a course of procedure. First of all, he was going to beg Leo's forgiveness. But now that he saw Leo in the flesh, he was dubious. Leo would think he owned Robert for life if he showed too much contrition. Robert could not help feeling Leo's amused contempt and cock self-sufficiency, and he became conscious of a vague resentment and a sense of injury. After all, Leo had served their father pretty shabbily all these years by keeping silent while Terry had no way of knowing whether he was dead or alive. Nevertheless, Robert was genuinely glad to see Leo. He grasped him by both hands, drew him inside, and urged him to sit down.

"Where in the world have you been all this time?"

Robert asked. "So *many* things have happened! Mother is dead. I just came home from the funeral."

"Yes, I knew she was sick, but I didn't know she'd passed away."

"Oh, Nell told you."

"No. I found out som'eres elset. Never mind how right now. How's the ol' man?"

"He insisted on staying and living alone. He looks bad. You should write to him at once, Leo, or go to see him. That'd be better. He took your leaving damned hard."

"I don't mind lettin' *him* know. It was the ol' lady. I couldn't bear t' have her knowin' where I was, and I couldn't let the ol' man know without her gettin' wise to it. So I jist kept mum."

"She never worried anyhow. You remember she was going strong with the Holy Rollers when you pulled out. She got worse, more violent, all the time. I had to leave home, too, on account of it. And when she got so sick with gallstones she couldn't stand the pain, she wouldn't have a doctor. She had Pastor Epperson and the saints praying for her, but she could never muster enough faith to get cured. Or so she thought; she thought she was at fault somehow, and that helped to kill her. She thought she must be lacking in some way as a Christian and a saint if she couldn't show sufficient faith to permit the Lord to heal her. So she died. . . ."

"Well, I showed ever'body I could make my own way and ask no favors from nobody," Leo said complacently, pulling open the pocket of his shirt, peering in it, and fishing out a half-smoked cigar, which he lighted. "I ain't had all strawberries and cream, but I made it, and I never asked no odds offen nobody."

"How did you find out that I was living in St. Luke, and where I was living?"

"It was funny. You know, Anna puts newspapers on the tablecloth t' save it from coffee stains and grease spots——"

"Anna? Then——"

"Wait a minute! Wait a minute! If you don't crowd

the monkey, ladies and gents, you'll see more of a show for the price of admission. Don't expect me t' spill it all in one gob. But might as well blow it. Yes. Anna Leischer that was. She's Missus Hurley now, and the mother of four kids and one miscarriage. All about that later. What I was a-sayin' was about the paper. You know, you take a want-ad section or the society and they ain't a damned thing in either I'd give two whoops in hell fer. After I look at the funnies and the sport sheet, you might as well take the rest of it to the bathroom. But jist as sure as Anna puts a sheet on the table and I'm settin' there drinkin' coffee and thinkin' about the day's work ahead, I get t' lookin' offhand at that paper and I'll see somethin' interestin'. Them little pieces 'bout so long maybe 'bout somebody uncoverin' some Indian relics or somethin' of the kind. Well, sir, last week I was settin' there and Anna hollerin' I'd be late and she was gonna take t' puttin' them papers on the table upside down so's I couldn't read 'em when I sees a teensy-weensy piece that all of a sudden jumped at me like a box car: 'Robert Browning Hurley, 16½ Traders' Alley, well-known St. Luke poet and one of the group affiliated with the magazine *Caliban* and the Green Dragon Café, rendezvous of St. Luke bohemians, is in Green Valley this week, where he has been called to the bedside of his mother, who is seriously ill.' So that's how I knowed it. It was sure funny. And nobody hardly knew where this out-of-the-way street was. Don't it beat the Jews how I happened t' run across that? I knowed I could depend on you t' keep mum about it. I'd made up my mind the ol' lady 'd never know what become o' me, and all these years I stuck to it."

Nell was embarrassed at having to listen to the brothers discussing their own affairs without noticing her, and she edged toward the door. "Excuse me," she said.

"Oh, yes!" Robert said. "I'm so excited, I forgot to introduce her. This is Nell Ravenel, and of course you know this is my brother, Leo."

"Pleased t' meet cha!" Leo said.

Robert hoped that Leo would catch on that Nell was his mistress, for this would serve to cast a wordly glamour about the little stranger, who could no longer be regarded by Leo as a softy and an innocent in matters of sex, anyhow. Leo would know that Robert had grown hair beneath his belly, and had managed to acquire a mistress without being put to the necessity of marrying her, while Leo was anchored to a wife and four children.

Leo looked at Nell with open admiration and hunger. Everywhere he went he saw women who were so much more trim than Anna, whose breasts had become heavy and pendulous. Leo often told himself that her hips were as broad as the rear end of a Mack truck. Her legs were knotted here and there with varicose veins, and it seemed that each childbirth became harder. Leo couldn't understand this; he had believed that once a woman was opened up good, it was easy afterward. But it was an undoubted fact that Anna's varicose veins became swollen and painful when she had to stand on her feet very long, and before each accouchement they were engorged and purple all the time. And every time a new baby came Leo was obliged to watch the whole horrible event. He could never feel the same toward Anna since seeing her in such a gruesome situation. He thought of his secret burial of the placenta; of the clotted sheets such as he had found in the closet after Robert's birth, and of Anna's ash-colored face with the blue lips curled back in agony, of her shrieks and moans. Leo knew that all these nauseating details must attend all women giving birth, but inevitably in his mind he had to associate these disagreeable things with Anna, for she was the specific woman he had known and seen racked and disheveled by parturition.

And, when he saw a narrow-hipped and erect-breasted girl like Nell, Leo could not help recalling wistfully Anna's fire and responsiveness those first times in the House of the Hand and the days before the second child came and wishing that she might be like that again. But she would never be. It was too late for her, but not for him. He could not get much satisfaction out of whores, however.

"Well, you might tell me just what happened after you pulled out that night," Robert said after Nell had left the room.

"It's a long story. First thing I done was t' go out t' the House of the Hand and I stayed there all night by myself. I heerd a thousand different noises that night—them limbs rubbin' against the comb of the house and groanin' till I thought ghosts and I don't know what all, and a bobcat yowlin' bloody murder outside, and somethin' sobbin' like a woman that may have been a panther, but naturally it would make a fellow think of the murdered woman that stuck her hand up out o' the well. But I stuck it out. I don't mind sayin' now that I needed clean underwear the next mornin', though.

"In the mornin' I went sashayin' around Leischer's and hid in the hazel brush. I seen Anna and give 'er our private signal, you know. Maybe you remember: Hoo ah! Hoo ah! Hoo ah! like a rain crow. I told 'er I was goin' t' St. Luke t' git a job; and then when she cried and took on so and I seen she couldn't live without me hardly, I made it up with 'er that I'd come back after 'er. I hopped a freight jist like an old hand. I'd been down to the jungles so many times and learned all about it. Gee! Them railroad yards looked big when I landed in St. Luke, but I was cool as a cucumber. I went scoutin' out among the factories, and I found a job right off. Had a hundred sence, I guess. I never have been out o' one over a coupla months at a time.

"When I come back after Anna, I got off the train at Kindro, so's nobody I knew 'd see me. I had it all planned to a 't,' and it worked jist like I figgered. Me and Anna walked back the ten miles t' Kindro, and got on the train separate and stayed that way till we got nearly t' St. Luke. We was only kids, but we acted jist like fifty-year-olds. We made it right from the start. I got an old gent at the shop where I worked t' take us in, and he helped me get a marriage license. Said he was my old man. He was a prince!"

"Were you in the army during the war?"

"No. Didn't have to. We had a kid by then, and I played a foxy trick besides. I got work in a plant that started makin' shells and munitions and there wasn't none o' the guys that worked there went. I made good money them days, but seems like it took it all. Not bein' a family man, I guess you don't remember when sugar was three pounds for a dollar, and hard t' git at that."

Robert and Leo talked a long time about the old days, and also about what had happened to each since they had last met. Leo did not mention their quarrel about Robert's tattling to Dogface and Robert did not feel obligated to say anything about it now. The experiences Leo had had were those that befall most working men whether they will it or not, Robert thought, and Leo need not feel so self-satisfied. He had nothing, as far as Robert could learn, save a wife, four children and some battered furniture. His job might play out at any time as many former ones had done. All the factories were cutting their forces daily, and, though Leo had learned a number of different jobs, machinery had so standardized production that thousands of other men could perform these tasks just as efficiently. But Robert was not just imagining Leo's air of semi-contempt and his sense of superiority. Leo had not forgotten Terry's scorn of clerks as he had expressed it on the way back from the hobo jungle that night so long ago, and Robert had turned out just as Terry said he would. He was a clerk, and the fact that he wrote poetry and had it printed made him all the more an ineffectual ninny.

Leo promised not only to write to Terry, but to take an excursion down to Green Valley to see him.

And this he did. When he came back, he said to Robert:

"It looked like it took ten years offen the old man's age when he seen me. But he had to admit I was in the right about that business, and that he hadn't done right by me."

"He took up for you," interrupted Robert, "and he looked everywhere for you."

"Well, he oughtn't t've let the old lady have 'er own

way. I said the first night Anna and me was married: 'Now, there's the britches on the foot of the bed. Which one's t' wear 'em? Me or you? So she said me, and I *have* wore 'em ever sence. . . . The ol' man he admitted you all done wrong by me, and I was in the right. . . .''

CHAPTER ELEVEN

Everywhere you turn it's a tale of woe, thought Robert. Everybody out of work; fortunes wiped out in the stock market, and a good many of the Green Dragon boys and girls had decided that it was not so necessary, after all, to live a wild, free life untrammeled by the strictures of puritanical relatives. The studios over the Green Dragon were being vacated. Even Gareth Shallore was looking long-faced and shaky. Alan Vass had lost his job, and, worse than that, his old man had all his money sewed up in a closed bank. The old man moped around a few weeks, sitting in a chair and cursing till he was blue in the face and the veins in his forehead stood out like ropes. Then one day he tried to rise to his feet while in one of his tantrums and found that he had lost the use of one side of his body. He lasted a few weeks more before the numbness crept across to freeze the other side of his body and then to still his heart. He cursed as long as his mouth would work, and after it froze, he cursed with his eyes until they glazed.

Robert had never before been especially interested in the cavernous building where the fires roared and the rivet hammers went rat-tat-rat-a-tat like woodpeckers drumming on dead tree trunks in Happy Hollow, but now he wandered anxiously about the shop, peering at the stilled forges and asking the few remaining men, who appeared to be dodging skittishly among the piles of steel and the machines, how much work they were getting. They always assured him emphatically that they were getting plenty, and he thought this queer until he reflected that these men regarded him as a spy from the office, snitching on them.

They would not confide in him; he was a "white collar" and a natural enemy. And he had never made any effort to talk to them when work was good.

Robert and Nell had visited Anna and Leo several times, but Robert never failed to feel uncomfortable there. Anna was not yet an old woman, but bearing four children and taking care of them had not helped her looks or her spirit. She had been like a spirited filly in Happy Hollow, but now she was a stolid, sad-eyed brood mare. Or so she seemed to Robert. When Robert and Nell came in, Anna ran about picking up clothing and toys from the floor, apologizing. And it was plain that she resented having to look at Nell's stylish attire and the attractive way in which she was able to keep her skin and hair and that she was never at ease as long as her visitors were in the house. The children were dogged and sullen, as though they had been threatened with punishment if they created a disturbance. But Leo enjoyed having Robert and Nell to talk to. He told of taking the winds out of his boss's sails, of convincing a fellow worker that he was not as tough as he first supposed, of punching more holes in steel plates than any other man in his department, and of the gang leader's praise at the accomplishment. Leo eyed Nell more than any one else. He wondered if all women did not prefer men who could fight, who really worked, and who knew something about life.

Nell picked up the baby gingerly, always feeling its bottom first. She was getting more and more crazy about children, and she often told Robert on the way home that Anna's kids would be lovely if Anna would only take some care of them. If *she* had that baby, she'd keep it clean and in cute togs if it took every minute of her time and every cent she could earn.

Robert had been staying away from the Green Dragon, and he was steadily piling up the sheets of his novel, taking satisfaction in the growing heap. But one night he took Leo inside to show him the place and to buy him a beer. Alan Vass came in and sat down at the table with them. He was less exuberant than formerly, for he had begun seriously to worry about how he was going to live. He had never been able to save any of his salary, and, though he did not need to worry about the rent on his studio above the Green Dragon, he was tired of eating meals with different fellows without being able to set them up now and then in return.

"Well, long time I no see you, stranger," he said to Robert.

"That's the name he had even before he was born—little stranger," said Leo, who had put away two cans of beer.

Robert told Alan that this was his long-lost brother whom he had mentioned so many times. Alan said this was an opportunity to get the real low-down on Robert's lurid youth, and as Leo called for beer after beer and his tongue became looser, Alan listened with incredulous delight. He had never been able to find a Negro who appeared to possess the qualifications of a man Friday or was willing to become one, and now he conceived the idea of attaching Leo as a disciple and a sort of court jester to re-vitalize the somewhat lugubrious air of the Green Dragon. The little fellow was so naïve, yet so cocksure. He had married at an early age, and had known nothing but a very ordinary life of hard work and skimping to make both ends meet. But he seemed to believe that his experiences, not of his own choosing and not unique from those of millions of other unskilled workers, had endowed him with wisdom which such punks as Robert and Alan could not own. It takes the practical knowledge; you have to go through the mill to know it, Leo thought.

Robert tried to get Leo away from Alan several times, but Leo objected so noisily that he had to let him be. Alan had engaged a Negro dancer to perform the cigarette dance, and he was anxious to find out what Leo might think about it. The lights dimmed, and one of the gang watched the door for cops or strangers. Then the lithe Negro girl, entirely nude, bounded out of the sanhedrin, an inner chamber often serving the same purpose as the one used by the Ancient and Mystic Brotherhood of Barbarians in the abandoned ice house at Boone. After the dancer came two unclothed Negro men, beating brass gongs and wailing an eerie chant. A spotlight ingeniously manufactured from a coffee can jerked after the girl, sometimes leaving her in shadow. But the audience yelled till she was flooded by the beam again.

"Look at them milk shakes! Hey, you want a milk shake?"

"Can you inhale, baby? Let's see ya!"

"Did you ever see one smoked like that before?"

"It's a Chesterfield! They satisfy!"

"Let's see you blow it through your nose!"

Robert was ashamed of Leo when he heard him breathing as hoarsely as he had when the two boys had lain on the hills watching the naked gypsy women. At times the spotlight touched Leo for a moment, and Alan glanced quickly at him. The father of four children, and sex-starved. See his eyes bulge out like glass marbles on a stuffed bear's head! And he's panting like a lizard on a sunny log with the temperature at two hundred in the shade. Here's my chance to study the sex impulses of the married male adult at first hand. What an unspoiled specimen!

At the climax the dancer ground her hips languidly for a while, then tossed her belly as the tempo quickened. The gongs clanged more loudly, and the dance ended with staccato snaps of the pelvis. The spotlight died, and only the cigarette bobbing up and down could be seen in the darkness.

Leo applauded till his hands burned, but the dancer would not come back. Even the cigarette had gone, and when the room became light again, the girl had disappeared. Alan tapped Leo on the shoulder.

"How'd you like a piece of that?" he asked.

"Not me!" Leo said emphatically. "I ain't *never* dressed it in mourning yet. Not while they's a single white woman left, even if she's a hundred years old and ain't got a snag in her head."

"But you seemed to enjoy the dance."

"Well, that's different. I usta enjoy slippin' out t' Hickey's breedin' stable in Green Valley t' watch a mare gettin' served, but I wasn't never anxious t' take the place of the stud. Say, did you ever hear the story about the fellow that took a cow t' the bull, and there wasn't nobody but a woman there?"

"No, I never did. Tell us about it."

And Leo sat telling one banal joke after another, Alan howling with mirth, not at the joke but at Leo's droll manner. At eleven o'clock Robert told Leo he could sit all night if he wished, but it was *his* bed time and he had to go to work if Leo didn't.

"Go on!" said Leo. "I only need three hours of sleep and I feel fresh as a daisy on a dewy mornin'."

"I'll see that you get home," Alan said, with positive affection. He could not get enough of Leo's talk.

"Save yerself," said Leo. "I ain't started yet. Wait till I get back. Jist now I wanta take a leak so bad my back teeth is floatin', and I feel like I could float a battleship with what I gotta get shet of."

It turned out, however, that Robert did not have to work the next day. The expected lay-off of clerks had come, and Robert was among those sent home. Then he had to endure a period of torture looking for another job. He grew tired of the inevitable answer: "Sorry, but we've just reduced our force here." He cringed each time he entered an employment office. At last he gave up the effort that seemed so utterly useless. While finishing his novel he would turn out some short stories to sell. He had had several printed in *Caliban*, and one of them had been listed in an anthology of best short stories.

When he worked in the office, he thought the deadly routine there atrophied his ability to create, dulled his creative sensitivity. But when he found the time all his own, he did no better. He sat and stared at the paper, found himself typing: "Now is the time for all good men to come to the aid of the party," and "Please pack with my shipment six dozen liquor jugs." These were practice sentences he remembered from the days when he studied typing. Then he'd rip the sheet from the machine and go down stairs to the Green Dragon for a while. He felt fidgety there, too.

Gareth Shallore had quit the place cold, and Robert was sure that this was because of the increasing number of touches for loans by the bohemians, most of whom had been forced either to go back home or to find refuge with more prosperous friends or relatives. *Caliban* was no more. The depression was even affecting Art. The magazine had never paid, and Shallore said his losses had been so heavy in the stock market and in a closed bank that he could no longer subsidize the publication.

Robert found Alan bottling a batch of home brew in the rear of the Green Dragon.

"You can cap them," Alan said. "It's getting so tough the gang can't buy malt, sugar and yeast much longer. I don't know what the hell I'll do next. You'll probably see me buttonholing sports in pool rooms and whispering hoarsely: 'Psst! Psst! How about some safeties, buddie, pal? Three for a quarter, and genuine Merry Widows. Won't rip, ravel, tear or run down at the heels.' Yes sir, it's getting almost to *that* point!"

Robert knew that Leo had been coming to the Green Dragon and that Alan had been making a fool of him ever since the night of the cigarette dance, but, as Leo seemed to be unconscious of it and having a good time, he reasoned that it perhaps did no harm to anyone. Some of the girls who used to sit about to discuss sexual psychology had been persuaded to come back to the Green Dragon for the purpose of baiting Leo. They told him their experiences and asked his advice, and he, feeling sure that the biological problems of women were ridiculously simple to a man of his comprehension, gave them grave counsel. But Alan did not stop at this.

One of the boys of the Green Dragon bunch was exceedingly clever as a female impersonator and used to take the prize almost every amateur night at the Garrick burlesque theater. When he found out that it was being whispered around behind his back that he was a queer, Sammy Mulvaney gave up his impersonating. But he could not resist Alan's scheme when the possibilities were outlined to him.

Sammy was introduced to Leo as Estelle LaVerne, a poetess, who had never married, but who wanted a child of her own to raise. And she wanted to make sure that she contracted with some one capable of the job. She had heard of Leo, still a young man, but the father of four children and a miscarriage. He must surely know what it takes.

Robert did not know that Leo was being baited by Sammy Mulvaney, and Alan was not anxious to have him know about it. Leo often came to the Green Dragon to spend an evening without seeing Robert at all, but at other times he came up to the studio for a few minutes.

"You coming down tonight?" Alan asked, as he poured sugar in the home brew bottles.

"No, I don't suppose so. Anything special?"

"No, nothing that I know of."

"I guess I'll work on the book tonight. I won't be down."

"Don't you worry," said Nell, as she had before. "I'm still working and maybe it's for the best if you can write something to sell. There's big money in writing if you hit the right spot. You may not have to go back to an office again."

Robert sat down and tapped rapidly and surely on his typewriter for about an hour. I'm getting into my stride, he thought, and felt quite festive about it. I'll go down and drink a can of beer to stimulate my imagination. It won't take but a minute.

The front door of the Green Dragon was locked, but John Davis, who had ceased to call himself Hjalmar Steffansson when he had abandoned the attempt to write a novel in the Scandinavian manner, opened up, and peeked out cautiously.

"Oh, Bob!" he said. "Come in. Thought it might be a cop."

"What's up?" asked Robert.

"Why, Sammy's got Leo in the sanhedrin. Hell, didn't you know about it? Maybe Alan wanted to keep you in the dark, but it's too late now. Just a little clean fun, eh?"

The peepholes into the sanhedrin were accessible only from the rear room, and when Robert came in nobody noticed him. Each one had a place, and all of the watchers were looking intently and tittering softly. Somebody kept hissing: "Shhh! Shhh! Pipe down!" Robert had not intended to spoil the fun, though he was a little resentful that he had not been told about it beforehand. But when he saw Leo looking so ludicrous he could not help recalling again the story in the Bible about the two men who had uncovered their father's nakedness and how he had been so penitent at uncovering Leo's nakedness by squealing to Dogface Epperson about the playhouse in Happy Hollow. If it had been one of the regular bunch in the sanhedrin, Robert would not have minded. But he felt that Leo was being made a clown of; that no one had any respect for him. Perhaps it was his own fault, but that did not matter. Leo would never be accepted as one of the bunch. He just didn't belong. To them he'd always be a fool—never a comrade.

"Be gentle with me, dear," sighed Sammy. "You're so strong and roughshod and I know so little. . . ."

"I know what I'm doin'," said Leo. "You needn't be uneasy, Estelle."

The sanhedrin was lighted by a dim blue bulb fastened close to the ceiling. It was arranged in this way so that the victim could not snap it out; there was no wall switch. Since there were no windows and the door could be bolted securely from the inside, there was seldom a complaint about the light that burned continually and could not be shut off. And the illumination, though dim, was of great assistance to the watchers at the peepholes.

The watchers stirred and giggled as the situation inside

grew more and more acute. Robert could not stand it any longer.

"You're making an ass of yourself, Leo," he said coldly, putting his lips close to the peep-hole. "That's a man you're loving, and a dozen people are watching you."

"Who's that?" said Alan. "Who had to gum the works right now? It was just time for the indignant husband with the revolver. Everything was working like a charm when somebody had to bray like an ass and queer it."

"I did it," said Robert. "That's carrying horseplay too far."

"The hell you say! We've done it before and you never chirped. No matter if he is your brother, he's no better than anybody else."

The moment that Leo realized how gullible he had been to fall for such an ancient trick, he began to maul Sammy unmercifully and to pull his female attire off him. The door was bolted on the inside, and Sammy could not manage to get near enough to open it. He beat Leo off as best he could.

"He's massacring me!" Sammy yelled. "F' Crissakes, break down the door or do something!"

Then Leo let up. He was sorry that he had allowed his humiliation and rage to lead him into such a display. He should have laughed it óff. Now he'd be branded a poor sport. He opened the door and Sammy ran out, his dress trailing in rags behind him.

"That's positively the farewell appearance of Samuel Mulvaney, the celebrated female impersonator," he gasped.

Alan tried to smooth it over with Leo, but Leo was not so easily placated. He stayed away from the Green Dragon almost altogether after that. He would drop in now and then when he came over to see Robert, but his value to Alan was over. Leo abandoned his rôle as adviser and philosopher and merely drank home brew.

CHAPTER TWELVE

I t's not so hard, and it's not so easy," said Leo. "Helper's job. They's men laid off, but I could git it fer you. I'm settin' purty with the boss and I'm a gang leader myself."

"Well, I don't know. I never did any work of that kind," said Robert.

"Of course, if y' think ye're too light in the poop, don't try it. It takes a little willy and elbow grease. You gotta have the ol' backbone."

"Maybe you could get some experiences to write about," suggested Nell. "You seem to be at such a dead end, and not able to get a thing done."

"What do you expect me to do? Work at writing like punching a clock?" said Robert, a little angrily. "I've got a lot of notes and stuff, a lot of things in rough shape. It takes some time to work them up." He was aware that he was exaggerating here, for he actually had accomplished little or nothing. He fancied that Nell was getting tired of supporting him. His money had played out, and he had never made a cent from his writing. The few things he had turned out recently had been rejected by all the paying magazines, but two of the non-paying ones had accepted stories. Robert liked to believe that he was getting a reputation in this way. But it required time. Nell had been hearing from her family, indirectly. They were all in tough luck—no work, and her mother needing an operation, or saying that she did. Robert suspected that the friends who came to report to Nell, protesting that her family knew nothing of their coming, were really requested to do so by the family itself. Though they had disowned her, she could not help feeling some responsibility for them. She mailed them a check for twenty dollars, and they did not return it, nor did they acknowledge it or answer the letter. But they cashed the check, all right.

"All right, all right!" said Robert. "Everybody thinks my writing doesn't amount to anything, anyhow. It's not how much art there is in your stuff, it's how it brings in the good old cash. If it doesn't, you're just out of luck in this world."

"Who are you throwing that at?" asked Nell. "If you want to make yourself unpleasant, go ahead. But you can't make me wrangle with you."

"Most of the hands here is Polacks and hunkies," said Leo the next morning, as he pulled open a small door set in a huge one and stepped inside the shop. Robert edged after him, and the door swung to and smacked him viciously on the back. It was weighted with a heavy piece of angle iron swung on a cord.

"Look out!" yelled Leo, after the door had hit Robert. "Hafta watch yer step around here. You'll get killed. You ain't peckin' a typewriter now."

This gave Robert an intimation of what he was going to have to endure. Leo was experiencing a great deal of satisfaction in coaching the little stranger who had gone to college and who was to have been *some* pumpkins. What did his book learning amount to when he had to get down and dig for it the same as anybody else?

The blue and black smoke was dense high against the roof of the building where idle cranes hung and the skylight panes gleamed dully in the weak morning light. Rivet forges were being heated, the helpers in goggles adjusting the air and oil. Sometimes the forges belched forth terrifying blasts as Robert passed by, and he caught the helpers laughing at him. They were purposely scaring him.

The shop was confusing to Robert before the whistle blew, and it was immeasurably worse afterward. All the forges bellowed loudly, there came the clang of struck steel, the whine and rattle of the cranes and the blue crackling on their trollies, the steady rat-tat-tat of the pneumatic rivet hammers. There was an undertone of slow rumbling from the heavier shears and presses.

"These hunkies," roared Leo. "Don't take *nothin'* offen 'em. Lay 'em out cold with a bolt or wrench if they get cocky. They expect it. You gotta do it or they'll think you're a-scared of 'em. Don't let 'em fill you full of bull, or they'll ride you like you was a gentle-broke work horse. You'll hafta work this mornin' with one named Stanley somethin' or other. I always sneeze his last name."

Robert grew more panicky every moment. A worker tapped him on the shoulder, beckoned. It was Stanley, the Polack. The job was to pile some angle irons on a truck with a hand hoist manipulated by a chain. Robert grabbed the chain and jerked at it rapidly. It twisted, caught. He was sweating, his face burning with exertion and embarrassment.

"No! No! No gude deesa way! Too fas'! Too fas'!" cried Stanley, a huge, dark fellow with thick, sullen lips and a dark growth of beard peppered with gray. "Look! Look!" he pleaded. "Eesa work! Eesa work! Look! Deesa way!" He pulled languidly at the chain, shutting his eyes. And the hoist *did* work better. "No gude deesa way," he said, jumping about and furiously yanking at the chain in an exaggerated imitation of Robert's manner. Robert knew intuitively that Leo was standing behind him, looking on, and he could sense his contemptuous grin even before he stepped up and Robert saw him.

"Hey, you squarehead Polack," Leo said to Stanley, "what's goin' on here?"

"I tell 'im too fast no gude," said Stanley sullenly.

"That's no way t' show 'im. It looked like you had the crabs eatin' on you or the St. Vitus dance. You gotta work it this way." He pulled the chain swiftly but steadily. "You're wearin' yourself out and ain't gittin' nowheres. All right t' hurry on the job, but you gotta git som'eres."

"Come with me," Leo said to Robert. He led the way out of the building into a yard piled with beams and girders. He signaled to an overhead crane; but there was no answer. Leo yelled more loudly.

"Sound asleep" he said. "By Jesus, if I had the say so, I'd can his ass so fast his head 'd swim."

Then a head poked out of the crane. "Yo!" called the crane man.

"Come on! Come on, sleepin' Jesus!" said Leo. "Layin' up there and dreamin' off. Around to number five!"

The crane came squeaking and grinding along its overhead track suspended from poles, halted over a pile of heavy channel irons, and let down a cable with a hook attached.

"We gotta send these inside. I'll show you how it's done," said Leo as he squinted at the beam and fastened the hook on it, motioning to the crane man. As the beam cleared the pile, it was found to be a bit unbalanced, and had to be lowered. But Leo hit the exact center the second time and the beam hung perfectly horizontal.

"I hardly ever miss the first time," said Leo modestly. And to the crane operator: "Inside, dreamy eyes! Drop it at the coper."

"Now you try it," he said to Robert when the crane returned. Robert was afraid of the hook, and he was timid about signaling the operator. He muttered "down" or "up."

"Hey!" Leo said. "He can't hear that, and wouldn't pay no attention if he could. Give 'im the high sign—this-a-way."

Robert placed the hook and gave the sign. When the hook clamped onto the beam it pinched his forefinger till he could not pull it loose. The pain was excruciating, but he was absurdly afraid to cry out, and somehow the pain made him forget to give the sign to lower. Then Leo noticed his twisted face and the beads of sweat moistening it.

"F' Go' sakes!" he cried, giving the down signal vigorously. "What y' done now? You got yer finger caught?"

Robert pulled off his canvas glove and there was the nail mashed to a red and blue pulp, and blood spurted.

He saw bright bubbles and points of light dancing and floating before his eyes, just as he had when the catfish skinned his hand in Happy Hollow. I'm going to faint, probably, he thought miserably. Jesus Christ, this *would* have to happen to me. He slid down across the beam, and when he came to, Leo was dashing him with water.

"Come into the office and get it fixed," Leo said. Robert could not help but resent the glow of satisfaction that visibly exuded from his half-brother. I can't stand this, he thought bitterly. I won't stand it. He held his finger with his other hand and followed Leo to the office, where there was a first-aid cabinet.

"D' ye suppose you can work?" Leo asked. "I never stop on account of a mashed finger, but mebbe you wanta."

"It doesn't hurt," lied Robert. The finger throbbed, and he wished that the bandage was off and nobody was looking so that he might ease it with his mouth.

"Well, come on over t' the coper then."

Behind the coper, a shears for trimming corners and edges off beams, a small metal locker was fastened to the wall. Leo went jingling a ring of keys and unlocked it, looked inside, pawed about. Then he yelped indignantly and strode determinedly toward the other end of the shop, Robert at his heels.

"That son-of-a-bitchin' squarehead! I'll learn him t' borry my tools and not bring 'em back. You can't trust them Polacks any fu'ther than you could throw a bull by the tail. You can't treat 'em like a white man. They won't let you."

He was talking about Stanley, and when he found him he halted and glared at him.

"Hey, Stanley!" Leo yelled. "When I loaned you that prick punch I wasn't givin' it to you t' keep. I left my locker open and told you t' put it inside. Why the hell didn't you do it like I said?"

"Wassa matter, Leo?" said Stanley, undisturbed. "I take 'im back, right away queek. No see?"

"Like hell you did!" roared Leo.

"C'mon, Leo," said Stanley, grasping him firmly by the arm. "I show you, right away queek. Maybe no see."

Leo was a great deal smaller than the muscular Pole, and he did not attempt to break loose. When they reached the locker, Stanley felt inside, explored under a pile of cotton waste, and shoved a prick punch before Leo's face.

"No see!" Stanley said, closing his own eyelids with a thumb and forefinger. "Wassa matter, Leo? Too much peachy. Too much poosh-'em-up, mebbe. Leetle bit, all right; too much, no gude. Crazy like hell." He stared steadily and challengingly at Leo, who finally dropped his gaze and muttered: "All right, Stanley. All right. Go on back t' work."

When Stanley was out of earshot, Leo said: "I laid him out with a wrench first week I worked here. I don't take none o' his lip." But this sounded like hollow boasting to Robert. He was secretly gratified to see Leo's bluff called, and he could not believe that Leo had ever dared to hit Stanley.

Leo set to work marking off a beam with a templet, a wooden piece with holes bored in it, which was laid over the steel as a pattern. Robert stood by awkwardly, not knowing what to do.

"One of the first things you gotta learn when you're f———n' the dog," said Leo, "is t' look like you're workin' hard enough t' make yer butt blossom like a rose. Rattle templets, beat with a hammer on a beam, but do *somethin'*. If the boss ketches you f———n' the dog while you're helpin' me, he'll eat *me* up blood raw. First thing I ever learned from old Willie, the sawyer, when I went t' work in the mill in Green Valley, was t' fool around doin' nothin' but keepin' busy at the same time. I tell you. Go down there and fetch that templet marked 9C1863 off that rack on the wall behind Stanley. If the Goddamn Polack says anything fresh, lay 'im out with yer hammer. I'll back you up."

Robert had lifted down the templet and had started off with it when he heard Stanley shout. He turned around and saw that he had inadvertently knocked down Stanley's coat, hung on the other end of the rack.

"Hey, pick 'em up! Pick 'em up!" yelled Stanley imperiously.

Robert picked up the coat and dusted it off carefully, hanging it back where it had been.

"I'm sorry," he said. "I didn't intend to do that. I didn't see your coat there."

Stanley appeared to be astonished. His face cracked in a sheepish grin.

"Oh, neva min'! Neva min'!" he said heartily. "Nobody sore. Nobody mean nottink. Beeg mout', das all. See?"

At noon Leo and Robert sat down to eat their lunches wrapped in newspapers. Robert had prepared his own, and he felt disheartened as he chewed the cold sandwiches. His muscles were aching, and he felt humiliated—that he was as completely under Leo's domineering thumb as when they had been boys. Leo could tell that Robert was dispirited, and, though he knew that Robert had not approved of Alan's making a fool of him in the sanhedrin, he felt a little sore at Robert for associating with such a bunch. And he wanted to show his half-brother what real men were like.

"You think you'll stick with it?" Leo asked, hoping that Robert would unbosom himself and confess his distaste for the job.

"Sure. Why not?" said Robert. Then he knew that he could not invite Leo's ridicule by quitting. And the prospect of staying on such a job indefinitely was one that he could not bear to think about. Better be dead. Better go down to Hooverville on the river front and live like a rat on the garbage the trucks unloaded into the scows for the hog farms upstream. He resolved to get right at some stories and to rush up his novel, too. Once he got a start, it wouldn't be such hard sledding. A guy with a reputation can dash off any old sort of crap and sell it for heavy money. But you have to get the reputation first, and that takes a lot of sweating and a lot of heartbreak and sacrifice. Danny Maupin never had any bed of roses to begin with, and look what the critics said about him when his second novel came out. He never came around the Green Dragon any more, and Robert did not blame him. The place was like a tomb. Gareth Shallore was talking of leaving town altogether. Alan said that none of the Green Dragon bunch could wring a sou out of him, anyhow; he was as tight as the bark on a tree. There was an old rundown Southern plantation he owned, and he was going there to escape the misery and woe that had come with the depression. He couldn't write poetry when he had to encounter hunger and dismal things like that on every hand in the city.

The general foreman and several of the under foremen and clerks ate in the glassed-in office, and as soon as Leo could gulp down his lunch, he hastened to the water fountain beside the office door. He sloshed some water around and around in his mouth for a while, all the time eyeing the group in the office. Then he slipped nimbly inside. He had not asked Robert to accompany him, and Robert would not have gone in, anyhow. The foremen and clerks reminded him of the office where he had worked as a payroll clerk. Leo could be seen laughing dutifully and obsequiously at all the jokes of his superiors. He must be ashamed of his lunch, thought Robert, or he'd eat in the office. He considers himself a foreman since he's a halfbaked gang leader, but only working three days a week and with a hell of a family to support, he has to watch his corners and can't afford to eat as much lunch as he needs.

While he was pondering over Leo's behavior, Robert felt a tap on his shoulder. It was Stanley, grinning widely and holding out a sandwich.

"Maybe you like," he said. "Too much. Can't eat all."

Robert bit into the sandwich and at first thought he had been tricked, it was so fearfully hot with pepper. But he managed to swallow it, and he told Stanley it was good. "Wait," said Stanley, and in a few moments returned with a thermos bottle. He rubbed his belly and rolled his eyes.

"Try," he said. The bottle held strong but pleasant-tasting home-made prune-jack, and Robert made the bottle gurgle twice. It soothed his burning throat. Stanley reached over to retrieve his bottle.

"Too much no gude," he said. "Leetle bit, fine stuff." He sat down by Robert and spat in the cinders, scraping with his calked brogans. He scratched with a heavy, blunt finger nail on the eye beam they were sitting on, and the rasping squeak set Robert's teeth on edge.

It was hard for Stanley and Robert to carry on a conversation, but Robert learned that Stanley had six children and that it was hard to keep things going on three days' work each week; there had been one five per cent wage cut and now there was going to be another the first of the next month.

"But we no take," said Stanley. "We got union, see!" He drew out a card and showed it to Robert. "Mebbe you join. I sign up fifty already. I sign up more than anybody else. We mebbe strike right away. Take vote right away."

Robert had not intended to say anything to Leo about the union and the strike vote, but on the way home Leo began to complain about the foreigners. They would work for anything they could get and whine thankfully for the driest bone. And they had no guts. They made it hard for the Americans who had guts enough to stand up for their rights.

"You'll find out when the strike comes," Robert burst out, and before he fully realized what he was about he had told all about the conversation with Stanley.

"They ain't gonna do nothin'," said Leo. "You wanta lay off them bolshevik unions. I'm fer a union, sure, if it's got the shadder of a chancet. You remember how poor old Monty Cass buggered hisself up so's he couldn't git no job nowheres. That's what comes from bein' too radical and a trouble-maker. And ever' one o' them Polacks and Rooshians git plenty fer stirrin' up trouble. They don't care whether they win the strike or not, the leaders don't. Their pay from Rooshia goes on jist the same. Ain't nobody with a fair mind could complain about the way the company treats us. They're hit by the depression harder'n we are, cause look how much more they got t' lose."

Robert felt stiff and sore when he climbed the stairs to the apartment. He had intended to do a little writing, but he stretched out on the bed and almost instantly fell asleep. When he awoke Nell was playfully removing his clothing and stopping now and then to fondle him. Suddenly he felt quite gay and important. I'm earning my own way, anyhow, he thought. He didn't feel like a sheep-killing dog any more. He had a right here. He surprised Nell with his ardor.

"I always heard that steel men were real men," she giggled. "It sure takes effect quickly."

About nine o'clock the next morning Robert was working with Leo at the coper when Stanley came up with his coat over his arm and carrying his dinner pail. Robert was alarmed at the black scowl on his face.

"Goddamn snitch!" cried Stanley. "You squeal like dirty rat; get me canned."

"What do you mean, Stanley?" asked Robert, but he knew well enough what was up and his shame must have reflected in his manner. Leo had been carrying tales to the officials, and had told them of Stanley's activity in organizing the union. Leo pretended to be very busy with a blue print, but Robert could see him anxiously watching Stanley from the tail of his eye. He appeared to be afraid, too.

"You know what I mean!" Stanley said. "Nobody else squeal what I say. You the one. You tell."

"I did not! I didn't tell the officials. Somebody else told."

"No! You tell!" Stanley said, but less firmly. He could not be sure of Robert's guilt, for a number of the workers had necessarily been acquainted with the news about the strike vote. He was sure of the loyalty of all the others, he thought. But he could not be too positive about it. Robert was a half-brother of Leo, who was thought to be a stool pigeon, and he talked like a college man. The college boys who came into the plant were usually finks.

"That was dirty of you, squealing," said Robert to Leo after Stanley had left. "If I'd known you were a stool pigeon, I'd have kept my mouth shut."

"Stool pigeon! Be careful what you're a-throwin' at me! I'm a gang-leader, and I'm supposed t' report anything I hear against the welfare o' the company. Besides, who said I told the supe anything?"

"I know damned well you did. They've evidently been talking about it for some time, and as soon as I spill it to you, Stanley gets canned. What else would a fellow think?"

"Well, what of it?" Leo snarled. "Youre a fine one t' bellyache about squealin'. Remember what caused me t' pull out from home? I didn't aim t' throw *that* up to you, but you brought it on yerself. You come in this shop two days and, by Jesus, you know more about it than a man that's been here fer years and worked on public works since he was knee-high to a grasshopper. You ain't quit yellerin' yer didies yet, and you think you know it all. You'll never get that smart that you know it all, not by a long shot."

"I didn't intend to get you in any trouble, and I was only a kid, and Dogface bulldozed me. You're old enough to know better, and you deliberately set out to get Stanley in trouble. And Stanley was trying to help his family and others as well as himself, while you were intent mostly on getting yourself bred down there in the House of the Hand. There's a difference."

"Why, you little prick! Who carried you around on two sticks, and spent half my money on you? And who fit Dogface fer you. That's the thanks I git. If a man's workin' fer a company, he's supposed t' work in its interests, not agin 'em. You got a lot to learn, my boy, and the first thing you oughta learn is t' stay away from these Polack bolsheviks. They won't git t' first base with their strike. They'll last about as long as a fart in a whirlwind, and they'll frig themselves and ever'body elset out of a job."

Robert was not sorry that he had spoken to Leo as he had, however. The more he thought about his words, the better he liked them. And he could tell that Leo was on the defensive, and amazed to find that Robert was no longer the timid little stranger who could be browbeaten into at least acquiescing to anything that Leo propounded.

They worked away in silence for a while. Leo signaled with his hand and Robert slued the beam around on the swinging chain hoist until it was in the right position for clipping off the edge. Then there came a change in the atmosphere of the plant, but Robert was so intent that he did not notice it at first. The roaring of the forges was dwindling to a hoarse whisper and clouds of black smoke were belching from them as the air was cut down. One lone rivet hammer, sounding like a solitary woodpecker in a forest of dead trees. The men were leaving their posts and converging on the office, where a riveter climbed on a keg and began talking. The coper rumbled so that Robert could not hear, and now and then Leo stepped on the pedal so that the beam jerked against Robert. Then the sharper sound as the jaws sheared off the steel. A man left the crowd and approached the coper.

"All right! All right!" he ordered. "Shut it off!"

"Who says so?" began Leo, but saw the gang of men about the office. He stepped back from the machine and allowed his hands to hang limply by his sides.

"The strike committee," said the worker, walking to the wall and jerking down the switch. "If you don't want a busted head, flag out of here."

"C'mon," Leo muttered. "This won't last. They'll be pullin' in their horns as soon as they get a few wrinkles in their bellies, and then it'll be too late. Somebody else 'll have their jobs."

As they passed the group by the office, Robert heard: "Pickets. . . . Meeting tonight at the Polish-American hall. Everybody out. Picket line tomorrow." The bosses and clerks huddled in the office, heads together, looking like a knot of chickens agitated by the approach of a hawk. They were afraid that some of the more impetuous strikers might take advantage of the situation to settle an old grudge against a rawhiding boss by shying a nut or rivet through the glass partition. But the men left the plant quietly enough, some scuffling and shouting, others tensely serious—these were the veterans of other strikes.

"Wait a minute. I'll be right back," Leo said, and Robert saw him rattling at the door of the office and tapping with his forefinger. A foreman walked over and opened the door. Leo thrust his head in the cluster of others and talked a minute; then he came outside. "Let's go," he said.

"They're gonna break it," Leo said as they reached the street. "They'll be protection here t'morrer fer anybody that wants t' work, and if you wanta work, be here. If you got any gumption, you'll be on hand."

"I'll not be a strikebreaker."

"Oh, you won't, hey? I guess you'll go home and lay around lettin' the flies blow yer pratt and pretendin' like you're a writer or somethin' 'bout as useful as poison ivy. You're lucky. You got a gal that's willin' t' support you jist because she's got hot pants and she likes the way you handle it. I gotta look out fer my wife and kids, and that's my first duty. I wouldn't be very much of a man if I didn't."

"You're not much of a man if you break a strike. The way I live with Nell is my own business and hers."

"Mebbe it is. But if I wasn't man enough t' support myself, if I had t' let a woman support me, I'd not be criticizin' a man that tries his best t' make an honest livin' fer himself and his family. I ain't wantin' t' take anybody elset's job. I jist want t' keep anybody elset from takin' mine."

"Oh, to hell with you!" Robert shouted. "Go on and be a scab if you want to. I hope somebody peels your knob."

"Don't come cryin' t' me if that gal kicks you out," sneered Leo. "You'll know it the next time I get a job fer you."

"Don't come crying to me if you get your head caved in," Robert answered, and he felt as though he didn't care what became of Leo. But by the time he had reached Traders' Alley, he was a little penitent. He did not intend to take any part in breaking a strike, even though he did not intend to endanger his body or his comfort in helping to win it.

CHAPTER THIRTEEN

The pickets were pacing back and forth before the gates, carrying placards. If a picket stopped for a moment, one of the many cops standing about yelled: "Hey! Move on there!" Across the street from the gates was a solid mass of strikers, jeering, cat-calling, giving the cops the Bronx cheer.

"All policemen has big feet."

"Burrrppp!"

"Hey, hey! Farmer Grey
   Hauled another load away."

"Boooooo! Booooo! Burrrppppp!"

"Hey, lardass, don't let that popgun go off in ya hand!"

"Bought me a scab fer fifty cents,
   Parley voo! Parley voo!"

"Bought me a cop fer twenty cents,
   Parley voo! Parley voo!"

Robert saw Stanley among the pickets, and started across the street with the idea of telling him just how the officials had learned about his union activities. He saw no reason why he should shield Leo. He had seen Leo and several others a block or so down the street a little before the plant's normal opening time, but Leo and the others had not approached the gate. They must have been frightened away by the pickets and the crowd of strikers.

"Hold on!" a cop bawled as Robert neared the sidewalk next the gate. "No more pickets here. You got all the law allows."

"I'm not a picket. I just want to speak to Stanley there," said Robert, pointing toward Stanley.

"You can't do it. An if youse people don't stop that

racket over there we aim t' call the fire department and give some of youse a good cold bath. Some of them lousy bolsheviks 'd die if a drop o' water touched 'em."

Stanley glanced at Robert coldly and briefly and resumed his steady pacing. He wouldn't listen to me, anyhow, Robert thought disconsolately. He recrossed the street and stood watching.

Presently the cops grew more alert, twirled their clubs, and eased their guns in their holsters. The pickets and the watchers on the opposite sidewalks stiffened to attention. Something was about to happen; everybody sensed it vaguely and uneasily. Then a police car could be seen and heard tearing down the street a block away, siren shrieking and wailing, a cop on each running board with club ready.

"Into the street! They're tryin' t' run scalies in!" somebody yelled. "Don't let 'em pass! Stop 'em!"

The police car did not halt as the strikers thought it would. It plowed into the living barricade and sent men reeling, but the impact stalled the engine. The policeman who was driving was flustered, jerked desperately at the choke, stamped on the starter button. The motor woke to life with a roar, and the gears clashed with ear-splitting noises. The two policemen on the running board had been dragged off, and a brick shattered the back window of the car. There was a stack of bricks left over from a paving job on the parking, and the strikers were grabbing and using them. The cops near the factory gates set to work with cool calculation, striking with precision. One of their most effective blows was a sharp whack across the Adam's apple. A policeman fell, downed by a brick, and his cap and club rolled ten feet. A striker grabbed the club and laid about him at every cop he could see until a blow caught him across the neck and he sagged and crumpled with a wheezy "auuugh!"

Inside the car Robert could see Leo in such a state of pitiable terror that he wished he might help him in some way, though he didn't deserve it. He should have known better, Robert thought with grim satisfaction. The strikers were struggling with the doors. Leo was yanked out.

Then came the crack of a shot, and a picket near the gate screamed and doubled, clutching his stomach. Blood dripped on the sidewalk, and the man opened up his hands, flinging them wide, spattering crimson drops on the concrete and on the fighting pickets and policemen. Robert had never been so sick and frightened in all his life, but he could not get out of the press. He felt a numbing blow across his mouth, and in astonishment and terror he clapped his hand onto his face. He first thought of his teeth and picked at them. They were all there, but they ached from the blow. Then Robert realized that he was not standing on his feet, but lying down and being kicked and stumbled over. Blood trickled down his throat, strangling him. He leaped to his feet and was carried along by a mass. The police were still firing, some of the bullets whining impotently into space, others thudding into a bed of flesh or wood.

By the time Robert fully comprehended where he was and what he was doing, he was trotting along with a bunch of perhaps twenty men and two of them were hustling Leo along between them. His hat was gone and his clothing was torn. Robert noticed that his hair was getting pretty thin on top; he had a bald spot as big as a good-sized orange.

They came to a skeletal structure, half built of raw steel and concrete, three stories high. The company erecting it had gone down to ruin in the stock market crash, and only a shell of the proposed building stood. Into this Leo was shoved, and hurried out of sight behind the walls and the huge pillars. Then everybody stood back to look at him. It made Robert think of the time when he and Leo with other children had played "Froggie in the meadow can't get out; take a little stick and stir him about." Leo was shivering and his jaw trembled. If he saw Robert, who stood back from the others, he did not give any indication of it.

"Well, what'll we do with the rat?" said one of the strikers.

"What do you usually do with rats. Bump 'im off. Hell, we croak him and hide him away down in the basement here and nobody'll even smell 'im. This part o' town stinks like a crappin' can all the time anyhow. Anybody got a knife? I'll slit his windpipe."

"You got me, boys," said Leo, trying to grin and making a sorry go of it. "And I guess you got a right t' do as you like. I know havin' a sick wife and five kids at home ain't a-gonna cut no ice in a time like this. But that's how I stand, and that's a God's fact if I die the next minute. I jist wish some of you gents could be in my shoes. But if you're gonna kill me, have it over with." His eyes roved wildly from face to face, begging for the least sign of sympathy or mercy, but there was none.

But now that the men had him away from the heat of battle, they could not just pitch in and kill him. They might have beaten the whey out of him, but neither did they feel like that now. When the fighting at the plant was going on, they would have put Leo out of business if they could have done so, but it was a bit different now. Everybody shifted and shuffled uneasily; some of the men lighted cigarettes.

"Let's beat the everlastin' holy piss out of him and then beat him for pissin'," somebody suggested.

"I deserve it, boys," Leo said humbly. "I ain't got a word t' say agin it." He bowed his head. His knees were wabbling, and he walked over to a pillar to steady himself. The strikers followed after him suspiciously, thinking he might have in mind a break for freedom. But Leo knew better than to attempt that.

The longer Leo's captors stood about, the more reluctant they grew. It just did not seem right to pitch into a man who wouldn't put up his dukes to defend himself and who would not sass back. It would be like pasting a cripple or a woman or a child. One of the strikers moseyed off, and others followed, one by one. Leo perked up.

"This has learned me a lesson," he ventured. "If the

good Lord lets me get outa this mess, you'll never catch me in another like it. I'll go on the city fer my keep before I'll try such a thing. And I'll never go near that damned plant agin. That is, if you fellers feel it's so you can give me one more chancet, though I'm not sayin' as I deserve one."

"Aw, g'wan!" spoke up one man, and his was the collective will. "You don't deserve it, and we oughta salivate you, but haul ass outa here. Don't you never try strikebreakin' again."

"You fellers don't know how I appreciate this, nor how my sick wife and five kids will," said Leo. He made his way rapidly out of the building.

That's the end of my job there no matter how the strike goes, thought Robert, and I don't know whether I'm sorry or glad. I couldn't go back if the union wins, Stanley thinks I'm a snitch, and I won't go back if it doesn't. His head ached and pounded and his teeth were sore. His tongue was swelling so that it felt several sizes too large for his mouth.

"What did you want to get in it for?" asked Nell.

"I didn't want to. I couldn't help it. I was just standing there."

"Yes, just as Mr. Harrison says. It's the bystanders and the poor dupes that the Communist leaders egg on. The leaders stand back and laugh at the poor fools that fall for their propaganda. But they're going to get a taste of it themselves tonight."

"How so?"

"I heard Mr. Harrison calling up a lot of business men that are members of the America First Vigilantes. He's the president. They're going to take axes and wreck that place out on Western, the Workers' Center. The police don't want to take any official part in it to begin with, but they'll be there to see that nobody gets hurt."

"That none of the Vigilantes get hurt?"

"Well, they'll be there to keep order."

"To keep order, when they know in advance that the Vigilantes are going to start a fight."

"There won't be any fight. They'll soon tuck their tails and run."

"Suppose they don't. What then? Will they murder them, or what'll they do with them?"

"They'll just play Carrie Nation with the furniture and chop it up and then they'll light a bonfire of the propaganda they find. That's what the bolsheviks produce more than anything else. Mr. Harrison says they always find a ton of pamphlets and books to make a bonfire of. If anybody interferes, they get a little rough, I guess, but I don't think they've killed anybody yet. They can always hold the ones they find on a vagrancy charge, Mr. Harrison says, and there are a lot of other laws about riots and conspiracies that come in handy."

Robert had heard of the America First Vigilantes, of which Mr. Harrison, Nell's boss, was the president. Whenever a strike occurred, the America First Vigilantes went about the city cleaning out nests of reds and foreign agitators. And the newspapers always patted them on the back, and sometimes there was a chance for a reporter to get some comic human interest stories about the reds, how they scuttled for cover, but weren't fast enough. The judges, too, could always get a few extra inches in the papers when they lectured the radicals about citizenship, which must be considered more of a duty than a privilege. And radicals have a lot of crust when they squawk for protection from a government they don't believe in and which they're always trying to overthrow.

The Workers' Center! Robert had not thought much about Sol Abraham and the others of late, but now his head was sore and his spirit wounded. He could not feel very amiable toward the cops or the vigilantes.

"Where were you all day? That riot was this morning, and you weren't in yet when I came in?" asked Nell. "You weren't around the union hall, were you?"

"Yes, I was. What's the harm of that?"

"Plenty of harm. You'll get yourself into trouble down there."

"I'm going down to the Green Dragon," said Robert quietly.

"Why, it's finally closed up for good. There's a padlock on the door."

"I'm going to run downtown a while, then," said Robert, and as soon as he had closed the door he bounded down the stairs. He fidgeted on the corner waiting for a street car; headlights began to blossom in the dusk and lights sprang out in the shop windows. It seemed as though the car would never get to Western, and when it did there was yet a long run to the Workers' Center.

Robert could see from the street that the hall was lighted. They must have raised enough to have the lights hooked back up again, thought Robert, as he shouldered open the door. He lunged into the arms of a policeman, and stood staring dully at the buttons, the club, and the red, triumphant face.

"Ho!" said the cop. "Here's another of the birdies flyin' back t' the old nest."

Robert looked about him in dismay. The room was a wreck. The bookcase had been chopped to kindling; the books had been savagely ripped to bits, and all the folding chairs had been smashed. Not a picture remained on the walls.

"How d' ye like the way the boys decorated the little red nest? Surprise! Surprise! But don't be grievin'. Comrade Abraham and Comrade Vinson and the nigger they call Fatfolks is down in the cooler, anxiously awaitin' you, and that's where you're goin'."

"What for?" asked Robert. "I haven't done anything. I was never here before in my life."

"Oh, no? What 're you doin' here then? Milkin' a goose?"

"I heard Abraham hung out here. I used to go to school with him, so I thought I'd drop around to pass the time of day."

"Where did you go to school with Abeski Solomonovitch? Moscow?"

"No, at Boone University. He was a student at Boone when I was there."

"Well, young fella, you may be shootin' straight and you may not. You got an honest, not to say dumb, look on that pan. But get this. You may 've heard of me. I'm Camera-Eye Norris himself in person, not a moving picture. And when I set my starry orbs on you—click!—somethin' in my brain just like a photographic plate, and it's there for keeps. They don't need no rogues' gallery in this man's town. Just call in ol' Camera-Eye and they got the culprit filed away. So I'll know you till hell freezes over and they build fires on the ice. This is a nest of reds, or it was one. I don't know whether you know that or not. The vigilantes just mopped them up. We got ten in the cooler and I was stationed here to nab any that shows up. But I'm gonna show you I got a heart as big as a whale. I'll only take your name and address and maybe I'll investigate you a little and maybe I won't." He jerked out a note book, poised his pencil.

"Name?"

"Bob Hurley."

"Address?"

"16½ Traders' Alley." And almost instantly Robert was sorry that he hadn't given a phony name and address. What a damned fool! There was no reason why he should have given his correct name and address. He was thinking, when he gave it, that he was entirely in the clear and had nothing to hide. The police could not possibly connect him with Sol Abraham's group. But how about Nell, with the police snooping down there? They were very lenient about the many couples who lived together without the formality of marriage until something came up. They raised the devil if they needed something to hang on a fellow. What a damned fool for playing right into the cop's hands!

"Traders' Alley," said Camera-Eye Norris. "Why that's where that nest of poets and artists is. The Purple

Snake, or somethin'. They tell me that they're all a bit queer down there. Is that right?"

Robert did not answer this question. He was eager to get away.

"May I go now, officer?" he said politely. You damned pus-gut, he thought. A lot you know about poetry and artists. Eddie Guest and obscene cartoon booklets, that's your speed.

"Yes, you may be excused, Rollo. Say, Bright Eyes, did you ever take it in your head to make money?"

"I never made more than enough to live on, and I don't want any more than that."

The cop was roaring and beating his knees with his open palms. "Oh, if you ain't a card, Rosy Cheeks! Do you stand or squat when you feel the call of nature? Clear out before I rupture a gut!"

Robert could hear his bellowing laughter a half block down the street.

CHAPTER FOURTEEN

Leo didn't get a chance to go back to work, so he had to keep his promise to the strikers. The strike continued for two weeks, and after the first morning no attempt was made to resume operations. Then the company announced that the union would be recognized, provided the non-union workers who had signified their willingness to go back before the settlement were not forced to join the union and were not terrorized. But Leo could not face the other men. He knew that they'd make life miserable for him, and he was confident that he could find another job.

When Robert saw in the papers that Sol Abraham, Sally Vinson, and Fatfolks had been given a sentence of three months for vagrancy, his half-formed idea of renewing contact with their group evaporated. He wanted now to find a little peace and quiet and security. The riot at the plant gate had sickened and terrified him. He had had a vague intention of warning Sol and the others that the vigilantes were going to wreck the Workers' Center, but when he saw the job already completed, he didn't see that there was anything else he could do. It was the same old story. The vigilantes had everything on their side, and the malcontents were as impotent as a straw in the sweep of a hurricane. The vigilantes had the support of the newspapers and the police, and Robert could not decide to wear himself away in a quixotic tilting against inconquerable odds.

He heard no more from Camera-Eye Norris, and he did not tell Nell where he had been on the night he had met the cop with a brain like a photographic plate. Nell came home often with stories of the plans and accomplishments of the America First Vigilantes, and from a dull resentment Robert grew to a bitter but concealed hostility for them. But he didn't say anything about it. He was afraid, that was the trouble. Afraid not only of the vigilantes and their strong-arm methods, but of Nell's disapproval. He could see that she believed everything Harrison told her, but he did not bother with trying to set her right. She was feeding him again, and with idleness came a desperate hunger for her body. He had nothing to do but sit around and think about such things. When he tried to put something on paper, he found that he couldn't get a thing worked out the way he wanted it. The sight of Nell undressing or displaying her form, which the years had not marred at all, in the provocative manner she knew so well was a powerful aphrodisiac that never lost its potency.

So for more than three years he lived in the little room about the dusty and cobwebbed place that had been the Green Dragon. The artists and dreamers were all gone. Even Alan Vass was living with a relative in the suburbs, and when Robert saw him, not often, he looked holloweyed and said it was hell having to sponge off people whom you used to ride and razz and who now took great delight in throwing it up to you.

When the winds were high and the air sharp and cold off the river, Robert snuggled in the bed gratefully, thankful for enough to eat, happy in the warm room, and appreciative of the soft womanflesh to enjoy. Sometimes he walked down to the breadlines and saw the dull-eyed men shuffling along for a bowl of stew and a slice of stale bread. Or he wandered along the river bank, near Hooverville, and saw the inhabitants wrangling and fighting over choice tidbits from the garbage that trucks were dumping onto scows for the hogs up the river. Across the railroad tracks from Hooverville was a loading platform, and when the truckers left a car for a moment the human swarm engulfed it. The truckers would not beat them off, and it was finally necessary to detail a squad of police for the vicinity. A car of frozen oranges was an event to be talked about for months.

Near Hooverville the city's sewers sent an odoriferous stream into the river, and in the shallow water Robert could see men panning the sewerage just as the forty-niners panned for gold. It had been reported that a diamond ring worth five hundred dollars had been discovered in this manner, and this helped the modern gold seekers to endure the cold and foul water, the backbreak, and day after day of hope deferred. Sometimes small trinkets were found, and then a shout could be heard from the lucky one. The other seekers threw down their pans and ran to examine the treasure.

So Robert came to feel a dogged pride that he was going on without being reduced to things like this. He read the reports of car loadings, the prophecies of business seers. He would wear out the depression yet. Just to be alive and in comfortable circumstances came to be a miracle with him. He would go back from the river front and open the cupboard doors, gloat over the food on the shelves.

He was sending out stories still, but he had ceased to be so keenly disappointed when the postman brought them back. At first he had awaited the mail in a kind of nervous ecstasy, hesitating between hope and despair, but that had passed. He had worked almost four years on a book, written and rewritten it until it was as good as he could make it. If he had anything in him, it was in that book. He kept putting off sending it away. He wanted to believe that it was as good as he thought it as long as he could.

PART THREE: *NOTHING TO LOSE*

CHAPTER ONE

Leo had learned to twist the dishpan in a circular fashion, setting the roily water to swirling in a miniature whirlpool. That erased the ring of grease that might have adhered to the sides. The pan was over full—it always was—and he stepped gingerly with it and tilted it at the sink. Something tinkled in the rancid depths. He plunged his hand in and groped in the opaque mess. When his hand emerged it grasped a dripping teaspoon, and globules of grease clung to the hairs on his forearm and wrist. As usual, he fouled his pants with the stuff as it sloshed over the edge of the sink. He couldn't remember not to handle things about the house in the same rough way he had pitched steel bars at the mill almost four years ago. Since the strike he had found a few piddling jobs, but nothing steady—not enough to keep a family the size of his going. They had been on the relief rolls for a time, but it was such a job to argue anything out of the visitors that it seemed a blessing at last when Anna had been able to find a job. Leo had not liked to see her go to work, but he finally had been forced to regard it as the lesser of two evils. It was better than living on relief. Anything was better than that, as Leo often said; he would rather get him a tin bill and follow with the sparrows after what the few horses left.

He was too impetuous for housework, as he had told

Anna when he started to work. He said he was too quick on the trigger. She wanted him to wear an apron about the kitchen, but that was going too far.

"Oh, *yeah*!" he had scoffed. "Get me some teddy bears and a *brashear*, too."

The kids were still asleep and he wasn't anxious to awaken them. The way they smeared eggs and glommed jam nearly made him puke sometimes. He liked to eat his breakfast while he had some appetite left. He tiptoed warily to the icebox and got a bottle of home brew. The rush of cold, stale air felt good to his steamed mug; it was equal to getting a Turkish bath to stand over the dishpan for a half-hour or so. His face felt like a boiled lobster looks. A small man, he was, with nerves as jumpy as a sore tooth, and his hair was going fast now, though he wasn't old enough for that, by rights. It was worry, he told himself. Baldness had plowed a wide furrow from brow to crown. He was still somewhat of a joker with all his troubles. Often he got off that one about having to tie a string around his head to know how far up to wash his face.

He sat down wearily at the littered table and poured himself out a glass of beer. The glass was not very clean; it had finger marks on it from the night before, but he'd rather use it than arise to fetch another. However, when a bloated fly that had been stuck to the bottom floated up in sight, it was a little too much. He carried the beer to the sink and emptied it, rinsing the glass.

He knew the kids would soon awaken, and he should eat his own breakfast while he could have a little peace. There would be hell a-popping with all of them yipping at once, struggling with their clothes, and their mouths flying open like those of hungry young jay birds. But the muggy air and the smell of cooking oppressed him. His stomach settled down so heavily it seemed to rest on the chair seat and spread out. Rather than eat, he'd sit and sip the cool beer, pitying himself and pondering cynically. He liked to feel sophisticated, aloof, somewhat like a scientist examining curious biological phenomena. It consoled him to reason with himself that not many people actually *think* about themselves and the enigma of existence. Why they were in the world and where they were going when they left it. "Life! What is it? Who knows?" he marveled, scratching his stomach where the belt was a little tight and heat pimples had raised.

At first, when he had had a little savings stashed away, he hadn't minded being out of a job. Standing around employment agencies and gassing with the boys was a pleasant way to pass the time. But after the first winter it got to be serious. It costs money to keep up a flat even in a Polack neighborhood, even if the house *is* shot to hell and crawling with cockroaches and bedbugs.

He wasn't one of those mossbacks who claim a woman's place is in the home and all that old-fashioned hooey, but he hated like the mischief to do all the housework. Now, he wasn't lazy; it was just a different kind of work—it wasn't a man's work. Changing the baby was the toughest job of all, and in spite of his constant scrubbing away at clothes and diapers in the bathtub, blue bottle flies got to buzzing around expectantly. They were not disappointed.

He hadn't been very sorry when the radio company took his set back. He had lost his heart for music, and, besides, the fellow next door was mighty generous with his set. He wanted everybody in the block to share it, and he made the windows rattle with its vibrations. Amos 'n' Andy rumbled like harbingers of a cloudburst and ecstatic sopranos shrieked like a pig caught under a fence. If the Bum Song was on the air, the neighbor could find it unerringly and tune it in. Leo was so damned tired of it he'd cover his head in the pillows and swear.

"EEEEP! EEEEP! ou ou ou ou! OU OU OUUUU! ou ou ou ou EEEEP!"

"Oh, why don't you work like other folks do?
Now, how can I work if there's no work to do?
Hallelujah! I'm a bum! Hallelujah! Amen!
Hallelujah! Give us a handout to revive us again."

Leo wished that the tubes might blow out or lightning strike the radio.

Anna's eight dollars a week had to be spread thin and then it wouldn't go around. Leo often had to play possum when insurance agents and rent collectors banged on the door. Perhaps a kid would start yelping and he'd feel like strangling it with a pillow. Of course he was s.o.l. then and had to open up and pull alibis he had used so many times before. Sometimes the collector wormed inside and gave the place the once over. Leo felt cheap when the rent collector told him to make the kids quit smearing the wall paper. The wall paper was already smeared when Leo and Anna moved into the flat, but a man couldn't shoot off too much lip if he owed a lot of back rent. You just had to take it and say nothing. You could always figure on heaps of dirty clothes lying about and plenty of dirty dishes to sort of set things off. At first Leo had apologized for the disorder, but the time came when he greeted visitors with a hostile and defiant stare, promising himself that he'd give them a mouthful if they so much as cheeped about the condition of the house.

It was a hard summer for both Leo and Anna, but it went its way, and the crisp fall weather reminded them of the coal bills and heavier clothing that would be needed. Leo was sitting worrying his head about this one morning in November when he heard a furious knocking on the door. The flimsy panels seemed to crack under the impact.

"Don't knock the door down!" bellowed Leo resentfully. The one outside hammered all the more insistently. Leo had tried to stifle the baby with a quilt, but the yells must have been audible beyond the walls. He jerked the door open and Anna stumbled into the room. She stood leaning against the wall and folded her hands across her stomach.

"What's the matter? You sick?" Leo hastened to place a chair behind her.

She turned and regarded him so bitterly, hopelessly—

and accusingly—that he was startled. An idea as to what was up sprouted.

"How could it? I don't believe it!" He was bewildered.

"It *is*, anyhow. I can always tell. I've been afraid for a week, and now I know. Everything went round and round and I nearly lost a finger in the punch press."

She sat down at the table and laid her face on her folded arms. Inarticulate sobs shook her shoulders. Leo stood helplessly by, squeezing his chin.

"Let's not get excited," he begged. "We can fix this up. I'll see Steve Kulakoski, the druggist. He's a good pal. He'll come across with something."

"Oh, we tried that before."

"We didn't try the right thing. Old Doctor Craig ain't had a new idea since Grant fit Lee."

Anna had had such a hard time with the baby two years ago that they had told themselves they *must* see to it that there were no more. They had tried before the baby was born to do something about it, so that the baby might not come into a home where there were too many already, but the information they could get was meager and unsatisfactory. If they had had enough money, possibly they could have tempted a doctor to induce an abortion, but they could rake up only a few dollars at best. They had been in the notion of going to a midwife who specialized in cheap abortions, but two of her patients had died, and she had been indicted and jailed even though she was past seventy.

They lived in constant fear and uncertainty, and Anna could not help thinking with horror of the prospect of another pregnancy and another mouth to feed every time Leo embraced her in the bed. And of course she would have to quit working. Leo, on his part, had come to associate Anna with the terrors and the red, raw unpleasantness of childbirth he had been forced to witness so many times. He still felt the need of a woman, though, and it seemed that the desire tortured him all the more now that he was confined to the house and worrying with the children.

Leo knew how it was with Robert and Nell, how they had lived together so long and how they had never had any children, but he could not force himself to seek advice from Robert. Though they had met and spoken since the strike, Leo's pride would never permit him to ask anything like this of his half-brother. He would hesitate about asking any sort of favor from Robert, but such a thing as broaching such a delicate subject, on which Leo, because of wider experience, should be a great deal better posted, was entirely out of the question.

It was several days before Leo found a chance to talk to Kulakoski. The girl at the soda fountain always had a bunch of sheiks horsing around and she giggled like a mare neighing at the approach of a stud. The boys would order ice-cream cones just to see her bend over the container at the rear of the room. Her short skirt would hike up, and the boys would bawl and paw like amorous bulls, embracing one another. Leo liked to josh her, too, but he was getting too old for that kid stuff. What he said never sounded as funny as it would have if a kid had said it. Sometimes when he'd order a creamy root beer he'd ask her in what he meant to be a devilish and suggestive way what time it was when she got in last night. "Who wants to know?" was the invariable reply, but in a mechanical tone inviting no response.

"Steve," whispered Leo when he had cornered the druggist at last and was sure the girl was out of earshot. "You know . . . the old lady. . . ." There was a bovine appeal in his eyes. "There's something wrong. Five kids is too many already for a poor bastard in these hard times."

Kulakoski stiffened and plucked at a button on his pea jacket. He was short sighted, and peered at Leo over his glasses. "I'm damned sorry, Leo. Maybe you're just a little scared and rattled. Maybe it's only a cold or something like that. You take this medicine I'm going to give you, give her a teaspoonful before each meal. But if it's anything abnormal, it won't do no good. You understand? They's a law, and a strict one!"

"Okay, Steve!" Leo said gratefully. "I know you gotta stay in the clear. I won't tell nobody. I ain't that kind of a skunk."

"I said it wasn't no good in certain cases, Leo," protested Steve. "Don't get no queer ideas in your head."

Leo was afraid he really meant it. A youth came in and ordered an ice-cream cone. The fountain girl brushed languidly by Leo, her bare arm warmly touching his hand as he lifted it diffidently to scratch his ear. He absurdly imagined that she must know what was in the package he carried. The aura of her cheap perfume and the acid scent of underarm sweat blended pleasantly and voluptuously. The boy was following her with anticipation, and Leo paused at the door as she bent over the container, having to reach lower than ordinarily.

"Some kid!" he exclaimed aloud to himself as he stepped into the stream of passers-by. And then inaudibly: "If she'd wrap them big white legs around a fellow, I'll bet she wouldn't let go till it thundered. Women! Women!" the blasé philosopher was in the ascendant again. "You can't get along with 'em, and you can't get along without 'em!"

"This'll do the trick," Leo exulted, handing Anna the package. She was sitting on the edge of the bed, scratching the baby's back. She seized the bottle eagerly, tipped it, darted out an inquisitive tongue. Despair extinguished the momentary flare of hope she had always felt when hearing of something new.

"It's the same! Just the same! Doctor Craig gave me that same stuff before the baby was born. There's nothing . . . nothing! Maybe for some women, but not for me. If I get something shook at me, I'm fixed up; and then you couldn't jar me with a pile driver."

The baby stirred in her sleep and shrieked in terror, agitated by a bad dream. Anna gathered her in her arms and hugged her tight.

"Precious mite!" she sobbed. "No matter how many you got, you love them all!"

"Yeah," observed Leo sagely, withdrawing from a mental pigeonhole one of his stock utterances. "I wouldn't *take* a million fer ary one, but I wouldn't give a continental cuss fer another."

He was racking his brain as he spoke. "I'll ask Mike Miljan. He's been married ten years, and they ain't got a single kid. Both healthy as fattenin' shoats and look like they're full o' git-up and vinegar, too."

"Well, Mike says fer me t' go t' see Dr. Patton at Cuba Center," Leo said the next evening. "He told me t' mention him and everything would be hunky dory. Dr. Patton's been in trouble several times, but I guess he's got enough backin' t' get out of it. Mike's goin' t' lend us his lizzie fer the trip, too. Mike's a good egg. And his home brew! Mama! What a wallop! I drunk a quart, and, believe me, good peoples, I felt it plenty. One more and I'd heard bells ringin' and birdies singin' tweet-tweet."

"I know what he'll do. An operation. Sometimes women die from that. Rosie Woods did, don't you remember? She bled for three days, and the neighbor woman that was in the house tending her said you wouldn't think there was that much blood in a human body."

"She went t' one o' them midwives that don't know their stuff. And she was four months gone. They ain't no danger if it's not too far gone."

Leo was able to reassure her and to quiet most of her fears for the time being. But that night she did not sleep until early morning, and then dreamed she was lying on a cot when a terrific pain struck her in the crotch and she could see the blood gushing, gurgling on the floor, raising a red mark on the walls till it began to trickle across the cot where she lay helpless.

The next morning as they bowled along the smooth concrete, Leo felt positively exuberant. It was such a change for him.

"They don't put motors like this in the new models," he shouted above the engine's din. "They only make 'em t' sell nowadays."

He felt pretty foxy. The air was sharp and invigorating.

It was glorious weather for November. Anna's sallow cheeks began to pink a little, and she looked around her at the fields and houses with interest.

"It's good t' get away from the kids like this," Leo yelled. "Seems like the old days before we had 'em. Do you remember when we went out t' Sand Point and I lost an oar, and we like to 've drifted down t' New Orleans? Or at least we was afraid we might. Them was the good old days."

"They're sweet!" Anna was thinking of the kids now. "They can't help being in the world. They didn't ask to come."

"Remember the first time I ever seen you at the House of The Hand? I thought you was a ghost, and you pulled me out of the well."

"Yes, and Robert was there, too. Poor little stranger! You ought to make up with your brother, Leo. It's not right. What if one of you should die? You'd never get over it."

"Well, the little snot thinks he's so all-fired smart. I speak t' him if I see 'im, but I'm not goin' t' honey after 'im. I just speak t' him, and that's all. If he had t' keep his nose t' the grindstone like I do, he'd get some sense beat into 'im. The old lady always made a sissy of 'im, and now that gal keeps it up."

They decided to take lunch in a restaurant at Cuba Center. It all seemed so strange. The white linen, the majestic splendor of the nickeled coffee urn, and the smartly clad diners coming and going. Anna felt suddenly old and bedraggled. Her frock seemed to pucker into a thousand wrinkles, though it was her best and she had thought it rather nice. Her hair, forgotten before, was remembered as being stringy and graying some. Leo drummed on the table with his finger tips and tried to act as though he ate in a restaurant every day. All he could think of to order was ham and eggs.

"Everything tastes *so* good," Anna exclaimed softly. "I wonder how they make this brown gravy so good." She looked around, and, seeing nobody's eyes on her, sopped up all the gravy on her plate with a slice of bread. "And it's nice to have clean dishes and spoons and knives and forks and no flies buzzing around and specking everything."

"Aw, they got everything t' do with. Guess they wouldn't do much better than I do if they had the same stuff to work with," Leo said, somewhat lamely. He was touchy about his housekeeping technique, and always took it that Anna was trying to reproach him about it when she complained of the food or the state of things in the house.

"Dr. Patton keeps his office in his house in the 400 block on Water Street," a white-bearded street-corner whittler told them. It seemed peculiar not to have to look for a place to park. They headed into the curb right in front of the house.

"You stay here till I see him. I'll call you," said Leo, fumbling with the door. It opened unexpectedly and he almost fell out.

"Be careful!" cried Anna. She was trembling violently again. Her lips were blue, and there were purple shadows etched under her eyes. Her almost joyful mood, confronted by reality, had fled.

As Leo opened the doctor's door he heard a bell jangle somewhere in the depths of the house. He sat down on a hair-stuffed sofa and picked up a magazine. He was surprised to find it a fresh one. He was thinking of the conventional jokes about doctors' waiting-rooms. By rights, the magazine should be years old. In a glass case against the opposite wall were racks of cold steel instruments. Some chilly blue bottles bulked on the lower shelves. They were the color of a headache, and bore legends such as *Cas.Sp.* and others that Leo had noticed in the back room at Kulakoski's where the boys sometimes gathered to drink bottled-in-bond and to tell jokes or to examine the latest French ticklers. Leo watched the instruments intently and in fancy he felt a dull stab probing under his muscles and tendons and a numbing virus inundating his veins. This place stank of pain and death.

It was marked with naked life, like a woman's body bulging and spreading to deliver its burden. The nymphs of romance assumed heavy sagging teats and bovine organs or melted into the harsh angular contours of the anatomical chart on the wall, smoked saffron and clouded with spider webs.

Dr. Patton pushed aside the portières and emerged from an inner room. Poised with his head sunk low between sharp shoulder blades, his long nose interrogating, he resembled the caricature of a vulture. Leo had been nervous before; now he was panic-stricken. The speech he had been monotonously rehearsing fled to the dim inner grottoes of his brain. Sweat sprang out in his palms and his collar tightened so harshly that his breath was expelled in a wheeze.

The doctor scanned Leo professionally. "Step this way, please," he rasped, and led the way to an inner office furnished with a cot and a chair. There were other cases of instruments and some stained rags in a pail that made Leo ill to look at them. It looked as though somebody had had a hemorrhage. He's been operating on some woman, all right, thought Leo, with hope.

"Take off your clothes," ordered Dr. Patton. "I always give patients a thorough examination first of all."

Leo thought of one of his favorite wishes. He'd like to be a doctor and whenever a peach came in he'd say: "I'm afraid I'll have to give you a good examination. If you'll just step in there and remove all your clothes, and lie down face up on the cot, I'll be right with you." But he had concluded that doctors were so used to it that it didn't mean anything. They had to look at women when they were at their nastiest and most disgusting, such as when they were in labor, and no matter how they primped and decked themselves out or perfumed up, a doctor couldn't forget the shapes he had seen them in.

"It's not me! It's my wife!" blurted Leo. He halted on the banks of the Rubicon and quailed before its seething current.

"Where is she? I can't tell what's the matter with her

by looking at you, can I?" The doctor was inclined toward heavy jocularity.

"I'm afraid . . . I'm afraid she's . . . she's goin' t' have a baby!"

Every word seemed to brace a thousand feet and to relinquish hold on his tongue reluctantly.

"Maybe you want to engage my services, then. I take care of obstetrical cases for my regular patrons only. See Dr. Lyons in the Empire Theatre Building. Tell him I sent you."

"It ain't that." Leo wet his lips. He had put his hand to the plow and must forge ahead. "We got five kids already. Five kids is too much for a poor man, even if he's got steady work. I got no job, and she's workin' t' support the family. Now that'll stop. I jist don't know which way t' turn. Mike Miljan sent me t' you. I want you t' help me out; I'm beggin' you t' help me out. . . ."

"There's no use for me to pretend I don't know what you mean," began Dr. Patton slowly. "But I can't help you, if things are as you think. I've been in trouble, had my license suspended for a year. The best I could do would be to give you some medicine, but in your case I'm afraid that wouldn't do any good."

Again Leo clutched at a forlorn straw. Perhaps the doctor only wanted to stay in the clear.

"Give it to me! Make it plenty strong, fer Christ's sake, doctor! She's a strong woman; it won't hurt her none."

Doctor Patton had been mixing something as he spoke. He was one of the old-fashioned doctors, and mixed his own drugs.

"I don't want to leave the wrong impression," he warned. "That'll be a dollar-fifteen."

Anna was leaning back in the car seat, her eyes closed, her hands folded. When Leo stepped on the running board and it squeaked she started violently and grasped the door catch.

"No use t' get out," said Leo with a sickly grin. "He give me this bottle." He cranked the Ford.

"Another bottle!" Anna was dubious.

By the time they nosed onto the main highway, she had unwrapped and uncorked the bottle. Leo, watching for a chance to pass a slowly moving coal truck, was dismayed by the sound of glass tinkling on concrete. Looking back, he saw the bottle smashed on the slab and its contents spreading a widening circle of orange hue. Anna was rigid as death.

"You should think of other people's tires," he admonished, but without spirit.

"It's the same!" Anna muttered, as though she had reached the jumping-off place at last and saw only a fog-shrouded abyss below.

"I want you to whip Nellie good and hard," complained the largest girl as Leo and Anna entered the apartment. "She's done nothing but bawl since you left and I couldn't get her to hush any way I tried. Missus Biloski said it looked like some people should stay home and take care of their brats instead of jazzin' around the country."

The baby rubbed her swollen eyes with her doubled fists, sobbing brokenly. She clasped Anna about the legs. "Mama!" she cried ecstatically. Anna's gaze ran around the cluttered room, recoiled from the tumbled bed, and winced at the unwashed dishes caked with stale food. But she picked up the baby and kissed it passionately, time and again.

CHAPTER TWO

Leo couldn't sleep. He rolled over and threw his arm about Anna, but the old thrill had gone. Something had been happening with the years, and it'd never come back. They could never recall the heaven-like moments in the House of The Hand and the first married days in St. Luke when they were so eager they sometimes went to bed before sundown. Her body now seemed a lump of misshapen dough, sodden and leprous. Her breasts were flabby mushrooms rearing from decay. The blanket tickled and he was tormented by an intolerable itching, now on his chest, now on his legs. The bedding had not been washed for a long time and he knew that pellets of sweat and dirt had rolled up. The cheap straw tick had burst and sent up lance-like wisps to pierce the bedding and the skin.

He felt a more pronounced sting and vaulted quickly from the bed, snapping on the bulb. He was in time to see three or four fat bed-bugs racing for cover. He squashed them triumphantly right on the bed. Purple blood stained the coverlet as he ground even the clinging, waving legs. The pungent odor made him slightly ill. One of the children began to whimper and he instantly turned off the light, forestalling a general uproar from the fitful sleepers.

As he turned about to climb into bed he was surprised to see Anna lying wide-eyed in the faint beam of light filtering in from the street lamp on the corner. Once her dark, luminous eyes would have reminded him of pansies, but now he thought of two fried eggs, sunny side up.

"I can't sleep," he told her miserably. "Think I'll go

down t' the drug store and buy a *Sleuth Story Magazine*. It's out today." Then he added defensively: "It's only a dime."

She did not answer, but he heard a faint rustle, as though she were shaken with emotion or weeping. The bedspring chirped like a hoarse cricket.

"Do you want me t' fetch you a *Love Romance Tales*?" he asked.

"Love! Love!" she mocked stridently and venomously, low so as not to wake the children but loud enough to peal against his eardrums like a thunder clap. Already she seemed to bulge portentously beneath the counterpane as she turned her face to the wall.

Damn it, it wasn't entirely his fault. What could he do? he consoled himself as he strolled toward the drug store. Couples hurried along arm in arm, dawdled before the White Eagle Motion Picture Palace where *Broken Hearts on Broadway* was being shown.

"Poor young fools! Don't know what they got comin' to 'em," he mused, and philosophic balm began easing his mental festers. Again he was like a biologist aloof on a haughty peak, amused at the small affairs and petty anxieties of comically earnest insects. Straightway he felt better. He tugged at his bootstraps and soared above the greasy flat, the sullen, crying woman, and the whimpering children. Maybe business would get better. Maybe. . . . O hell! A lot of things *could* happen.

When the soda-fountain girl handed him his magazine he reflected that she looked devilish attractive. He wondered how she'd look if. . . . But the inchoate idea skipped away. When he asked her how late it was when she got in last night, she sprang a surprise. "It wasn't *late*, it was *early* in the *morning!*" she chirped, with a vein of archness. This deviation from rote encouraged him to believe he was making headway. He wished that he had sponged the dishwater stain off his pants. He produced a nickel and handed it to her.

"Gimme an ice-cream cone," he requested wistfully.

He hoped that the ice cream was low in the can as he followed her to the back of the store.

Leo knew that Anna could not work much longer even though the coming baby had not yet begun to tighten up the slack in her stomach, which had hung in a pouch since the third child, an unusually large one, had been delivered. Nobody had advised her to bind up her abdomen afterward; she had been without the advice that women usually get from their mothers or relatives. She laced her stomach in and kept it under partial control, distributing it rather evenly as long as her girdle was on, but when she removed her corset the loose muscles allowed it to sag as though it might be a flesh-colored rubber sack weighted with a stone. Even though she had not begun to bulge noticeably, she could hardly keep at work. The vibration of the punch press she operated kept her constantly ill. At first she hoped that this would induce an abortion, as it had for several of the other women who worked there, but no such thing happened. She awoke in the morning with the nausea gripping her, ran to the cupboard, and nibbled a bit of bread to still the retching that tore at her stomach without bringing anything up. But in spite of everything she could try—peppermints or patent soothing draughts—she gagged and strained till her stomach was sore from the impotent tugging at it. She was already weak when she started handling the thin strips of steel through which she had to punch holes.

It was not very pleasant for Leo, either. He had to work as hard as ever, and he had to try to cheer Anna up. She was always stricken with melancholia when she was pregnant, but this time it was worse than ever. She sat about with tears streaming down her face, or lay face down on the bed, quivering with sobs. They could seldom buy coal, and Leo walked along the railroad tracks each morning looking for the few slaty cobbles to be found. He had to get there before daylight, for there were always others seeking feverishly for the chunks of coal as though they were black diamonds, indeed.

They moved to a cheaper house, a frame building with sagging doors leaving a great crack at the top. In the bitter winter weather they all had to huddle together in one bed like animals for the collective heat—Anna, Leo and the baby at the head, and the other four somehow managing to crowd across the foot. Their bowels rumbled and vented gas from the cheap navy beans they were compelled to eat daily. Nothing else was as nourishing and as cheap. Leo said the air was blue with the gas till he was afraid to strike a match. And when the mercury fell below zero it was almost that cold in the house after the fire died down. The wind soon sucked the flame from the meager coals up the chimney, and the cold seeped in through the cracks over the doors and in the spots where the plaster had fallen. The rafters and joists cracked and the cold increased so steadily that Leo sometimes wondered if this were not the end of the world, if it would not just keep getting colder till everything froze into an icicle. They were compelled to keep their heads beneath the ragged quilts even though they strangled from the foul exhalations and the sour stench of their bodies. There were days and days in that house that one could not bear to bathe in a washtub even beside a roaring fire. The cold nosed in everywhere.

Their nerves were as raw as hamburger. Disputes were always arising and the first thing they knew they were shouting and even throwing things. The children would scream in terror and bring Leo and Anna to their senses.

"I'm afraid I'm losing my mind," Anna would sob. "I can't stand it! I can't stand it! A person can stand just so much, and then they've got to pop somewhere just like an electric fuse goes out: pouf, and leaves everything still and dark."

Leo wrote to Terry almost every week now. He could not help thinking wistfully of the comfortable house as he had known it. He had sworn as strong an oath as he knew never to go back there to live, but he had broken a previous oath just as strong when he set foot in the house again on the occasion of his visit to Terry four years ago.

He had never been able to see his way clear to go back since then, and Terry had never come to the city. Leo wondered now if he had not complained too much in his letters. He was always writing how hard up he was—how difficult it was to keep a large family going. And perhaps this had dissuaded Terry from coming to St. Luke.

The more Leo thought about the pleasant and comfortable house as he recalled it in Green Valley the more he wished he might know its security and placidity again. He could not get it in his head that Green Valley might possibly have changed as much as St. Luke. He knew that Terry had not worked for two years, but he supposed the old man had some money saved up. There were only taxes and food for one to pay for, and that didn't take much. So he wrote to Terry, hinting that he'd like to pay him a visit some time. The old man did not answer at once and Leo was afraid that he'd been too brash. After all, not many people want to entertain a family of seven, even for a day.

CHAPTER THREE

When Robert at last decided that he must do something about his book manuscript if he was ever going to, he hunted up Alan Vass to ask his advice. He had some difficulty in finding where he lived, but he met one of the Green Dragon bunch by chance and learned that Alan was still living with his uncle in the suburbs. It was a long ride before he stood on a cocoa doormat before the door of a squat, conventional bungalow.

"Yes, he's here," said a sourly handsome man of forty-five or so, answering the bell. A Masonic charm dangled from the heavy gold chain festooned across his only slightly protuberant belly. He exercises to keep it down, thought Robert. He's the sort of a fellow who would go grimly and conscientiously through radio setting-up exercises and worry over B. O., pink toothbrush, halitosis, and athlete's foot. Oh, mighty Alan, hast thou sunk so low? Are all thy triumphs, spoils, victories shrunk to this small measure, living with and dependent upon an uncle with Philistine engraved all over him? And he was the sort of man to break a guy's plate if he didn't toe the chalk line. Poor Alan!

"I've been thinking about you. Was going to drop you a line," said Alan, obviously delighted to see Robert. But he was ill at ease; his neck seemed too small for his collar and his shaggy hair no longer made him look like an artist. There was a pinched and petulant look on his face to replace the cynical quirk that used to ride it. The uncle undoubtedly knew of the hectic saturnalias of the old

Green Dragon days, and he did not trust Alan too far. He lurked near, his ears cocked and alert.

"Let's take a walk and I'll tell you about it," said Alan.

The uncle stomped off toward the back of the house. "Don't stay out after nine and expect me to get up in the cold to open the door for you," he ordered.

"I won't," said Alan meekly. "I'll be back in less than an hour."

"Well, what's the good word?" said Robert as they paced down the concrete walk.

"Christ! It's hell here. They know they got me with my pants down, and I have to take it and grin and pretend to like it. Show me a job where I can make enough to eat on, and I'd soon enough flee from Uncle Jinglebollicks' hospitality. But I've tried everywhere till I'm sick of it all; begging till I'm blue in the face. Too much competition even to sell safeties and smutty cartoon booklets around pool halls and public comfort stations."

When Robert told Alan about the book manuscript, he said the best thing to do with it would be to get Danny Maupin to look it over. He could fix it up. In fact, Danny had a check coming in a week or so, and he was going to throw a New Year's party for three or four fellows.

"He's not doing so good lately," said Alan. "But he wants to have a good time for once and to make somebody else feel good. He told me to pick them out, and I thought of you. I thought about Leo, too. I never felt quite right about that business at the Green Dragon, and I'd like to make up for it. There won't be any horsing around this time. The poor little chap would enjoy a bat, I'll bet."

"Well, I don't know. Leo and I don't get along so well. We speak, and that's about all. It's all right, only I don't know how he'd take it."

"Aw, nobody ought to hold any hard feelings in this joyous holiday season. Danny's even going to rent a car, and we'll make all the new joints. We'll start in early, and never quit till the last dog is dead. What do you say?"

They had reached the end of the street, and faced a cemetery, dismal and bleak in the grip of winter. Metallic wreaths were still lying on some of the graves, and the stalks of the hardier flowers had resisted the frost enough to stand like lances, but the ground was blackened by the more fragile leaves. In the low iron fence soiled newspapers and wisps of blown grasses had caught.

"Sometimes wish I was in there with six feet of dirt on my pan; I do for a God's fact," said Alan gloomily. "When the weather's good I come down here and sit for hours among the dead, lucky stiffs. They don't have to swallow insults in order to get their bellies filled. Dead guts never growl for groceries that cost money. . . . Well, we'll have to mosey back or Uncle Jinglebollicks will get suspicious that I'm hatching some sort of plot to rape a virgin or bust a safe. And I am after a virgin, for that matter."

"Where'd you find a virgin?" asked Robert incredulously. "How old is she? Three?"

"It's true as you stand there. Listen! You remember how I always wanted a disciple in the old days; first a man Friday, then a disciple. Now I've got something else on my mind. I've got acquainted with a girl out here who is a devout Catholic. She looks in the Index Expurgatorius or whatever the hell it is to find out what she should read; she doesn't go to the movies for fear of seeing something indecent. The old stud-horse has had to be pretty docile since he came to set his brogans under Uncle Jinglebollicks' pie board, and I'll be damned if I ain't made an impression on the gal—a strong impression. Now, here is a chance for an interesting experiment in psychology. I'll work in a wedge, plant a seed here and there, till I break down all her inhibitions and prejudices. Damn it, I'll bring all my heavy artillery of literature, philosophy and sex appeal into play till I'll have her a frank and unashamed pagan, giving of herself as freely and shamelessly as I wish. I'll quote such things as this to her:

> 'For sweet, to feel is better than to know,
> And wisdom is a childless heritage.
> One pulse of passion, youth's first fiery glow,
> Are worth the hoarded proverbs of the sage.'

"She'll never feel a pang of conscience or nostalgia for her former condition of servitude; she'll love her new and absolute master. I feel I can do it, and that's my life's ambition now. Damn the writing! I just bite off my finger nails when I try it, and from what Danny Maupin tells me the game's not worth the candle, anyhow. But when I remold my pretty bigot into a glorious pagan queen, I'll be willing to curl up and die contented."

"Well, you have a hard job cut out for you."

"Watch little Alan when he gets in his stride, pleading like angels, trumpet-tongued, till I bend her to my will like a potter thumping his wet clay."

When they reached the house Robert said he could not spare the time to come in. Alan looked relieved. "I'm still nesting over the sad sepulchre of the Green Dragon like a demented hen trying to hatch a doorknob," he said. "I'm the last of the Mohicans."

"Ah, yes," Alan sighed, and not mockingly. "Them was the good old days. Say! I won't dare to come home the night of the bust. I'll have to cook up some sort of story for Uncle Jinglebollicks. Tell him I'm staying somewhere. He won't believe me, but I don't give a damn. Let him paw and scrape. You remember the song the Barbs used to sing at Boone:

'Hell! Hell! The world's all wrong.
Ain't had a drink for so *God-damned* long!'"

CHAPTER FOUR

Danny Maupin's childish face looked like putty, as though you could sink your thumb in it and the hole would stay. He sat glumly in the back seat of the car, taking off his glasses now and then and wiping them with a wad of toilet paper he carried in his pocket for that purpose. Alan was driving and Robert sat beside him. Robert had not felt like broaching the subject of the little celebration to Leo single-handed, and Alan's misgivings grew. He did not know whether Leo had ever forgiven him more than formally. It might be that the grudge had been festering all this time.

Robert did not know that Leo had moved from the apartment, but he found the correct address from the janitor. Leo was living in the working-class district near the Workers' Center. As they passed the hall, Robert screwed down in his seat and looked up. The windows were dark. Perhaps the place was deserted. Sol Abraham's name was in the paper now and then. He had led a delegation to the city hall, taken part in the strike of Negro nut pickers, had been given a lecture on citizenship by a judge who liked his own peroration so well he had allowed the America First Vigilantes to print it in a pamphlet which they distributed gratuitously to the employees of almost every factory in the city. Mr. Harrison had worked Nell overtime addressing a batch of them, and she brought one home for Robert to read.

"There's a row going on," Robert said as they stood on the skimpy porch of the house in which Leo lived and heard the sound of stormy voices through the thin door panels. When Leo opened the door his face was flushed and angry, and they could see Anna lying face down across the bed.

"Well," said Leo awkwardly. "Well, this is a surprise. Never expected to see *you* fellows. Well!" They stood on the porch, looking at one another. Now that Alan and Robert were here, they scarcely knew how to begin.

"Come in, fellows," Leo said at last. "Have t' excuse this house. You know how it is with a bunch o' kids. Or I guess mebbe you don't, at that. You're lucky, that's all. Anna ain't been feelin' good, and I guess I ain't much of a housekeeper."

Anna arose without speaking to Alan and Robert and walked into the other room, keeping her face averted.

"Well," said Alan. "Might as well cleanse the stuffed bosom, as old Shake puts it. I've felt kind of dirty about that trick we played on you ever since it happened. And Danny Maupin is out here with a car and a little dough. We thought you might like to go out for a few drinks, and maybe a little tearing around. New Year comes but once a year."

"You can't expect a sucker t' bite twicet in the same place," said Leo.

"This is on the level, Leo," said Robert. "No skylarking. The depression knocked that out of us. We want one more go-round before we dry up and blow away. We're being consumed by dry rot, year after year waiting for ships that never come in."

Leo could not help believing them, and he was so sick of this little house, the harsh food, the shivering under torn covers, awake almost all the night, the squabbles of the children, and the fusses with Anna. It seemed they could not say two words any more without becoming involved in a wrangle.

"Well, I might," he said. "Only I don't want no more shenanigans."

They could hear him in the next room talking to Anna.

"I'm goin' out with Alan and Bob and another feller."

"How long'll you be gone?"

"I don't know. You oughtn't t' care. You act like you're sick o' the sight o' me, anyways. Looks like you'd be glad t' git shet o' me a while."

"What about you? You're such an angel; never a cross word out of you, to let you tell it. Who started it tonight?"

"There you go! Rave on if it does you any good! Have I got a clean shirt?"

"I don't know. I can't work all day and keep the clothes washed up, too. I guess you don't know or care that I'm sick as a dog almost every minute. If you want clean shirts you'll have to wash them yourself."

"All right! All right! You don't have to keep throwin' it up t' me about you working. It ain't my fault that I ain't workin'. God knows I'd give anything on this green earth if I could work and get out o' this hell hole, messin' with a bunch o' kids all day long, and worryin' about what's the cheapest grub t' buy, makin' one dollar stretch as fer as five ought t' go, fightin' off bill collectors, and tryin' t' scrape up coal where there ain't even a smell o' coal. A railroad bull took after me t'day, and I had t' run like I was a pussy cat chased by a bull dog. Yes, I got a swell time. That's what *you* think. You seem t' think because I don't work I'm jist layin' around here and livin' off you. By God, I got to a place where I don't care whether school keeps or not. I'm goin' out with the boys t' make a little whoopee if it's the last thing I do."

"Go ahead. I wish I could go some place once in a while instead of just to work."

"It ain't gonna cost me a penny. Don't be afraid I'll squander any of the money you make on havin' a good time fer myself. I know you have t' feed me, and that's enough. I get it throwed up t' me often enough."

"When did I ever throw it up to you? That's as black a lie as a man ever let out of his mouth."

"Plenty of times. . . . No buttons! I ain't got a shirt with a button on it to my name."

"Sew some on, then."

"I will. Nobody's askin' *you* t' do it."

"Looky, brethren! Looky down the street. Let's give the girls a break here. Seventy-five beautiful girls; ten cents a dance." Alan whipped the car against the curb. He could see the Golden Beetle sign winking a half block down the street, but he knew that parking space was at a premium and he had better nab a place while he could. Everybody who had the price was celebrating the return of legal liquor. Alan and his companions got out and Alan locked the doors, pocketing the keys carefully. He didn't want to lose them, and he didn't know what kind of a shape he'd be in when he came back. So he chose the deepest pocket and thrust them as far as they'd go.

Leo had not anticipated coming to such brightly lighted places where all the men and women were well dressed. His own black suit had been patiently patched by Anna at the knees and across the seat, and it was frayed at the cuffs. Every time he turned his head a horse hair popped up from his coat collar to jab him in the chin. The suit had cost only $10.98 to begin with, and he had worn it seven years. His shirt was anything but clean, and his string tie had had the same knot in it for five years. Leo merely loosened it and slipped it over his head when he wanted to take it off, and when he had occasion to wear it again, he lowered it onto his neck and beneath his collar and pulled the knot tight.

But they had had a few drinks already, and the warmth was pleasant in Leo's stomach, which had grumbled so long over potatoes and beans without even salt pork in them. He had eaten five hamburgers on Danny Maupin, taking one every time Danny asked him if he wanted one, not noticing that the others were not eating so much. He had never eaten anything that tasted as good as the juicy hamburgers with plenty of hot relish on them and the cool creamy beer washing them down. He had not put such beer to his lips for what seemed many a weary day.

The Golden Beetle taxi dancehall was upstairs. As

Alan, Robert, Leo and Danny climbed the steps, they met a drunk descending heavily, dropping his feet with a lurch that forced him to hug the wall to keep from falling. "I'm tellin' everybody Merry Easter. Merry Easter!" he cried. "Be different. Same old stuff, Happy New Year. Merry Easter! Everybody likes a change once in a while."

"You want company?" a girl usher said to them as they entered the ballroom.

"Sure," said Alan. "We want everything you got."

Each one sat down at a little table behind the railing encircling the dancing floor. Leo did not like it here. He felt out of place. It had been all right in the little hot dog joints where appearance did not mean so much.

The usher brought a woman to Leo's table. "This is Tess," she said. Leo looked around and saw that the other boys were talking to girls who were sitting at their tables.

"This sure is a swell night," Tess said tentatively, tapping her cigarette on the ash tray. Her finger nails were blood red and her eyebrows were heavily shaded, Leo saw. She had put on the lipstick to make it look as though she had a much larger and more symmetrical mouth than she actually possessed. And she wasn't young. You could tell that in spite of her kalsomined face and dyed hair. When she smiled the wrinkles at the corners of her eyes and mouth cracked the enamel of her make-up like an eggshell shattering. Bet she's as ugly as a mud fence with her war paint off, Leo thought critically.

"Yeh," Leo said. He didn't feel like bantering with this floosie. All the while he had been eating the hamburgers or soaking in the warmth of the well-heated buildings like a grateful cat he had not been able to get Anna and the cold, shabby house out of his mind. No wind that blew in that direction was ever deflected over or around the house; it could find plenty of crevices in which to thrust its cold tongues. Anna had to work so hard and she grew so deathly sick each day, yet tried to hide it from the foreman. She would have to quit some day soon, but she wanted to postpone as long as she possibly could the crisis this would bring into their home. And Leo did not know why he had to shout at her the way he did. Sitting here forlornly with the taxi dancer he could see Anna's side of it.

"You ain't married, are you?" asked Tess. "I don't like to fool with married men; they can sure make you wish you was in hell with your back broke."

"No, I ain't," said Leo. He was not feeling very receptive, but he did not know what might turn up. It was always safer to deny being married.

"You wanta dance?"

"No. Don't feel like dancin'."

She screwed up her mouth and winked her mascaraed lids. Each lash bore a pellet of wax like a black tear drop.

"You wanta little drink?"

"Yes. Whisky."

"I'll order a little highball t' keep you company if you don't mind."

When the drinks came and the girl stood by with her tray, Leo did not know what to do. He had in his pocket the greater part of Anna's pay for the week, but he could not spend any of that. It would barely buy groceries for the next week. But he didn't want to walk over to Danny to ask for money; that would look pretty cheap after all the hamburgers and beers. He grew red and cursed himself for ever coming. The girl waited impatiently, leaning her tray on the table; Tess rested her sharp chin on her clasped hands and stared at him. Hell, no other way, thought Leo. He drew out a dollar bill and handed it to the girl; she plinked fifty cents change on the table and started off.

"Don't forget; twenty cents," said Tess.

"I won't, kiddo," said the waitress.

Tess fingered with her cocktail a moment, then suddenly dashed it down without a grimace. Jesus Christ, she didn't bat an eye; bet she can hold enough to float a battleship, thought Leo, dismayed.

Leo was feeling glum about this, but as the night wore on he was given a snort out of several bottles belonging to fellows who insisted upon sharing them with everybody.

He began to feel cheerful and warm, forgot his patched clothes, and petted Tess half-heartedly. She pecked him swiftly with her hard, dry mouth.

"You're a sweet little devil," she said. "But I bet even if you are short and don't weigh much you're big in lots of ways." She nudged him sharply in the ribs and tittered.

"Now, what do you mean by that?" Leo asked, grinning.

"Oh, big heart, and so on," she giggled.

"You know the old story. If a woman's got a big mouth she's big in every other way."

"Oh *yeah*! How you know, sonny boy? You musta been peekin'."

"You tell 'em, corset. You've been around the wimmen."

Leo felt her leg under the table. It was bare, but it was cold. All the time something inside him was crying: She's lying there in the dark after a hard day's work, shivering with nobody to warm her back, and you're here feisting with this floosie.

I must be drunk, and good and God-damned drunk, he thought an hour or so later. He realized at intervals that he was spending money, and spending it fast. He saw that Tess now took a dime out of every quarter he spent. The girl handed it right over to her, and she slipped it in a pouch hung to her garter, baring herself to the crotch each time. Nobody noticed, for the celebrating had begun in earnest. They think I'm so drunk I won't get hep that she's getting a rake-off, thought Leo. She couldn't drink that much and navigate if they're real highballs. He reached across and grabbed her glass, managing to down a few drops before she jerked it away. "That's sody pop," Leo said. "No wonder you drink so much at two bits a glass, two glasses t' the five-cent bottle."

"Why, you cheap sport," said Tess. "You spend about a buck, and get ten dollars' worth of free feels. You can't get your batteries charged for nothing. What do you expect for a measly buck? You want a mortgage on it? Maybe you want it wrapped up so you can take it home with you."

She looked as though she'd like to desert Leo, but not many new customers were coming in, and she could not expect a man to spend money on her as readily as he would on one of the younger girls. She tried to keep up an appearance of pep and ginger, but it was more than she could do when the hour was late and she wished so hungrily for her bed, even though she might have to share it with one of the customers.

"I'll be damned if I dance with 'im! He stinks like a sewer rat! He stinks! I'll not dance with that lousy bum if I have to clear right out of this place and never come back." Leo thought at first that the girl was talking about him. She had backed against the railing next him, and when he turned around he struck his nose against her hips.

"Who stinks, you four-bit whore?" he shouted, jumping to his feet, his chair falling over backward. When he reached for it, he fell and bruised his mouth till it bled.

"Pipe down!" said Tess. "She ain't talkin' about you, sonny boy."

Then Leo saw a grizzly fellow dressed in overalls and a hickory shirt trying to grasp the girl by the arm. She beat him off with short flapping blows. She scratched viciously at his face, matted with curly red whiskers.

"For God's sake, get Charley!" screamed the girl. "I won't dance with 'im. He stinks like nobody's business."

"I paid my dime," insisted the man. "I gotta right t' dance. Lookit, here's my ticket. And I got more dimes where that come from."

"You stink!" shrieked the girl, stamping her foot.

"You stink!" chorused a gang of dancers that had congregated to see the fun.

The manager had come, pushing through the crowd. The angry customer told him the girl would not dance with him, even though he had bought a ticket.

"Well, brother," said the manager soothingly. "It's like this. I ain't no slave driver. I can't make the little lady dance with you if she don't want to. Would that be fair and square? If she won't trip the light fantastic with you, maybe they's other ladies here what ain't so pickish."

"Then take yer crummy dance hall and yer gals and shove 'em t' the promised land," snorted the customer, as he made toward the exit like a bull charging.

"I guess I got as strong a stomach as the next one, but I couldn't stand that. Phew! He'd stink a dog off a gut wagon. I'll bet he ain't changed his underwear since the Civil War. I guess he thinks he's cuttin' quite a dash comin' here and wantin' t' feel up somebody, when he ain't fitten t' slop hogs in that outfit."

"He's from the stock yards," somebody said. "I'll bet the heifers ketch hail Columbia tomorrow. They tell me them guys out there had a special sheep they named Bessie and tied a blue ribbon on 'er so's they'd always know 'er. They kept 'er in a separate pen, too. But somebody played a joke and took Bessie's ribbon off and turned 'er in with the rest. 'Jeez!' one of the stockyard cowboy yaps. 'Now we've got a job as *is* a job. Now we gotta go through that whole five thousand sheep t' find Bessie again!'"

There was a raucous shout of laughter, then the orchestra, which had ceased playing during the altercation, burst out again. Leo remembered that his own underwear must be pretty dirty, and he had not washed his feet recently. It was just so cold in the house and he was so tired after another hopeless day that he did not care. I've got a lot of business in a place like this pretending I'm a sport, he thought.

At midnight he could not see very far, but he knew that somebody clapped a conical dunce cap on his head and thrust a tasseled horn, striped like a barber pole, into his hand. Blaa! Blaaa! Blaaaa! The horns bleated crazily, and the master of ceremonies pranced to the center of the dance hall, waving his hands for silence, and standing in the middle of a widening circle as the dancers retreated from the floor. He had a small microphone with him, and his voice rumbled and echoed in every corner.

"Ladies and Gents! Ladies and Gents! Lend me your ears, or, if they're too big, lend me your bottles. They're empty, anyhow. Happy New Year, folkses! And many of 'em. Let joy be unrefined, as the old poet said. I got a little special treat for you tonight, or rather this morning. This is 1934, folkses, and a brand New Year and a brand New Deal, so let's everybody make whoopee. Whoopee! So, as I started to say in the first place, I got something you'll all enjoy. Andy McCoy, the singing waiter. You didn't know that black-haired heartbreaker that concocts them delicious cocktails and draws them beers for you could wiggle a wicked tonsil, did you? He draws flies, too. Well, I'll let you in on a secret. He comes by it honest. The singing, I mean, not drawing the flies. His real name is Hoochie Kuchi, and he's Galli Kuchi's youngest brother. She learned him the song he's going to render now. Get your handkerchiefs ready, folkses. It's plenty sad. All right, Andy, take it!"

A white-aproned waiter with patent leather hair had been standing by and smirking. He thrust his red face close to the mike and sang nasally:

"My sister took castor oil,
  Then went in the garden to sit;
  And after she sat there five minutes
  The ground was all covered with——
  Sweet violets! Roses that bloom in the spring, tra la!
  Covered all over from head to foot,
  Covered all over with s-s-s-s-SNOW!"

The customers joined in the singing, the master of ceremonies hopping about like a monkey, pertly interweaving a word now and then. The horns blared flatulently.

"My brother died in the country,
  He died in a terrible fit;
  And just to respect his last wishes
  We buried him six feet in——
  Sweet violets! Roses that bloom in the spring, tra la!
  Covered all over from head to foot,
  Covered all over with s-s-s-s-SNOW!"

Tess had left Leo, and he did not care. He was feeling sick, and his shame at leaving Anna and the way he had spoken to her had lain like a dark hard core in his mind all the evening—had swollen till there was room for nothing else in his head.

He saw the other fellows coming toward him, and he arose, steadying himself with the table.

"Happy New Year, hell!" said Danny Maupin bitterly as he felt his way down the stairs, not because he was very drunk, but because his eyesight was getting worse all the time. His childish face was screwed up as painfully as though he might have bitten into a sour pickle while afflicted with the mumps.

"Merry syphilis!" he said to Alan.

"Clappy new year!" Alan said.

Robert had been telling Danny about the book manuscript.

"Bring it over," said Danny. "I'm being rushed for a new novel, and I have to eat while I'm writing it. I'm turning out westerns, Godawful stuff. I may not get to look at your stuff for a month or so, but I'll do it as soon as I can."

Look at Leo, thought Robert. Drunk as a boiled owl, and he sat there with a fatuous grin on his pan fingering that worn-out taxi dancer.

Leo tried to walk steadily down the stairs, but he could not judge the distances accurately. He reached out with his foot for what he thought should be a step, pitched forward on his face, and rolled to the bottom of the flight. "I'm not hurt," he said, but his leg felt as though it might have a bone shattered in it. He could not keep from limping.

When he let himself in the house he could not avoid any of the chairs, it seemed. He stumbled over them all and made a great deal of noise. When he made a light with the kerosene lamp, there was Anna with eyes as big as the moon and as placid and emotionless. Dead and cold as the big white moon slipping like a spook through the clouds, thought Leo. She wouldn't believe me if I told her I'd been thinking of her most the time. What a fool I've been to think there's any chance for me; I've got a fat chance when boys of eighteen and twenty get what few jobs are vacant. A man of forty might as well get ready to curl up and die.

He sat down on the edge of the bed and began to untie his shoes. Suddenly he started as though somebody had pricked him with a pin. Of the six dollars and a half he had had when he started out, a measly quarter remained. He was sicker than ever then. He did not care for a moment whether he lived or died, for death would be preferable to the kind of life he had been living. He crawled in beside Anna without saying a word to her. Lying there, he resolved that he would not stay in this town a single hour longer than necessity demanded. Things *must* be better in Green Valley; the house there was warm and it was large. There was plenty of cordwood to be had for fuel; it was so much easier to live in a small town, anyhow. Things couldn't be any *worse* in Green Valley. With the determination to leave St. Luke came a kind of exultation.

"We're goin' t' Green Valley t' live," he said to Anna. His tongue was thick.

"Are we?" she said tonelessly.

CHAPTER FIVE

Leo did not falter in his determination to return to Green Valley, and he wrote Terry that he was coming home. Terry answered the letter this time: "You and yours are allways welcom as the flours in May." But how to get there? Leo had seen whole families traveling in box cars, and they could go this way for want of a better if they had to do so. But it would be hell trying to load a pregnant woman and five kids into a box car. "You couldn't bother me," Anna said, but with less than her usual bitterness. The last days at the factory had been torture for her, and the boss had reprimanded her more than once for slowness when her eyes blurred and her head swam for five minutes at a time. She had not dared to sit down, and she had to cling to her punch press to keep from falling. "You couldn't bother me. You couldn't knock it out of me with a sledge hammer." They were all excited now that Anna had quit her job; they had to leave now whether they wished to or not. It seemed as though they could not have existed a week longer on her wages, anyhow. Leo went about telling all his friends about the trip he planned, and all of them said it was a good thing to get the children away from the city. The city was a poor place for children in these times, or for grown people, for that matter. The people in the country towns, living close to the soil, were not feeling the full impact of the depression.

Just as the public will complacently view semi-starvation on a mass basis without doing anything about it, but immediately respond to the call of some major catastrophe such as a fire, flood, or earthquake, Leo's friends stirred about to help him clear out of St. Luke. Mike Miljan gave him his old Ford, the one which Leo had driven to Cuba Center when he and Anna had gone to see Dr. Patton; John said he could not afford license plates or gas for it, anyhow, but there were a number of miles' travel left in the old bus yet. Others gave money or clothing, and on the night of the Hurley family's departure for Green Valley there was a party at which everybody wished them Godspeed and good luck in their new life.

Why can't we always be like that? thought Leo as he steered the Ford down the highway toward Green Valley. But most of those people were not too flush themselves, they couldn't be helping somebody like that every day. There are so many of them. Well, the old man still has the house, and I can go down into Happy Hollow and cut land on the Jones heirs' land. That white oak brush will still be there, and white oak will burn as good as anything if you have something to start it off. Maybe some of the drift mines are running, or I can start one of my own. But I wouldn't like to be bunged up like poor old Monty Cass. I don't want to die with a thousand tons of dirt and rock squeezing the stuffing out of me just the same as if I was a juicy apple in a cider press.

As they passed the sawmill where he had first worked, Leo was disheartened to see most of the kilns gone. Those that remained were falling apart, and last year's weeds were standing among the piles of warped and weathered lumber. There was no smoke coming from the stack, and the stack itself was rusty; the top section had broken off and hung creaking from its guy wires. It hasn't been used for years, I'll bet, Leo thought uneasily.

"Can this be the same place?" Leo said, as they pulled up in front of the house which had once been Martha Darrell's pride. Scarcely a window pane was left unbroken, and the cavities were stuffed with rags or patched with cardboard. Terry saw the car stop, and came limping out, leaning on a cane.

"Rheumatiz," he said. "Always gits me in the damp days these late years. Welcome home, me bye. Welcome,

Anna, and the kiddies, forbye. I got a job fer ye, Leo, a'ready."

"Where's that?" Leo said, his heart leaping.

"I been wantin' t' climb up there on the roof t' see about some tar paper I put on. I couldn't cover the whole roof, and I couldn't strip off the shingles. I kin hear the paper flappin' whin the wind's on the rise, and I'm afeared the whole shootin' match 'll go sailin' off like a kite some o' these fine nights. The old rotten shingles wouldn't hold nails, and the roof still leaks, even where I put the tar paper. The nails pop up out of the shingles and the paper like a jack-in-the-box."

"I'll fix that," Leo said, a little disappointed that he did not have a real job. He had half-expected to hear Terry tell him of some job that was to be had in Green Valley.

In spite of the desolate condition of the house, Anna and Leo felt more secure than they had in the city. A sort of hysteria had laid hold of them the last few weeks in St. Luke, and they had wanted to get away as frantically as a person in a burning building, looking about for some avenue of escape.

Leo soon learned that Terry had nothing to live on. He had no money. He had not worked steadily for years, and the last two years he had not hit a lick. He was getting a few groceries from the Welfare.

"But it's like pullin' a log chain through a body, and ever' other link a swivel, t' go down there and stand wi' hat in hand, sometimes comin' away wi' nawthin', sometimes wi' a loaf o' bread and some navy beans averagin' five farts t' the bean. And whin that's eat, divilish soon, it seems, it's the same song and dance agin. I been thinkin', me bye, about the old days afore we come here, you and me. I was niver out o' work, I always had a pocket jingling full o' silver and a roll o' greenbacks and yellowbacks fat enough t' gag an elephant. Lord, but we did have a time whin we started in Saturday night t' celebrate! This country here is as dead as a door nail, me bye, and I can't think that it'll iver come back. I'm too old t' wait. I sent out t' Butte fer a copy of the *Post*, and, sure enough, I sees lots o' ads fer men. Ads fer men in the copper mines, and that's where I shine. I asked about you, too, when I writ Tuck Saunders, an old pal o' mine at the Golden Plume mine. He may be dead and gone, or he may not be wi' the Golden Plume, but if he is, he'll answer. He was niver one that would be changin' jobs, like I was, more fool me. He'll answer if he's alive and still wi' the Golden Plume. He'll not be forgettin' ol' Terry Hurley; we been on too many sprees."

Leo did not like Terry's idea of pulling out of Green Valley. He was weary of uncertainty, and the old house was a haven of security for a while. He knew, though, that Terry would have difficulty in getting any increased allowance from the relief authorities. They would not take kindly to the idea of transients blowing into town, particularly when there was an automobile. If they can afford an automobile, they can feed themselves, the relief authorities thought, and often said.

The next day Anna and Leo loaded the children into the car and started down into Happy Hollow, but before they had bumped along among the ruts very far, they found they could never reach the creek bottom. The corduroy road had rotted out and there were sizable cottonwood and elm saplings blocking the road. The mines are all closed; nobody has been through here with a wagon or a car for years, Leo thought. He walked down the road a hundred yards or so and stopped when he saw an almost impenetrable wild plum thicket rooted in the dimming path. They did not feel like walking the long distance when they had to worry with the kids, so they gave it up. It was only a foolish notion, anyhow, going down to look at the place where the House of The Hand had been and the site of Leischer's cabin. Those days were gone forever, and wandering around in the hollow could not serve to recapture any of their lost flavor. Leo had to back out of the lane, craning his neck to see the deep rivulets washed in the clay. The wheels chugged into them now and then in spite of Leo's tugging at the wheel. They hoped that the jouncing might have some effect on Anna, but it only roiled her stomach enough to make her sick. She had to lean over the side and vomit even after they reached the highway. People rolling easily by in cars eyed her curiously.

Each night Leo, sleeping upstairs with Anna and the children, could hear the tar paper on the roof flapping and bellying like a sail taut with the wind in it. Now and then shingles were ripped off, and he could hear them rattling as they blew off the edge. The next morning they would be gathered for kindling. Leo would walk down the street and into a vacant lot to gaze anxiously at the top of the house. The yellow pine sheeting could be seen through the holes in the shingles, and a black void in several spots told him that the first heavy rain would inundate the attic and soak all the plaster off the ceilings. It had been a dry winter, but when the February and March thaws came and the equinoctial storms broke, there would be hell to pay if the roof was allowed to remain in its present condition. He could not sleep for thinking of this, and when the tar paper slapped onto the loose shingles with more than ordinary force, he winced as though he had been struck a blow. He knew he should climb onto the roof, but it was so high and the winter wind so chilly. Perhaps it would last till a warm day.

Then a night came when he knew the worst had happened. There was a terrific ripping noise, a scraping, and then pattering as though ten thousand rats were scampering across the shingles. He sprang from bed and ran for a step ladder which he placed beneath the hatch leading into the attic. He butted the covering out of the way, dust and cobwebs sifting into his face. He could see the stars through the uncovered holes in the roof. At least part of the tar paper had blown off the house altogether.

"The old man oughta knowed better than t' put tar paper right on top of old shingles," he said to Anna, who had awakened. "But it costs less that way. He hadda do the best he could. I'll have t' go up on the roof right now, that's all. Hear that flappin' and the nails tearin' out. The whole kit and kaboodle 'll go sure as God made little apples if it ain't took care of *right now*."

Terry had heard the commotion, and came upstairs. He protested against Leo going onto the roof.

"Not t' night, not wi' the wind howlin' like a thousand mad divils. If it won't wait till mornin', let it be. T'hell wi' it."

"No," said Leo. "It has t' be t'night. It'll all go."

The only ladder to be found was one that would reach the roof from the top of the front porch. Leo set this ladder against the edge of the roof and started up. He had found a hammer and nails. As his weight pushed it, the ladder's foot slowly began creeping toward the edge, ruffling the decayed wood.

"Hold it, fer God's sake," Leo yelled.

Terry climbed out of the window and pushed for dear life, bracing his feet. The ladder stopped slipping. Terry stood shivering with the cold as Anna looked out of the window anxiously, drawing her nightgown tight about her.

When Leo started worming his way up, his foot slipped and he scooted almost to the edge. He was sweating with terror in spite of the bitter wind. It was so queer and scary up here with only the stars above and the demoniac night wind tearing at his thin clothing. Then a violent gust burst upon him and the roof lifted and sailed like an aeroplane. It seemed as though everything was going, but Leo saw that only the tar paper had blown away with patches of shingles clinging to it. Then the wind tore at the loose shingles and sent them whirling. Leo climbed dejectedly down.

Leo was down in the dumps for days. His throat was raw and sore, and he could not help worrying about the roof. He knew it was no use, however. They had a little money left over from the amount collected by their friends in St. Luke, but it was melting like snow in April. Getting something to eat was more important than patching the old house.

Then Terry came in one morning shouting exultantly over a letter from Tuck Saunders. Leo knew what to expect, and he was not sorry now. He knew it meant leaving Green Valley, but it seemed that he was having to worry here fully as much as he had in St. Luke.

The letter from Tuck Saunders put them all in high spirits. Terry could always have a job there as long as he had anything to do with it, Tuck said. He would find something he could do, even if the old joints were a little stiff. Terry could bring Leo, too.

"I am glad to hear from the little shaver," wrote Tuck. "But it makes me feel old to realize he is grown up and has a family. The last time I saw him Lupe left him here with us while she went to a fiesta or something the spicks was having, and she didn't come dragging her tail in till after one. That was when you was off in the Powder River country looking for work. She was drunk as a fiddler's bitch that night. You was always too good a man for her, Terry. I could have told you she was putting it out to every Tom, Dick and Harry that wanted it, but, you being my pal, I wanted somebody else to spill it. I knew all about it and so did everybody but you, I guess, before you moved to Seattle to get her away from her old sweethearts. Then you walked in and caught that big Swede lumberjack between the buggy shafts and there wasn't no use for anybody to tell you. You knew what to do. Terry, old pal, I am sending you fifty dollars expense money, and I want you to get yourself right out here and bring the boy and his family. The Golden Plume Mining Company don't forget its old hands. I am now supe instead of just bottom boss. I am a little up in the world to what I was when you last seen me, but I wouldn't want to ever get anywheres if I had to forget my old pals, which I ain't. What is the boy's name? Leon, you said? I do not have your letter here, as I am writing this at the mine. In fact, I am sleeping and eating at the mine now, business is that good. We are working six days a week. I'll be looking for you, old timer."

"Aw, that's the place," said Terry joyfully. "'I'll be lookin' fer you, old timer,' he says. Good old Tuck! I well remember the night we cleaned out a whorehouse in Butte and had the girls runnin' ever' which way wi' nawthin' but kimonos t' their pretty backs, poor creatures. We wouldn't 'a' harmed a hair o' their dear heads; we was only sore at a couple o' wooden-head Swedes that thought they was the cock o' the walk."

They locked the doors as best they could, boarded up the ground floor windows. Leo knew that the spring rains would soak off all the plaster, but it could not be helped. Like as not, they'd never return to this house. It was about bare inside. Terry had sold all the furniture he could dispose of, and almost all of the books had gone the same way. It was hard to sell the books in Green Valley, but Terry put the price so low that anybody who cared for books at all could not resist. It was good riddance if they never saw the house again, Terry said. Let the county have it for taxes. You couldn't eat a half-rotted house and a patch of clayey soil not big enough to whip a cat on.

Within three days they had equipped the Ford with a short truck bed, loaded the children and a few effects on it, and were headed for the West. Leo felt as much excitement as he had when he heard the bums telling their travel stories in the jungle near Green Valley so long ago. He would get to see most of those places now, and, being older, he'd appreciate them more.

At the first glimpse of the Rockies, Leo cut off the engine and steered the machine to the shoulder. They stood up and cheered at the snow-capped peaks. Terry was the only one who could remember seeing a full-sized mountain before. Leo must have seen some, but he had forgotten. It had been a long time since then, and so many things had happened. So much had happened to both of them since he and Terry rode a freight train east to Green Valley.

"If a man's foresight was only as keen as his hindsight," mused Terry, "I wonder how he'd lay his life out. What would 'a' become of us if you hadn't took the scours and I had rode on through wi' ye, instead o' droppin' off? Or I might 'a' stayed in Seattle wi' Lupe if I'd 'a' had all these years behind me 'stead of afore me. Poor girl, she would lay down and spread her legs fer any man that whistled, it seemed to me thin. Yet she was not all bad, and she had many endearin' ways about 'er. I've been doin' some thinkin' these last lonesome years, and I believe now a man should niver be blamin' a woman fer what's put in them afore they iver come around. I well remember Lupe whin I caught 'er wi' the Swede, her big eyes fair swimmin' wi' tears whin I told 'er good-bye and she knowed certain sure she'd niver see aither of us again. 'Tis no doubt at all, at all, in me mind now that she loved us both in her way. Some women has it in 'em like a candle flame, puny and easy put out, and others like a ragin' volcano that never cools. And Lupe was one o' thim that a dozen men pourin' all their love into 'er couldn't drown 'er fire. Poor Marthy's candle soon petered out so there was only the ashes left, and then she was cold as an icicle and couldn't endure me nigh 'er. She couldn't help it, poor soul. And I should not 'a' pestered 'er so whin she was that coldish to'rds me she shivered at the touch o' me hand. But by the time a man learns these things, it's too late. Aw, I don't know what t' make o' things. The longer I live, the less I be knowin'."

Leo had learned that Anna's passion for him had burned out already, and her body could never warm him again. She had been torn so many times in parturition—had suffered so much pain, humiliation, and fear—that she shrank from sexual embrace with him, though she had an idea it was her duty to submit. And she knew that Leo was aware of her frigidity and was disturbed by it. She tried to deceive him by employing the whore's device of feigned ecstasy, but Leo still missed something. When he came at last to understand her feeling about it, he grew more considerate. There were other things to occupy his mind. Soon he was taking a small measure of comfort in the thought that their sixth child might well be their last. There would be no more anxious watching of the calendar, no more frantic appeals to doctors, and no more spending ill-spared money for mail-order nostrums guaranteed to "relieve the most stubborn cases in forty-eight hours."

CHAPTER SIX

"Yes, I finally got to read your book manuscript," said Danny Maupin. "I'm sorry that it took me so long. I promised to finish the novel before Christmas, but I spent two weeks staring at the typewriter platen and not able to finish a page. I had to tear everything up. I spent the advance on the novel months ago, so they've got a right to be sore, I guess. Let me show you something funny. You'll laugh."

The room was small and stuffy. Danny kept the blinds down all day long; he could see better with the light turned on. Often he did not know whether it was day or night, and the bedding was always awry. Papers were strewn all over the floor, and Robert noticed that many of them had the prints of dusty rubber heels stamped on them. Others were burned where cigarette stubs had lit.

Danny had been fumbling among the litter on his table. His hands shook, and some of the papers slid to the floor. He sank to his knees and riffled the sheets that had fallen before, then arose with two typewritten pages to which a photograph was fastened by a wire clip.

"Here you are," said Danny. "The latest photograph of Chinook Mavison, the cowboy author. The editor of *Western Yarns* writes me that the fans are panting to know what their favorite ink-slinger looks like in the flesh. Do you see that bold, eagle eye, and that rugged jaw that looks as though it might be about to fly open wide enough to let out a few bars of 'Roll along, little dogies'?"

It was a picture of Danny decked out in a cowboy hat

and bandana handkerchief. The childishness of his face was accentuated by the big hat and flaring neckpiece.

"What's this?" asked Robert. "What's the masquerade for?"

"Just as I told you. I am none other than Chinook Mavison, and the populace clamors for a peep at my map. Hence a request, even a command, from the editor of *Western Yarns* that I send a photo in costume. I had it taken at that penny arcade down on Seventh Street where the rangy giraffe-necked blonde tries to date you or sell you French postcards or Merry Widows when you ask for pennies in exchange for a nickel or dime. They got a new slot picture machine in, 'Night in a Turkish Harem,' but the light fades out just as the Sultan gets down to business like it does when you look at 'First Night of the Honeymoon.' There's more pictures to it, too, because you can hear the cards still falling after the light goes out. I often wonder if a man would take a flashlight. . . ."

"That's where you had the picture taken?" Robert asked. He was anxious to know what Danny thought of his manuscript.

"Yes, he had all the props. Even a lariat, but the editor just wanted a head, so I didn't have to change my pants, even. I couldn't make my sloping chin bulk out squarely and bellicosely to save my soul from whatever devils there may be in that land where they don't shovel snow. I know damned well I don't look as virile as Chinook Mavison should look, and my readers will be disappointed."

"Well, why didn't you get somebody else to pose for it."

"I suggested that, but the editor said it wouldn't be ethical. You understand that? It would not be ethical to deceive the public that way. Unethical. And he knows what I look like, for when I first started submitting to him and had sold him a few, he asked me for a picture of myself for his own private Rogues' Gallery of contributors. He said he always liked to know what his authors looked like. He said he would never use it in the magazine, and he kept his word. He's a man whose word is as good as his bond; he knew that wouldn't be ethical, it wouldn't be

Rotary, it wouldn't be cricket, old son. No sir, he never used it. Now listen to this. This is rich. He wants a little autobiographical note for his Contributors' Round-Up department, all in character. It'll run with the picture. Read it. You'll bust a gut laughing."

Robert was not much interested in the autobiographical note, but he looked through it dutifully. He wanted to keep on the good side of Danny, for he was a successful writer and knew all the ins and outs.

"Mr. Walden ask me fer a little info about myself," Robert read. "He told me you folks has been kind enough to write in and want to know all about me after you read my yarns, and he wanted a chromo of me, too, to print along with this. Well, here's one that's been hangin' out in the corral to scare off the buzzards. It was snapped by Ogalalla Slim, the most ornery hombre that ever pulled leather, just as I made fer the mess house and the musical fruit and jerky after a hard day in the saddle on the range spurring my pinto after them cantankerous dogies. I look like a sad accident that had started out to happen but hadn't happened yet. But I ain't much of a hand to have my picture tooken, so it will have to do. Well, they ain't much to tell about me, folks. I'm just a cowboy, and I reckon I'll always be a cowboy and nothing else but. They was times out there on the range with the big silver moon overhead powdering the earth and the restless backs of the herd waving before us like a sea and us singing songs of the range to keep them quiet. The moon was pouring down dream dust them nights and I got to thinking about my life and the places I had been and the things I had seen, and the time come when it seemed like I had to get it out of my system and put it down on paper for other folks to read. So that's how I come to write these yarns you-all people has been good enough to write in about. As I said in the first place, I'm just a cowboy, and I always was a cowboy since I can first remember. I forked a bronc before I was knee-high to a horned toad, and I seen some of the western country when a man had to be mighty fast on the draw to keep healthy, been in a dozen revolutions in old

Mexico and Central America, but had to come back when I run out of greasers to shoot at. I've seen some mighty tough times when I didn't have a dime in my saddle-pockets and I ain't got a sou in them right now, but I reckon if I had my life to live over I wouldn't have it much different. All I got is my memories, but they're worth all the gold that ever come out of Cripple Creek, folks. I ain't got a single hard feeling only for one ornery pup that I'll sure make claw for his holster if I ever meet up with him. That's the hombre that started that cussed lie that I was caught herding sheep up Montana way with a false beard on. I've done many a thing I wouldn't like to see in print, I've got a few notches on my gun, and I ain't no sky pilot nor even close to one, but they's a few things I draw the line on, and sheep-herding's all of them. Well, ain't no more to tell, folks. Adios to all."

"How does it sound?" asked Danny, grinning wryly, his face shuddered in distaste as a belch rose. "I'll have to take out that musical fruit part and make it beans. You can have the he-man talking a little Rabelaisian, but there's a limit. After all, these western magazines go into cultured homes of Legionnaires, Elks, Lions, Rotarians, and Owls. The horror and detective stuff doesn't go so good for me, but I've been fairly successful with the westerns."

"It sounds all right for that kind of a magazine, but I thought you'd be busy writing novels and more serious stuff."

"I am, but I have to eat the while, my boy."

"Don't the novels pay so much?"

"None of them has ever earned more than a few dollars above the advance, and that's never been more than three hundred dollars."

"You always get swell reviews."

"You can't fry them. The green and never fading bays bestowed on your brow by the critics look pretty and feel good, but spinach or mustard greens will stick to your ribs longer. The lightning strikes a few books each season, and they bring their authors big money, but so many are published. Each year since twenty-nine it's been getting worse."

"Well, about that manuscript of mine. . . ."

"The first time I got anything printed I thought I'd dirty my pants I was so elated," said Danny. "Then I sold something, and I was in the clouds for weeks. I sold more, and then I thought I'd like to spend a little time in Paris; that was the place to learn how to write. It gave you something, an atmosphere, a flavor, you couldn't get elsewhere. I was in heaven for a while again after I got there among the berets and velvet pants. I was always running across some new and quaint *bistro*, and I saw life in the raw—savage, elemental emotions—in those joints furnished with peepholes about the walls, and the guy inside don't know he's making an ass of himself for a dozen pairs of eyes. Then there were the mirror rooms to be rented for a few francs an hour where you can see yourself and your bed-partner in a dozen places and from every angle. There was the absinthe, and the American tourists conscientiously exploring the Louvre. I brought back the syph, empty pockets, and a head full of fool notions, but not a page of writing worth a tinker's damn."

"I'd like to see Paris, anyhow. Maybe you found a lot of typographical bugs in that manuscript of mine. . . ."

"I used to think a writer was only a notch below God in anybody's hierarchy. He could actually create life, and shape it as he willed. That was before I had to sit here with a headache and a sour stomach and drag across the keys, wearily writing a tremendous climax, an emotional orgasm, no less, arching and wiggling the backbone of my mind, moaning in a mental ecstasy. And all the time my belly is griping, my groins paining me, and my nose running. I always put off writing till I can't put it off any longer, and when I'm not writing, day or night, I always know I *should* be writing. I'm always spending an advance or two ahead, on books I haven't written a word of, and if I should die before I wake, I pray the Lord my soul to take, the firm of Noel and Lassiter would be holding the sack. One book didn't even earn the advance on it, but they didn't make me make up the balance. They have their troubles, too. That was the one that some critic compared to the work of Dostoyevsky, another to that of Zola, another to Hardy, still another to Balzac, and God knows what other comparisons were made. But you get so it don't mean a damned thing but the headache and the sleepless nights and the nerves raw as hamburger all the time."

"I worked hard on that stuff there. I know," said Robert, trying his best to get Danny's mind onto the manuscript.

"You're damned right it's work, and hard work, and there's never a whistle to tell you when you can knock off and forget about it till it blows again in the morning."

"I know how it works on a man's nerves. Well, what do you think of the novel? I guess it's not much; I don't like it so well myself."

"Yes, you do, Bob," said Danny smiling gently till his tiny yellow teeth showed momentarily. His smile was ordinarily tight-lipped and acid. "That's the hell of it. We all like our own stuff, and we can't stand off and look at it as though it was a stranger. We have to dress it up as prettily in our minds as a mother idealizes an ugly and mediocre child. Don't try to write, Bob. Your story is pretty bad—pretty lousy. It's not about life—the sort of life that matters to anybody. Old Thoreau was a nut in lots of ways, but he was right in saying one should not pay a high price to live what is not life, and a life that's not very important to live isn't very important to write about. That was a not-life down there at the Green Dragon. I don't think you'll ever be a writer who can turn out salable stuff or even good stuff, but that's nothing for you to worry about. It's more honorable and satisfying to be an efficient truck driver. He really does something; he amounts to something. Writing at its best is only a pale imitation of life, and it's always distorted like those concave and convex mirrors down there at the penny arcade where I posed for my cowboy picture. The best writers show things too fat or too thin; it's always grotesque and out of shape. Don't be sore at me, Bob. But I won't feed you any bull to tickle your vanity. I don't know everything, and somebody else may tell you your stuff is swell. Maybe it is, but I don't think so. It smells of the Green Dragon; there's no sun, air, earth, water, flesh or blood in it."

Robert listened to all this calmly. He had expected it, and he never questioned Danny's judgment. The little fellow was only solidifying and molding into definite shape Robert's own nebulous convictions. That's that, that's the end, he thought, with a certain degree of relief.

"I wish I *could* be a truck driver," he said. "I can't be anything." He was ashamed of the tears in his eyes. Before he could wink them back or dash them off with the back of his hand, two big drops slid onto his nose. Crying like a baby. Now Danny 'll think I'm bawling because he panned my book. "I'm tired of living the way I am, half alive and half dead. Not enough to really live on, but a little too much to die on. There are thousands of grown men who have never had a job in all their lives. This can go on for years, till I'm gray-headed, and still no job. Do you know that?"

"Sure, I know it. We're all in the same boat and it's floundering badly with nobody at the pumps."

"All of the people are not in the same boat. Some of them are still sitting on top of the world."

"Yes, and they'll stay there till Gabriel toots his horn to call them to their heavenly home, too."

"Why should they? I've got as much right to live as the next one. I want to work, but I can't work. Nobody will let me work."

"You'll have to *make* a job for yourself, there's always room at the top. It's only at the foot where the fellows unpolitely tramp one another's fingers and try to kick one another off. I heard a guy telling about it over the radio. You've got to pack some sort of message to some sort of Garcia somewhere, you've got to cook and serve a juicier hot dog in your roadside kiosk, and be a friend to man. Or get a job in a filling station; but to be a filling station attendant, or gastician, as some of them call it now, you have to be at least a Ph.D. nowadays. And those who are lucky enough to get a filling station have to wipe the windshields brighter, smile more widely, and exemplify the Spirit of Service. One guy I know follows his customers into the neat little room marked 'Papa' or 'Jiggs' just across from the one marked 'Mama' or 'Maggie' with a roll of tissue in his mitt. It ain't the kind with splinters in it, either, not the kind the ads warn us against."

"Well, I guess I'll be toddling along," said Robert miserably. Danny could never be serious over a few minutes at a time.

That's all of that, all of that, all of that, thought Robert as he closed the front door and walked slowly down the street. I guess I knew it all the time, but I was wanting to believe the best as long as I could. I'll not stand her coming home in a huff and asking me how much writing I've done. Since she sends nearly all her money to her folks and I have to cook for her, even, then endure her reproachful looks when I tell her I haven't sold anything yet, I've been in hot water continually. There's going to be an end, and it might as well be now. Better go down to Roosevelt Roost along the river front and hole up in an abandoned houseboat with the rest of the bums. That's where I belong. I've kidded myself too long as it is.

He strode along with the manuscript under his arm. The stream of pedestrians thickened; he was in the district of shops and theatres. He felt a tug at his arm. A husky youth of twenty with butter teeth and straw-colored hair sticking from beneath an overseas style cap stood grinning, with a bundle of papers under his arm. He wore a military blouse and trousers, and his legs were encased in shiny puttees.

"Buy an *American Wakener*, mister," he said. "Read all the inside dope about the Jew bankers that caused the depression. Lookit!" He shifted the bundle around to show a picture of a group of bearded and sinister Jews hovering over a prone and naked body from which they were sucking blood through quills. "That's the way they do a Christian when they get a chance. Only you don't hear of it half the time; most of the big papers is owned by Jews, but in the *American Wakener* you get it all straight. That ain't the half of it. Read what they do with the foreskins they save from circumsizin'. How they kidnapped a young Christian girl out in Los Angeles and stuck a big firecracker up her and set a match to the fuse. If you want something to make your hair stand straight up on your head, read the Protocols of Zion. I got it in a nice little book, only three cents. It costs more than that to print it, but the America First Vigilantes made up the difference."

"I'm flat. An elephant stepped on my purse."

"Well, take one if you ain't got the price. They just slapped a teensy-weensy price on it to make people respect it. Any give-away stuff is always throwed around and not read. We just want to get the people next to the Jew plots before it's too late."

"Naw. Thanks all the same, buddy. I can't read. I never went to school but two days, and the first day the teacher was sick and there wasn't any school, the second day the school house burned down. So I never went again."

"I never went only till the third grade. I've learned more since I joined this outfit than I ever did in school. Well, if you can't read you can see, I know. You can look at pictures. Come here." He drew Robert to the entrance of an unoccupied store. "Git where the light shines through. Now, these is pictures of Jews rapin' good-lookin' Christian girls. They show ever'thing just as plain as day—it's natural as life. Here's one shows how she looked after they all got through—fifty-three of 'em."

"Aw, go peddle your papers. These were taken in Paris before the war. Look at the hour-glass waists. That gal doesn't look as though she'd been damaged much. She knew how to pose to let the camera catch everything, too, didn't she?"

"Hey, don't you want *anything*?" the youth called angrily as Robert stepped away.

"No."

"Why did you look at 'em so hard for?"

"You asked me to. I didn't damage them by looking at them. Besides they give me a belly-ache and so do you."

"Maybe you're a Jew sympathizer. Maybe you're a sheeny yourself. You got a long enough beezer on you."

"I am. My name's Isidor Levy, and I want your foreskin! Come on!" Robert plunged his hand into his pocket.

"You asked for it, sheeny, now take it!" shouted the youth. Robert was astonished to see him deftly jerk a blackjack from a blouse pocket. He threw his head sidewise, and the blow tore at his ear. The blackjack swung again, and this time caught him on the left shoulder, numbing that side to the waist. He put all he could muster into a straight blow with his right arm and saw the uniformed youth stagger against the plate-glass window, crash through it. His putteed legs waved as he yelled for help.

Robert stooped to pick up the bundle of *American Wakener*, and ran down the street. He heard somebody call to him, and, turning, saw a policeman. His first impulse was to stop, but he decided against it, rounded the corner, and was soon dashing up an alley. Three blocks away he halted in another alley and tore the copies of the *American Wakener* into pieces no larger than a dollar. He blew on his skinned knuckles as he emerged sedately into the street again. It seemed funny at first, he thought, but it's serious. You can call them crazy or whatever you like, but they're here and they're at work. The next time she says anything about doing extra work for the America First Vigilantes, I'll walk out on her. I can eat breadline stew if I have to; and there's always a place to sleep. I hear that a bunch of down-and-outs have broken into the old piano factory on Tenth Street and sleep there snug as a bug in a rug. Nobody bothers them. The factory hasn't worked for years; not since the victrola first became popular.

He stopped abruptly, and pounded his right fist into his open left palm. Jesus Christ! He did not have the manuscript with him. He must have lost it in the scuffle with the youth; he did not remember having it after that. It did not matter about the manuscript itself—he'd intended to destroy it, anyhow, but his name was on it. Or was it? He had wanted to publish the book under the pseudonym of Raoul Rawlison, and this name was written underneath the title. Perhaps he had not typed his own name and address on the title page, after all. Danny had had the damned thing so long he could not remember. What the hell! It didn't matter. Come one, come all, this rock shall fly from its firm base as soon as I! Bring 'em on one at a time! He sidestepped and waltzed daintily along the sidewalk, shadow-boxing. What a night! He felt better than he had for years.

CHAPTER SEVEN

Fillmore Taylor surged up from the depths of sleep like a swimmer bobbing to the water's surface after a long dive, exhaling with a sobbing gasp. He fought with the quilts, threw them on the floor. He had been sleeping with a pillow over his face, and was almost smothered. He panted like a spent runner, knuckling his bleary eyes. On the foot of the bed his funereal white shirt hung rakishly, and his tuxedo could be seen crumpled against the far wall, weighted with a shoe. . . . Fool! Fool! He flayed himself bitterly. Had to pass out and spoil everything. He had had sweet little Beulah Horley, the keenest piece from Silver Springs to Salt Lake City, all hot and bothered with his blarney. She had been swallowing his really masterful line of bull as avidly as a hungry trout leaping for a gaudy fly. The first few snorts of liquor had lent him a subtle tongue, had overcome his natural timidity, but he hadn't known when to stop. He remembered that somebody found him in the bathroom, his head hung over the can. Somebody bundled him in the car. In the big Buick, the motor roaring, the gravel pinging on the underside of the fenders. The sudden fear sobering him momentarily as he had to paw desperately and jerk at the wheel as the big machine took the curves on two wheels. The empty windows of a vacant farm house reflecting the headlights like the angrily blazing eyes of some sinister pre-historic monster squatting in the darkness. Then the beet dump and the travel-scarred Ford parked beside it; some figures reclining on blankets under the platform. Maybe dead, he thought with terror, maybe murdered. He remembered the bum that had been found dead behind the billboard flanking the highway south of Silver Springs. He had caught a strong whiff of that bum more than once but thought it was a dead animal somewhere afield. Maybe somebody putting up a load of coal. The darkness warmed with voluptuous images which always had to be incomplete, for, with all his questing, he still had to imagine a lot of things about girls. And by passing out in the bathroom he had missed learning a lot. As he neared home his head cleared a little, though it still felt as though it had a tourniquet about it and somebody twisting it with a broomstick. He stopped the car, leaned against a silver poplar with ghostly, rustling leaves, and puked into an irrigation ditch. The air from the canyons of Bear Mountain, where snow lingered, was pleasantly chill against his forehead. He drove the last few miles to home at a moderate rate of speed and managed to put the car in the corrugated iron garage which his father, Bishop Maroni Taylor, had built onto his granary.

And now it was the morning after the night before. He slid from bed, searched for mints in his tuxedo pocket. Perhaps the scent of liquor persisted on his breath. He blew against his hand, sniffing as he did so. But it was hard to tell exactly. He crunched all the mints left in the package. If the bishop ever got wise to his carryings-on . . . good-night! . . .

Bishop Taylor was without his shirt and his faded suspenders were slung over the shoulders of his Mormon undergarments as Fillmore opened the bathroom door.

"Good-morning, father!"

"Good-morning, Fillmore." The bishop turned quickly, his lathered brush cutting a semi-circle on the glass. Great blobs of lather hung on his chin and half way up one side of his face. He thrust a look at his son, neatly dressed in an orange and green sweater and golf knickers, and turned to his shaving.

"Who are the folks in the kitchen?" asked Fillmore, indicating over his shoulder the direction from which came the buzz of unfamiliar voices.

"Poor people," mumbled the bishop through his soap.

"Transients. They came in this morning and I hired 'em to help in the beets. Better than hirin' Mexicans, I reckon. Plenty of the saints need work, but most of 'em are too lazy to work in the beets. Besides, the woman needs to see a doctor. They've five children with them, and they can work in the beets the same as the Mexican children, I guess. That's the way lots of the white families work it when they want to lay up a nest egg for the winter. Only the two littlest ones would only be in the way and ruin more than they'd thin. With them and the Goode boys we kin finish soon enough, providin' the rain don't stand us off."

"You'll miss Don," ventured Fillmore.

"Ummm!" mumbled the bishop.

As Fillmore entered the kitchen there was loud talk at the long, broad table. James, the hired man, had come in, and was talking animatedly with the two men for whom the bishop's wife was frying pancakes. The woman sat buttering pancakes for five children, and talking to them in low tones, evidently trying to restrain their wolfish bolting. The eldest girl was almost a woman now, and Fillmore regarded her speculatively. People with no place to stay couldn't be too stand-offish, he thought; he'd have to do some sly maneuvering. He had heard of male flivver tramps pimping for their daughters and wives; the women putting it out so they could buy gasoline and food. The children were gobbling down the pancakes so fast their mother couldn't get a bite, and she was shaming them for their bad manners, aloud now. "These people will think you were raised in a hog pen." But she was so hungry on her own account that she could scarcely refrain from snatching up a cake and devouring it.

It didn't take Fillmore long to discover why she was in need of a doctor. She was in the family way, and it looked as though she might have twins. Sitting as she was, there was such a contrast between the loose flabby skin of her cheeks and the rotundity of her belly that he knew she was nearing her time. She had deep blue puff-balls under her eyes, and pain and worry had creased deep furrows in the corners of her mouth.

"It was nigh Miles City, on the N. P.," James was saying. "Me and the boy rid that gondola for twenty-six hours 'fore we got off and warmed ourselves by a big fire some boes had built near the tracks. Beatin' it back to Paducah, the boy was. 'What time does the train get into Paducah?' he'd ask every time the train stopped and somebody come walkin' up the tracks. Even dicks and yard bulls, he was that green. He was as green as grass, that kid. 'What time does the train get into Paducah?'" James chuckled and scratched the inside of his knee. "I don't know whether he *ever* got to Paducah. We parted at Aberdeen. The kid takes to the highway, and I goes on into Minneapolis."

Fillmore caught the younger man staring contemptuously at his orange and green sweater and golf pants. He turned aside and walked to the kitchen door, leaning against the jamb and breathing the morning air. Outside, near the granary, he saw the dilapidated Model T Ford that had been parked beside the beet dump. So the two men, the woman, and the children had been asleep under that platform. He wondered if the Buick bore any evidence of last evening's carouse. He'd have to go down to inspect it right after he ate.

"Fillmore," his mother called. "These are the two Mister Hurleys and Missus Hurley and the children."

The woman had begun eating at last, and seemed to be struggling to keep herself in check. She didn't want to make a show of her hunger. She kept on eating, but raised her eyes briefly. The men mumbled something unintelligible and their faces wrestled with a brief attempt at amiability.

"They're goin' t' help yo'r pa in the beets," his mother continued.

"That we are," spoke up the elder man, "though it's divilish little we know about the thinnin' o' beets."

"It's easy to learn," replied Fillmore, making an effort toward conversation. "All you need is a weak mind and a strong back." He did not know that this was an almost universal witticism which the two flivver tramps had heard in a dozen states and on a score of jobs. He had heard the beet workers saying this. He could not keep his eyes off Anna's swollen body, and wondering about her, trying to re-create in his mind the embrace that had caused her condition. His "facts of life" had been learned from roadside petting, never progressing beyond hot kissing, and from the conversation of friends who had done a lot more and seen a lot more, to let them tell it. But he didn't know. He boasted of his own amorous adventures when he was out with the boys. Bishop Taylor had a large buckram-bound volume named *A Guide to Marriage, or an Encyclopædia of Sex,* and every time he caught his father far enough away from the house and his mother occupied, he would hastily steal into the forbidden front parlor, reserved for funerals, visits of church dignitaries and other state occasions, and jerk down the heavy volume from its resting place atop the melodeon, thumbing rapidly through the book till he came to the chapter on *The Female Organs of Reproduction.* There were diagrams of the sexual organs, but they were as skeletal as a blue print and Fillmore had to exercise his imagination a great deal.

The bishop entered the kitchen just as Anna was finishing the last hot cake, and Leo was removing a sack of makings from a soiled shirt pocket. James tried to catch his eye before he'd begun to pour the tobacco out, but Leo didn't understand his veiled gestures.

"No smoking in *this* house, my man!" The bishop's stentorian voice rolled across the large kitchen. It was the tone with which Bishop Taylor dominated his little congregation of Mormons, as well as the monthly meetings of Providence County commissioners, and it tended to command obedience, but not good will. Fillmore saw that Leo's growing good humor had vanished. The flivver tramp poured his tobacco silently back into the sack, careful of the precious grains, and crumpled the rice leaf into a ball which he dropped onto his plate.

"Outside, if the vile habit has enslaved you," continued

the bishop, a little more mildly as he noted Leo's unhesitating compliance, "you will find room enough to smoke. Never has tobacco been smoked in *this* house."

James and Fillmore exchanged knowing glances. With the presence of the bishop in the kitchen, the atmosphere changed. Arrangements were made for Anna to see Dr. Wooten in Silver Springs. The bishop was going to foot the bill, and the men and the larger children were to work it out in the bishop's beets. Anna was plainly thankful and did her best to show it by attempting to help the bishop's wife clear up the dishes. But Mrs. Taylor had a certain place to put everything, a certain way to do this and that, and Anna only muddled up her routine. She sat down miserably, and was afraid she was going to go into a crying fit as she had so often in the last year. The bishop's wife sensed her mood, and gave her a tall glass of warm morning's milk, then told her to lie down in the front room and listen to the radio.

Neither Leo nor Terry had ever thinned sugar beets before. The process consisted of cutting a space twelve inches in length out of the row of budding beet sprouts, and the spacing was done with a short hoe held in the right hand, while the actual thinning was done with the left. After several spaces had been cut out, corresponding clusters of sprouts were left in the row. Thinning meant merely to pick all but one of the small plants from such clusters. The work had to be done in either a stooping or kneeling position, and soon Terry was complaining of a stabbing pain in his back when he stooped, while his knees felt as though they were covered with boils when he attempted to kneel. The dry clods of the beetfield ate through his overalls and soon drove bits of dirt and dust into his tender skin. Leo stood the work better and found that he could make better time by watching for thin spaces in the row and then doing all the thinning with the hoe. The fingers of his left hand were already sore and stained from picking at the sprouts. He pulled gradually away from Terry and hurried down his row. They were being paid by the acre; the field was a large one, and eight rows took up an acre of space. If they could each thin four rows a day, with the help of the children, they would be ahead four dollars. But the children were not much help. They could not understand that they must keep humping away, and they stopped to look around at the strange sights—the snow on the mountains, and the families of Mexicans working on adjoining plots. In most cases the entire family was there, the babes wrapped in blankets tended by smaller children or amusing themselves alone. Their beady eyes glistened, and they sometimes grinned or waved a fat brown hand as the entranced Hurley children gathered around them. Mexican children of five or so were working silently, swiftly and gravely in the fields. The season was short, and enough to keep the family the rest of the year had to be made within a brief period.

Four dollars a day! The thought roweled Leo to more furious exertion. Jesus! If he could only get Anna back to Green Valley before her time. But they had been delayed too much—begging for work, for gas, the inexorable days passing, Anna's belly filling more and more. And she sometimes looked as though she would rather face death than parade her swollen body before strangers. She reminded him of some wild animal that yearned to hide away unseen in the brush to bring forth her young; she was pained and frightened as curious eyes poked at her protruding abdomen, ashamed as though she were already lying exposed in the throes of delivery, encircled by a gaping crowd. If the doctor at Silver Springs thought she could make the trip at all. . . . The old truck was so bouncy. . . . It was clear now that Terry's working days were about over, but the old man was game to the core. Nobody could *try* harder than he did, and he never beefed. The children were not getting all the weeds out. Well, no use worrying or waiting. He'd just have to hump-te-diddy on his own hook, and then help the others.

When a train, rounding a bend on the far side of the valley, announced that noon was not far off, Anna appeared with lunches sent out by the bishop's wife. Hot, home-made sausages, sandwiches, and a generous slice of apple pie for each person. Anna had wanted to come out and help with the weeding, but the bishop and his wife objected to that. The Mexicans in the next field had their women and girls working with them, but there appeared to be some difference between Mexicans and white men in the eyes of the Mormons. Anna had wanted to carry water for them, but neither did Mrs. Taylor like the idea of that.

"The radio music is nice," Anna told Leo, "but I almost go crazy just sitting there and thinking. Thinking how it'll all work out. If I was out here, I wouldn't think so much." So she stayed in the field until after the noon hour was over, and, with Leo, listened to Lem Burt talking. Terry went to sleep with his hat over his eyes, in the shade of the grass near the canal, but Leo and Anna liked to listen to Lem Burt talking about Utah and the Mormons. Lem's family wasn't religious, and Lem swore that he wasn't a Mormon because he hadn't been baptized. The work he and his brother were doing in Bishop Anderson's beets would save the church from supporting his family for at least two or three months during the coming winter.

"It was early in the spring the year that I worked for Bishop Anderson," he was saying. "Old man Anderson is first counselor to the boss in Melbourne Ward. I remember standin' at the head of a row and wishin' to God it was five o'clock. Some of the fellers was goin' to work after supper, but they was fellers that hadn't been workin' long and wanted to do an acre in one day. I remember thinkin' it was kind of purty down at the end of the field where the slough cut across the bishop's place. I could hear some kids in swimmin' and it made me twicet as hot and tired knowin' *I* had to keep right on workin'. The bishop had been kickin' at some of my work, and I was purty mad. I was sort of mad, anyway. You see, the bishop is kind of religious. Whenever he walks out in the fields and any of the boys is smokin', he looks dirty-like at 'em and purty soon no one smokes when he's around."

Leo grunted, shrugged, and began to roll a cigarette.

" 'Course, that's all right for the Mormons," continued Lem. "They ain't supposed to smoke, anyway. Well, and then he lectures Bill Bogard for sayin' 'Jesus Christ!' while he was filin' his hoe. We didn't mind that so much, either, and kind of cut down on the swearin' when the bishop was around and quit shootin' craps in the cowbarn on days when it rained and you couldn't work. It wasn't all that that made the fellers mad. Some of 'em really wanted to cut down on the swearin', and I'd been losin' too much to worry about the craps, but one day the old bastard says that we all got to go to church on Sunday if we want to keep our jobs. No one said much when the bishop told us about goin' to church until finally Skinny spoke up and said, 'Jesus Christ, do you think we're gonna waste the one good day in the week listenin' to you preach when we might lay around or go in swimmin'?"

"Now, that made the boss hoppin' mad and he fired Skinny quick as a cat could lick itself with its tail raised and its tongue out. It's the only time I seen the bishop get real red-hot mad. He's sort of an easy-goin' old guy and don't get excited, not very excited, anyway, even when he's preachin' to us about smokin' or swearin', but this time his face went red and he talked to us straight and fast for a couple of hours. Finally, after he'd finished spieling, and sort o' calmed down a bit he took Skinny by the arm and led him away and we went back to work. We was kind of mad at losin' the time, but we all felt sorry for Skinny 'cause we knew jobs was scarce and he was tryin' to go to school in the fall. Some years it was easy to get jobs and you didn't have to take no old man's slack, but this was the year an extra gang of spicks come in and there wasn't much water in the mountains. Lots of the beets dried up and was plowed under."

"What about the Mormons? Do they shout and dance in church like the Holy Rollers? That's the way the Holy Rollers do in Green Valley, where we came from," said Anna.

"Well, now," said Lem. "I can't say that I've ever seen any of 'em take fits but they do bless with oil. Administerin', they call it, and they go to the temple."

"In Salt Lake," said Leo, knowingly.

"Yeh, and here, too," answered Lem. "You see that?" He pointed a long finger toward the spot where Silver Springs could be seen huddled on the very foothills of the Wasatch Mountains, seven or eight miles to the north and east. "You see them two tall spires a-shinin' from that second hill?"

Leo and Anna could see them as soon as their eyes became accustomed to the distance. The air was dry and clear, not like the heavy air of Green Valley or the smoky atmosphere of St. Luke.

"Well, that's a Mormon temple. That's where the Mormons get married and baptized and all—in them temples. If they don't they go to hell when they die."

Leo laughed, but Anna was serious. "What do they do in those temples?" she asked.

Lem humped his shoulders. "I donno. It's a secret like a lodge or somethin'."

"Like the Masons?" suggested Anna.

"Yeh, I guess so. Like the Masons."

While they were talking, Bishop Taylor was walking back and forth across the field. Leo saw him kicking into the soil with his toe, and now and then he would pull a large mustard weed and lay it carefully between the rows of beets. It was easy to see where the thinners had worked —the soil was darker and the small shoots did not appear to be in long rows as they had before they were hoed. As the bishop started toward them, Leo pulled the leg of Terry's overalls, and the old man got up painfully and slowly. Stiffness was already beginning to settle in his joints. It was time to begin work again, and the men, followed by Anna, started down the row toward the bishop. It was Terry that Maroni was waiting for.

"You been crawlin' on your knees?" he asked sternly.

"Me?" answered Terry. "Sure, and one look at me

knees and there'd be not the least o' doubt in yer mind." He rubbed his swollen joints as he spoke.

"You're wipin' beets out with your toes. Be more careful," said the bishop.

Terry nodded comprehendingly, and they went on toward their work. Anna walked behind them with her hands in the pockets of a sweater Mrs. Taylor had lent her. The pockets of the sweater were exactly below and to either side of her stomach. With her hands she supported the child that occasionally stirred within her. Once she stopped, staggered, and almost fell, her face blanching. Small silver specks floated in the air in front of her and disappeared like spray at the bottom of a waterfall. She was behind the men and they didn't notice. She was glad of that.

About four o'clock Leo had slackened his pace and had begun to worry about the time. He had been watching a Mexican woman from the next field leaving her work frequently and walking to the bank of a large irrigating canal near which he had eaten his own lunch. He supposed she was going to relieve herself, and he was not as curious as he had been when the two boys, Leo and Robert, lay on the hills above the gypsy camp in Happy Hollow to see what they could see. The canal cut diagonally across both fields and was used to water all of the acres in this section of the valley.

Leo heard the Mexican woman scream. Turning, he saw her, a bright shawl fluttering from her shoulders like a banner, a bundle in her arms, running toward the men in the field, shouting words Leo could not make out. She stumbled and fell, but, instead of raising herself, just laid in the middle of the beets and threshed about, howling. Occasionally, she talked rapidly. The Mexicans were all on a dead run for the woman, their voices droning across the hot valley air like a hive of bees with now and then a staccato bark of bastard Spanish.

Lem, two or three rows off, called to Leo: "Let's go!"

By the time they reached the Mexicans, the men had

taken a bundle from the woman's arms. Holding it in his arms, one of the Mexicans threw two folds of blanket to one side and exposed the face of a dark Mexican baby about three months old. The blankets were alive with large red ants, and the child's face was puffed and swollen until it resembled an overripe strawberry. Both eyes were swollen shut and a small round hole was the only indication of what had once been the mouth. It was clear that the Mexicans were struck beyond reason, and could do nothing for the child.

"Aw, what a pity!" said Terry. "Look ye, gi'me the child." The baby was reluctantly yielded by the women into his arms. A slight whine was all that escaped the swollen lips as Terry laid the child upon the ground and began unrolling fold after fold of bright dirty blanket.

The Mexican woman at last succeeded in getting the mother to rise from where she lay, her face rooting in the hard soil of the field. Sobbing hysterically, she couldn't bear to look at the child who by this time had ceased its whimpering, apparently unconscious.

Terry gave the child to Leo, who started across the fields on the trot, two of the Mexicans following. The small body had been partially protected by the blanket covering, and a few bites on its brown belly were the only signs of the ant horde that had swarmed into the improvised cradle.

By the time Leo had found the bishop and driven with him to see Dr. Wooten in Silver Springs, the baby was apparently dead. Its tiny tuft of black hair was sitting on the top of its puffed head like a skull cap. The doctor explained that the poison had entered the bloodstream, first affecting the eyes and later the small heart. Maroni took charge of arrangements and assured the Mexicans that the church and the county would see to the burial. While the bishop was calling the undertaker in Prairie City, the Mexicans went into Hilda Nelson's joint and got rip-roaring drunk.

"That's the way they mourn," said the bishop, tight-lipped. "Such people should never have children."

I know why they got drunk, and it ain't because they're not sorry, thought Leo. A lot you know about it.

That night while Leo was massaging Anna with the olive oil he'd bought in Silver Springs, she was stricken with terrible pains and he was afraid the baby was going to be born then and there. But it wasn't. Anna asked Leo if he thought the sight of the Mexican baby would affect the looks of her baby. He told her she was too far gone, and she finally went to sleep. He could hear her moaning and feel her uneasy limbs as they threshed about, almost the whole night through. He could not sleep.

All the way to Montana Terry had been singing and cutting-up, sure of the good job with his old friend, Tuck Saunders. Then the first hint, rumors of a strike. "But Tuck Saunders was always in favor of the union," Terry argued. Then pulling into Butte, and a man in overalls running up to the truck and handing them a four-paged paper, *The Golden Plume Striker.* "Unfair! Stay away from the Golden Plume Mine. Don't sell yourself as a scab." The militia was guarding the mine, and the paper reported that, "even the scarlet women of Butte are not vile enough to cater to the sexual needs of the scabs behind the gates of the big mine on the hill. However, the scabs are getting too restive, and it is reported that a large delegation of scarlet women from Helena are going into the stockade, heavily guarded by the militia. We wish them luck in their pleasant occupation, but feel sure that sooner or later they will see that they have made a false step and will follow the example of their sisters in Butte by refusing to satisfy the desires of the creatures now penned like craven wild beasts behind the stockade at the Golden Plume."

Terry would not even attempt to see Tuck Saunders. They might have known there was something fishy about sending half across the continent for men when so many were pounding the pavements. But Terry and Tuck *had* been great pals once.

Then the rumor of work in California in the lettuce fields, and finding a strike when they arrived there. They saw the vigilantes rounding up strike leaders and sympathizers into a cattle car for shipment out of the state. Trying for odd jobs, desperate, trying to get back to Green Valley, the only place they knew to go now, and all the time Anna nearing her hour.

CHAPTER EIGHT

I told him that I could build a houseboat that cheap, too, if he wanted me to skimp on the material and slap it together so lop-sided you couldn't keep it inside the banks," said Garfield Potter, citizen of Roosevelt Roost, formerly Hooverville. "After all, you only get what you pay for. If you pay for trash and a botched-up job, you get it and you deserve it. And if you give a man good service, he's comin' back and he's gonna tell his friends about you and they'll be comin', too, and that's the way it goes. If you hornswaggle a man, it's goin' to come back on you sometime and somehow. Yes, sir. I never knew it to fail. My old mother taught me that thirty years and more ago, and I ain't *never* found that she told me a thing wrong. I'll never forget her last words on her dyin' bed: 'Garfield, anything you do, God's got his eye on you, and you can't travel far enough or fast enough but what he'll be seein' you. So do unto others just like you'd like them to do unto you.' Yes, sir!" He sighed heavily.

He tapped his pipe on the decaying bridge timber serving Robert and himself as a seat. Across the river swifts were circling about the dead chimneys of a foundry, chasing invisible insects. Into a pile of sand enclosed by a bin close to the water's edge a clam-shell steam shovel had bitten heavily and lay with extended jaws, its cable slacked. It had been in the same position for days; no human being or wisp of smoke or indication of life could ever be spied among the buildings flanking the bank. Everything was suspended, frozen in a vacuum, waiting for some word or some event—for something, anyhow—just as Robert had been waiting for years now.

He had come down to Roosevelt Roost to escape the sight of people who were still able to wear good clothing and eat the sort of food that had tantalized him from restaurant and grocery windows everywhere he turned—to escape the cold or pitying eyes of strangers. Pity and contempt disturbed him equally. In Roosevelt Roost he came into contact with others as ragged and forlorn as himself, and when slumming parties came down from the city he had fled, he hid beneath the boat house where he had made him a nest in which to sleep. Though it was now early summer, the river cooled the air before dawn, and Robert sometimes burrowed deeper into the rags of his bed. He had never scrambled for the garbage when the trucks unloaded it into the scows for the hogs up-river, nor had he panned the black residue of silt and excrement from the sewers. He could get by for two or three more weeks on the money he had realized from the sale of his typewriter, ring, and watch. He had it all figured out precisely. Twenty-five cents a day for food, and at times he used less than that. This was when he managed to salvage a few moderately sound oranges, bananas, onions, or potatoes from the refrigerator cars across the tracks. But he never pushed others out of the way or betrayed undignified haste in making for the cars after the truckers had finished unloading them, and thus he missed a lot the more agile and forward ones bagged.

Shabby and lean with hunger at times, he nursed a melancholy pride in his ability to live on here. He lay under the boathouse filled with masochistic gratification at the pangs in his stomach and the knowledge that he was suffering stubbornly for a principle, when he might have stayed comfortably in the little apartment above the vacant room where the Green Dragon had been. Nell didn't believe me when I said I was through. This living like a holy Christian hermit is better than trying to save pennies of somebody else's wages at the cash-and-carry, hoarding bacon grease to avoid buying lard, peeling potatoes, and listening to her wondering how she could squeeze out a dime here and a dime there to help her folks, to whom she really owes the first allegiance. Thoreau had the same idea that I have. He didn't like to wash dishes or sweep floors any more than I do. And I haven't heard a word about the America First Vigilantes and the redoubtable Mr. Harrison since I've been down here.

The colony had grown since a change of administration had necessitated changing its name from Hooverville to Roosevelt Roost. It was full of bustle and hurry which never seemed to accomplish anything tangible. There was always a great deal of nailing going on, the rasping of saws, hurrying here and there with second-hand planks. The citizens of Roosevelt Roost worked with a feverish energy, stuffing cracks against the winter wind while the sun was scorching, piling up wood in neat stacks. Scheming, scheming, anything to make a dime or a nickel. Baling paper, gathering bottles and washing them in the river, tying up bundles of kindling split from driftwood in the hope of making a few pennies. But nobody ever bought. Robert saw that these people were fighting frantically against the despair that would surely creep like paralysis over them if they lapsed into inactivity and brooding over their lot. So they worked at something, no matter what, for work's sake, but Roosevelt Roost changed only in the increasing number of hovels. Garfield Potter had been sawing, hammering, nailing and shoveling about his place, the remains of an ice wagon, for months, and Robert could not see that it had changed in any way. Perhaps there were more wooden strips and tin advertising signs tacked to it.

He wondered what would finally become of him. Sometimes he entertained the idea of looking up Sol Abraham, but he knew that the people at the Workers' Center would believe that he had been driven to them only by his belly. As long as he had had a snug place to stay, and food to eat, and decent clothing, he had not felt enough interest to attend any of the meetings. He could not bear to face anybody who had known him in his more prosperous days. The cardboard innersoles he fitted into his shoes wore out within an hour or so if he walked around much. The bottoms of his feet had never toughened, and the cinder ballast on the railroad tracks made him wince at every step. So he sat around listlessly most of the time, and his only satisfaction was that days were passing and he was still alive with his stubborn principles intact.

Garfield Potter, the houseboat carpenter, had not found anybody with the inclination or the money to engage his services, but he kept himself busy figuring, and often measured on the ground the dimensions of a boat he planned, and it would surely be a jimdandy, a pisscutter, if he could only find somebody who would pay him to build it, or if he could contrive to rustle up the materials on his own hook. Time was wasting on his hands, and the material was all he needed. He possessed the brains and the time. He frequently heard of old buildings to be torn down, the wreckers taking their pay in lumber, but he could never be at the right place at the right time, or the lumber was not suitable for houseboat construction. He told himself that he would not use shoddy material if he never built a houseboat. Nevertheless, he liked nothing better than to talk about the houseboats he was capable of building and to argue with other houseboat carpenters who were just as confident of their own skill. Day after day they basked in the sun beside the river and wrangled over the fine points of their theoretical crafts.

Then there were the treasure seekers who panned the sewer's muck near the mouth of the black stream pouring into the river. They talked of their queer finds, laughed about the rubber tubes, inflated like sausages, floating away toward the Gulf of Mexico. No one had found a five-hundred-dollar diamond ring like the legendary one everybody had heard of but nobody had seen.

All of these people Robert endured as part of his self-immolation.

Garfield relished talking to Robert, for he was lonely

and a good listener even though he didn't know much about houseboats.

The sun was going to rest, projecting shadows of the low structures along New Deal Avenue into grotesque shapes. Here and there among the city's high spires and towers a light bloomed.

"Well, meetin' tonight," said Garfield, rising to his feet and holding his back for a moment before he stood erect. "Always feel a little better, a little closer to God, a little more like the man my old mother wanted me to be, after I go to a meetin'."

Robert was not interested in the meeting, but as he passed by the church he heard the preacher shouting more vehemently than usual. He stepped inside and sat down on a bench against the rear wall. At the front there were pews salvaged from a dismantled church in the city, and some of the stained glass windows had been brought along, too. It was much like any other church—girls were giggling at boys, and mothers were bouncing infants to quiet them. Everybody was shabby, and many of the worshippers were dirty. There was only one porcelain bathtub in Roosevelt Roost, and water for it had to be carried from the river. The minister stood behind an ornate pulpit of oak, incongruous on the unvarnished pine platform.

"I'm not asking you to take my word for it," the preacher said, quietly. "Do you want better authority than the word of God? The devil tempts you more when you are needy, as many of us are, but if we resist him and walk in the way our Lord laid out for us, what a glory will shine on our lives and all men will rise and call us blessed. I call your attention to a passage in the Book, to be found in the first book of Peter, the second chapter and the thirteenth verse:

"'Be subject to every ordinance of man for the Lord's sake; whether to the king, as supreme, or unto governors, as sent by him for vengeance on evil-doers and for praise to them that do well. For so is the will of God, that by well-doing ye should put to silence the ignorance of foolish men.'

"So when this evil messenger of the race which crucified our Lord and Savior on Calvary's tree came down here in this peaceful community, trying to stir up strife and resistance to authority, trying to tempt us into a violation of God's command, I am proud to say that we escorted this fine gentleman across the railroad tracks and told him his presence was not wanted here. The handbills he brought with him, paid for by a nation beyond the sea that has mocked our Lord and Savior and persecuted his people, we consigned to the flames, where they belong.

"If any man in this peaceful and law-abiding community feels like taking part in this proposed march on the city hall to present entirely unreasonable and unjust demands in defiance of law and order, I hope he or she—forgive me, ladies for even hinting that you might be un-ladylike enough to do such a thing—I hope you will arise and let the rest of us know it, so that we may pray for you.

"And if some of you have been misled by the cunning lies and serpent tongues of these agitators, I hope you will take home and read carefully and prayerfully the little book I am going to hand each and every one of you at the close of this service. Mr. Harrison, commander-in-chief of the America First Vigilantes, an organization pledged to preserve those sacred liberties for which our forefathers fought at Valley Forge and Bunker Hill, has donated entirely free gratis two hundred and fifty copies of this invaluable little book ripping the mask from the Jew atheists in the pay of the murderous Soviets that are stirring up trouble here in this country by pretending to be on the side of the working man, getting him to take a stand for the devil by following their law-breaking tactics, and then he will burn in hell for ever and ever till time shall be no more. Think of that, brothers and sisters, ponder over it carefully, and read this book. It's an eye-opener. And we have another reason for being grateful to Mr. Harrison and his organization. Next Sunday we'll have a hundred and fifty brand new song books to replace the dog-eared half-dozen we've been struggling along with. So we ought to all come out and use these fine new books Mr. Harrison and these good friends have so thoughtfully donated us to exalt the Lord in song. And I think it would not be amiss at this time to offer up to God a little humble prayer for this good friend and his splendid organization. Shall we pray. . . ."

Robert made his way out as the others were bowing their heads. The preacher raised his eyes and gave him a reproachful look just as he began: "Our Heavenly Father, we come before Thee this evening asking. . . ."

Robert lay in his nest of rags under the boathouse thinking of Sol Abraham. He must have been the Jew the preacher was talking about. Poor little Sol, brave little fellow, still at his futile shouting into deaf ears or into the unsympathetic ears of those who were ready to crucify him for his efforts. He could not get away from Mr. Harrison and the America First Viligantes even in Roosevelt Roost.

"Yes, Alan Vass, I'm certain sure. That was the name he give all right," said Garfield Potter. "He told me to be sure to tell you to wait for him here tonight. He'll be here at six; says he's got an extra special message for you. Good news, he said. Maybe a job."

"Yes, I've got a picture of that. Jobs will soon be as scarce as earmuffs on the Sahara. If you get out of a job now, you're out of one from now on."

Nevertheless, he was eager to see Alan and to find out what was on his mind. At six o'clock he had been waiting half an hour by the pile of bridge timbers. He had borrowed a second-hand razor blade from Garfield Potter, and, according to the houseboat artisan's instructions, had attempted to whet it inside a water tumbler. Garfield said he had used the same blade for a year, and a little stropping inside the glass made it cut like new. But Robert could not get a very keen edge on the blade, and he couldn't see himself very clearly in the dim and blackspecked sliver off a mirror that Garfield had found somewhere and tacked up beside his door. Every stroke with the razor made him cringe with pain, and when he had finished, tufts of whiskers still sprouted on his face and there were bleeding nicks where the dull blade had bitten.

"How did you find out I was here?" was the first thing he asked Alan.

"Process of elimination, my dear Watson. A simple case of deduction. I could not find you anywhere else, at none of the flop houses or missions, and Sol Abraham had not seen you. Ergo, you must be in Roosevelt Roost. I thought maybe your troubles had affected your mind, and you had decided to jump off the deep end and join Sol's radical reds. Now, what in the hell *is* the matter with you? Why are you pouting and sulking down here like a naughty schoolboy?"

"I'm not pouting. I came down here for a definite reason, and a good one, too."

"Why?"

Robert, when asked directly, found it difficult to explain just why he had come down to Roosevelt Roost to live. He said that he could not stand it any longer—Nell supporting him when he knew her folks needed help and he was only a millstone around her neck. When he had at last become convinced that he had no future as a writer before him, he had just felt like crawling off somewhere like a wounded rabbit to die.

"Yes, and left Nell in trouble up to her neck. You never thought of her side of it, I guess. She can't go back to her folks, even if they do accept the money and speak to her again. You ought to know that. She came out to Uncle Jinglebollicks' abode and demanded to see me, eyes all red from crying, all worked up, and showing it. And this circumstance caused me to get the Riot Act read to me up one side and down the other. Dear uncle thinks I had seduced her or something. Now what the hell *are* you doing here? What good are you doing? What do you represent?"

"Well, it's the principle of the thing. I can at least feel free here."

"Free to starve and to freeze, come winter. You'll be arrested for indecent exposure of body and person before long. If a wind comes along, those rags'll whip you to death. But have your own way. I'm not arguing with you. I'm just telling you. She swears she'll gargle a quart of Lysol and curl up in the bathroom if you don't come back. If you want *that* on your mind, just stay away, and watch the papers. She'll do it, too, as sure as that sewer down there is not belching attar of roses into the river. I tell you, she's wild—simply wild. She's going to crack up like the wreck of the Hesperus in the midnight and the snow, and you'll find her laid out stiff and cold. How'd you like that?"

"It's surely not as bad as that," said Robert. He felt deeply touched to hear that Nell had missed him so, and that she would rather take her own life than live on without him.

"Yes, it is. Here's a letter from her, and two or three others that have come while you've been down here punishing yourself. Your hair reminds me of the old Green Dragon days, but you need a Windsor tie and a beret. You're a masochist, for true. Have you got a bed of sharp ten-penny spikes to lie on, like a Hindu penitent? I'll bet you keep tacks sticking up in your shoes so you can walk on them and make yourself suffer."

If Nell had upbraided Robert in her letter, he could have resisted going back. But she was pleading, and asking him to come back to tell her where she had been wrong, and how she could do better. When Robert thought it over, he had to acknowledge to himself that she *was* in a trying position. Moreover, his self-imposed martyrdom was getting less and less endurable. Try as he might, he could think of no vital issue at stake save the preservation of his own pride. And if she should actually swallow the Lysol, the fault would be his own. Along with the realization that there was something to be said for her side of the matter and that she must want him back rather desperately, he thought of the cupboard and the good food with which it was always stocked. And of the bed, and her warm body in it.

The other letters were from Leo, and told of their discovery of the reason behind Tuck Saunders' generosity and his eagerness to send for men across half a continent; of the trip to California and the lettuce fields; of the halt in their journey near Silver Springs, Utah, where they were working in Bishop Maroni Taylor's beet field. The doctor had told Leo that Anna could not stand a trip in the truck. The jolting would surely cause her to miscarry; it was a wonder it had not happened long before. Robert read Leo's letters to Alan.

"Couldn't stand the jolts, eh?" said Alan. "I wonder if that's a fact. Wonder if that would work in the first stages."

"It depends on the woman, I guess. Some of them have only to jump down from a chair, and it's all off. A fellow that worked with me in the office told me that when his wife got the calendar worry he just took her for a ride out Prospect Boulevard, where the pavement is full of chug holes. It was hard on the springs, but it never failed to accomplish the desired result."

"It's funny about the difference in women. The more I fool around them, the less I know. What makes them tick, what motivates them to do this and that. Psychologists can only guess, after all. They can try to classify them and analyze them till the cows come home, and then can't make head nor tail of them. Well, head, anyhow."

"How are you coming along with your experiment with that devout maiden whose resistance and moral scruples you were going to break down? You don't seem to be in a very optimistic mood about women in general. Can't you bend her to your will?"

"Sure, in some ways. Yes and no. She was willing to go the limit with me after I convinced her it was a case of forever and ever with me. Aw, what's the use? Might as well spill it. I'll be going around buttonholing everybody to tell them about it soon, I guess. She came across, all right, but she's knocked up higher than a kite this six weeks gone, and the hell of it is, she won't do anything about it. She says we've got to marry whether or no and give the child a name. At first she begged, but now she just demands—terrorizes me with her ham-fisted brother and elephant-footed papa. Her religion won't permit her to submit to an abortion, and I'm flat as a flounder, if she would. The times are out of joint, O cursed spite! I could never find a Negro who would make a suitable man Friday, and Leo petered out as a disciple. I'm just on the verge of being disinherited, cast out into the cruel world, by my fond Uncle Jinglebollicks. He evidently thought I'd had carnal relations with Nell when she came out there with eyes raw from weeping and wronged innocence written all over her."

When Robert came in, Nell ran to meet him, sobbing and laughing, clinging to him and stroking him.
"Oh, my poor boy! What *made* you do it? I never believed at first that you'd stay away more than a few hours. I've been crazy. Day after day, and poor little me crying myself to sleep in the bed all alone. I'd wake up in the night dreaming of you and reach over to love you and I had an empty feeling in my stomach and every other place when you weren't there."
"I told you I couldn't stand it any longer."
"Let's just talk our troubles over together after this, and share them. I meant what I said about killing myself, and I'd have done it, too."
"I couldn't stay another minute. I had an idea of breaking something loose, of starting something. Day after day here and knowing all the time you were feeding me while your family needed help."
"Oh, can't you see that I've queered myself for keeps with my family? They always told me you'd pull out and leave me and no other man would have your cast-off plaything, knowing how it had been all these years between you and me."
"I don't like your fooling with that America First

Vigilantes business, and I don't want any more of those circular letters and pamphlets around here."

"Oh, I don't know anything about politics and business and all such. Only I wish you could have a long talk with Mr. Harrison and let him explain things to you as he did to me. He knows that things are not as they should be; the poor are getting the dirty end of it. But he says we can solve our problems in an American way, not a foreign. The international Jewish bankers in every country. . . ."

"Aw, nuts! I've heard all that. You've got to give up all that work if you want to get along with me. I'll go back down to Roosevelt Roost before I'll see any of it around where I am."

"But, honey, be reasonable. I've *got* to work, and I've got to do what my boss tells me. If you believe in unions, you wouldn't like to work in an open shop, but sometimes a man has to to get along. And I don't exactly believe in the America First Vigilantes. Only Mr. Harrison is the grandest man to his office force, never a cross word from him, and he can make exerything so clear. I wish you could talk to him. I'm just dumb about all such things, though, and I'll not bring any more of it home if you say for me not to."

"He couldn't convince me. I've seen their stuff."

"Be patient with me, then, and teach me. If I'm ignorant, that won't stand in the way of our love. We've belonged to each other so long; ever since that day in Probstville, out past the cemetery. I just read in the paper the other day where even Stalin says nothing to his old mother when she still goes to church, and if anybody could be more fanatical than Stalin, I don't know who it'd be. Mr. Harrison says he. . . ."

"Don't tell me what Mr. Harrison says about anything!" shouted Robert. "That's the first thing I want to teach you."

It had occurred to him that he could not tell her why Mr. Harrison was wrong, or what was right, for he himself had only the most nebulous notion about such things. You didn't have to be able to dissect the chemical components of a rotten egg or to explain in detail just what spoiled it to tell it was rotten and stinking.

"What's there to eat?" he asked, opening the cupboard, saliva flooding his mouth as he gloated over the bright-labelled cans of food, a crisp bunch of celery, and the lean-streaked bacon showing through its cellophane wrapper. Boy! How he'd eat! And there was the soft bed and her warm and loving body would be in it.

CHAPTER NINE

When Leo and Terry first started working for Bishop Taylor, they felt that the way was now, finally, paved for their return to Green Valley. The trip from Oregon had been more difficult than most of their traveling because of the distances from one town to another. Flivver tramps are seldom welcomed in any town, and it had been with difficulty that they had found gas enough to get them across the Blue Mountains of western Oregon. Blue Mountains! Cache Valley! Leo remembered how such names had fired his imagination as he listened to the stories of the hoboes back in the jungle near Green Valley, but at close range these places were not so romantic. There was the constant and agonizing fear of a breakdown—he winced at every strange squeak of the chassis or unfamiliar knock of the engine. He and Terry knew so little about gas engines and their ailments; and the old Model T was suffering badly from the thousands of miles it had traveled since they had first left Missouri. They could not spend a cent for repairs.

Leo had been through an unforgettable experience in Pocatello. On the main street the engine sputtered and died, and they had to push the car to the curb. They had seventy-eight cents in cash. So Leo accosted several men in overalls, begging them to look at the engine. "Could it be the spark?" he'd ask, flinging back the rusty hood and glaring helplessly at the tangles of wires. "Take it to a garage," was the almost invariable advice. Some of the men stepped aside as though they feared contamination from the wild-eyed, bearded little man, avoiding his grease-stained hands clutching at their sleeves. Then the round of garages, telling a hard-luck story. At last, a kind-hearted mechanic came to look at the wreck, tinkered with it, and soon had it belching out the poisonous, sooty fumes from its exhaust. "Better jack up that tail light and fasten a new car to it if you want to save yourself more grief," he advised. "Mebbe it'll take you past the city limits."

One night in the desert country bordering the Snake River they had been forced to detour because a road gang was re-surfacing the highway. It was raining mistily, and they had slipped off the road. At first they hadn't minded much. The children were huddled in their usual place inside the truck body at the rear, under an old army blanket, playing "circus tent," telling stories to one another, laughing softly at the novel experience. Then the rain started pelting against the flimsy top of the cab, and Leo felt cold drops seeping through, then a steady trickle. The blanket kept out the mist, but was soon soaked through by the downpour. A cold wind came racing down the river as soon as the rain storm had subsided, and soon they were all so cold that anything seemed preferable to sitting till they froze stiff. So Leo had almost burned the motor up in an attempt to get back on the road. It had been useless, however, even with Anna at the wheel and the two men and larger children pushing. The car had slid deeper and deeper into the sticky mud of the barrow pit, and they had had to wait until morning when a bread truck from Burley came by and pulled them out. It had been cold, shivering in a knot in the car, waiting for the sun. They had slept only in short and fitful snatches, waking often to listen to the wind as it moaned across the sage that grew thick on either side of the road.

Once during the night a large Lincoln sedan had gone weaving by at an astounding rate of speed. Terry had tried to hail the occupants, whom he could see hunched in the front seat. Two men wearing heavy fur coats, cigars stuck in their mouths. But they hadn't slackened their pace at all. It was only by a desperate leap into the ditch that Terry managed to get out of the way of the heavy car as it careened roaring by, its tires whining like a wild bullet.

Now, working for Bishop Maroni Taylor, they felt comparatively safe. Working in the beets, they had averaged almost four dollars a day between them. This had seemed an enormous amount to them until Terry had figured out just how much of this they would owe the bishop. They were to pay him a dollar and a half a day for board and room. This was what he usually charged for board alone, he had been careful to assure them, but his wife had felt sorry for Anna and the children. James had given up his room to Anna and the children, and had made a bed in an empty beet rack in the yard for Terry, Leo and himself. This he had done by carrying straw from the barn and spreading it over the bottom of the rack. The rack was placed upon two logs behind the granary. It would not be placed upon the wagon till fall, when the beets would be ready to haul to the dump. Beside the charge for board, there would be doctor bills. These would probably amount to ten dollars, depending upon how long they stayed. The work in the beets might possibly last three weeks. The bishop's patch wasn't a large one, and the men daily saw the rows of unthinned plants diminish in numbers. Mrs. Taylor wanted Anna to stay on till the child was born.

"The men kin stay on here and help pa with the hoein'," she argued. "Maybe they kin get work in the pea factory; then they could earn enough for you to have your baby in the hospital over in Prairie City."

The idea of a hospital accouchement, with white cool beds and clean sheets, appealed to Anna, but Bishop Maroni Taylor was more practical than his wife, and pointed out that Leo and Terry could not earn enough, even working the seventeen-hour shifts, to pay the cost of hospital care for Anna.

So Leo, Terry, and Anna decided to leave Cache Valley in about two weeks, even though Dr. Wooten had advised against Anna doing any more traveling before her child was born. All of the bishop's beets would be thinned within the fortnight, and Anna was sure that nothing could ever happen to make her miscarry. Leo figured out that they would then have, providing they were not kept from work by the rain, between twenty-five and thirty dollars clear. They would have preferred cooking their own meals over an open fire in the fields as the Mexicans did, but neither the bishop nor his wife would consider this. It wouldn't look right, they said. Leo could not help but notice that the bishop had plenty of milk and vegetables going to waste, and it was much more profitable to him if the Hurley family ate their meals at the house.

By the beginning of the final week in the beets, Leo began to realize with dismay that his figures had been entirely too optimistic. During all of his married life with Anna it had been this way. They would lay out a foolproof plan on paper, and check it over carefully, but somehow or other they inevitably came out at the little end of the horn. Dr. Wooten billed them for twelve dollars, and they were held up for two days by a heavy rain that kept them from the fields and made the work slower for a couple more. They slipped about in the mud, shaking it from their fingers and cursing bitterly. Terry's knees creaked like rusted hinges from the damp, and each morning when he arose he felt he would rather descend into hell than to kneel down with his twinging knees on the damp soil of the beet field.

Leo now reckoned that they would be lucky to leave the valley with fifteen dollars. This, they hoped, would get them to Denver, where, if they couldn't find work, they might at least get a "floater" into Kansas. He and Terry considered stopping in Salt Lake City, but in the end they settled upon going right on through rather than chance losing what little money they had in looking for something to do in the capital of this Mormon Zion. They could save about sixty miles by driving up Willow Creek Canyon and then cutting across Wyoming, a barren sage-covered desert dotted with small railroad towns all the way to Cheyenne. There had once been work in the oil fields, James told them, but now there were several men for every job. If they wanted to try the mountains of central Colorado, he had heard that there was a miniature mining boom in the country near Leadville and Fairplay. And thousands of city people had taken to the hills to pan out the dumps of abandoned and gutted gold mines. Sometimes a lucky one had found a hundred-dollar or even a five-hundred-dollar nugget, but most of the prospectors rocked their pans all day, standing in the icy waters of the mountain streams, and washed out only a few flakes for their pains.

They might find something, somewhere, somehow. A man could always hope and try. That's all a little red bull could do—try. Leo and Terry remembered the positive assurance they had had of a mining boom at the Golden Plume Mine, and shook their heads dubiously. They were tired of wild-goose chases, and if they could ever step out of the Ford before the old house in Green Valley, they'd never get in a car again without feeling uneasy. "I bet I'll cry ever' time I see a Model T if I ever git shet o' this one," said Leo.

"Pa *wants* me to use the car," said Fillmore. "He needs some grease for the mower."

"Well, Mr. and Mrs. Hurley want to ride to town with you. She has to see the doctor again," said Mrs. Taylor.

"Well, all right. Only I wanted to make a quick trip," said Fillmore, scowling. He had intended to pick up some high school girls in Silver Springs, and now Anna and Leo were going to queer it.

"It won't take long. Just long enough for her to see the doctor."

When he went out to the garage, Leo and Anna were already seated in the Buick, and he climbed disconsolately in. He would try to shake them in town, and then he could claim he had had a blowout to explain his long absence. He intended to make them good and tired of waiting while he was entertaining a bunch of girls in the car.

The road from the farm to Silver Springs, due partly

to the bishop's influence as a Cache Valley commissioner, was wide and smooth. The valley in this section, however, was low, and part of the land was swampy and wet. As a result, the road surface was built high, with large concrete culverts about every one hundred yards. The swamps dried out early in the summer, but there was still a pool of water here and there along the highway.

Fillmore was feeling resentful toward Leo and Anna for butting in and spoiling his fun, and as soon as he was out of sight of the farm, he pressed the accelerator to the floor. The large car roared as it picked up speed, and Anna's hand reached involuntarily for the handle of the door. Leo didn't like so much speed, but he did not feel like protesting. It would afford Fillmore too much satisfaction if he knew he had Leo scared. Young smart alec, showing off, thought Leo.

Nearing the high school, he noticed that the students were leaving the building for their noon hour. The highway led past the school, but Fillmore always took the lower road into town, and he didn't slow up for the turn that would have kept them on the better road. He knew where he was going, so he turned his head to see if he could recognize any of the students. The car was turning onto the familiar lower road. Fillmore could follow it blindfolded. But some premonition caused his eyes to fly back through the windshield to the way ahead just at the instant when the radiator struck a low-cross bar intended as a warning that the culvert was out. He heard Anna shout and Leo yell, felt fingers grabbing his shoulder. There was a sickening thud as the car nosed into the dirt. He heard the tinkle of breaking glass as he catapulted against it. The steering wheel was wedged against his chest. Oh, Christ! he thought. I've cut my throat from ear to ear. I've cut my jugular vein and I'll bleed to death like a stuck hog. He somehow contrived to wriggle through the door. Then the machine tilted slowly and pinned him to the bank. He felt no pain in his lower body, and tried moving his toes. His body below the waist seemed gone, and he looked down wildly to see whether he had been halved. Blood was trickling down his face and onto his neck, down his chest and belly. Then he screwed his head about and saw Anna sprawled on her back in the ditch beside the road, her legs wide apart. Leo was bending over her and ministering to her, and Fillmore wished he would stand aside. When Leo moved, Fillmore's heart leaped till it almost choked him as he took in what was happening to Anna. Her dress was pulled up and her underclothing removed; she was bared to her hips, her stockings hanging loosely about her ankles. Fillmore was seeing what he had often wondered about, and he forgot his pinned and helpless body and the bishop's coming wrath over the wrecked car.

"Oh, if somebody'd only come by! If I could leave you, I'd fetch help. I'd run like the wind," Leo said to Anna. "The kid's hurt bad, mashed against the bank like a caterpillar on a pavement."

"Don't leave me," she begged. "I can't stand it. It's coming *now*. The water broke as soon as the car hit."

"I'd better go fer help! I'll be back in three shakes of a dead lamb's tail!"

"Don't! Don't!" She could scarcely gasp out the words. "If I had something to pull on. . . . Ah! Ah! OH! Oooooooo! Oh, God! Oh, God, have mercy! Oooooo! Ou! Oooooo!"

Leo could scarcely hold himself from running blindly away. This sort of screaming had had the effect of throwing him into an unreasoning panic ever since he had cowered in the library of the old house in Green Valley to listen to Martha's weird shrieks and moans as she delivered Robert.

"I'll hold your hands. Pull on my hands," he said, bracing his feet in the earth and grasping her wrists, but she did not grip him with her fingers.

"No! No! You'll have to do like the doctor. Can't you remember how the doctor does? If only I don't faint! Ahhhhhhhhh!"

Leo found a clump of fibrous weeds, but she was too far away. He lifted her shoulders and dragged her within reach of it. But when she pulled on the weeds, they uprooted. Then her hands began clasping and unclasping, digging into the ground, compressing the earth into lumps under her agonized squeezing. She muttered "hah!" "hah!" during the last throes, and kept her head clear enough to tell Leo he'd have to cut the navel cord with his pocket knife. The baby's face was blue, and it felt icy cold to Leo's touch. "Blow in its nostrils and mouth! Blow in its nostrils and mouth!" whispered Anna, her voice dying. Leo breathed in the babe's face, but it did not stir. It's dead, all right, thought Leo bitterly. Poor little fellow! Poor tiny chap! You got a fine start in this world, but you're better off, God knows, you're better off than the rest of the Hurley family.

Then for the first time he saw that Fillmore was not only conscious but staring goggle-eyed at all that was going on, and, what was worse, there was no pity or horror written on his features. . . . Why, I'll kill him! thought Leo. Why, the dirty son of a bitch! And he ran to the car for a wrench or tire tool with which to brain the bishop's son. . . . But: Easy! Easy! That won't do her any good. She'll *have* to go to the hospital now. The bishop's got money and influence; you'll need his help now as never before. But he's not a bit sorry for her. He's *enjoying* it, by God! . . . Leo jerked out the rear cushion and propped it up as a screen between Fillmore and Anna.

The sight of blood had always made him sick as a dog, and now he could not stanch her at all. That's her life coming out of her, that's her life! I got to stop it! I got to stop it! But he couldn't, no matter how he tried. He tore up his shirt, rended her clothing, but nothing stopped the terrible warm red flood. It was everywhere, creeping sluggishly toward the ditch, staining her stilled feet. She can't lose that much and live; she'll die anyhow if I don't get help here! She's unconscious! She's dying! Yes, sure as shooting, she's a goner. . . . He scrambled like a mad animal on all fours up the bank and fled shrieking and bellowing toward the town.

Bishop Maroni Taylor suggested that Anna be given a Mormon funeral, and Leo assented numbly. He wasn't grateful to the bishop; it didn't matter. As yet, he couldn't assemble the fragments of his world into any sort of intelligible pattern. Accompanying James into Prairie City, he had selected the cheapest casket possible for both the mother and the stillborn babe, which would lie on her arm as they were lowered into the grave.

Bishop Taylor and his wife had practically moved into Prairie City, where Fillmore had been taken to the hospital. He was badly bruised, but all danger of internal injury or concussion had passed. Leo and James had gone into the hospital to find Maroni, but had been forced to wait because Fillmore's bed was surrounded by slick-haired, bright-sweatered fraternity brothers. Leo was worried. He knew how funerals cost, and he didn't know how he was going to pay for the casket and the burial.

"The bishop'll fix it up," James assured him. "He's a big shot in the county. Course, if you want t' take 'er home. . . ."

"How in the hell 'd I take 'er home?" said Leo. "Besides, we ain't got no more home than a rabbit."

There hadn't been much said after that.

Inside the chapel there was a low rhythmic murmur of country gossip being exchanged. The eyes that followed them down the aisle to their seats made Leo flush, and he wanted to cry out that this whole thing was a fake. What was Anna to these red-faced, pious Mormons? Or what was he to them? A short man with a bald head and an immense, spongy red nose ushered them to their seats.

"Right 'ere, brother," he said to Leo in jumbled Cockney English, touching his elbow.

Leo pulled his arm away, and took his place on one of the hard, heavy seats. A small organ above the pulpit began to play as the casket was carried down the aisle and placed on a stand just below the spot where Bishop Taylor, an old man with a spreading gray beard, and a tall Scandinavian farmer were seated on a raised platform. Leo caught a whiff of the flowers, and the cloying scent sank beyond his nostrils and into the pit of his stomach, heavy, oily, and unsettling. The organ ceased, and the bishop arose and stood before the rostrum.

"Brothers and sisters," he began in his heavy, rasping voice, "we have gathered together to pay tribute to one, not of our faith, who, in pursuit of the noblest calling of her kind, has shed her worldly garment and gone forth to interview her Maker. On behalf of the relatives of the deceased, I wish to express my gratitude for your attendance here this afternoon. Originally from that section of the country that once cast our persecuted people from its doors, these strangers have come into our midst to ask for bread. We, in return, shall give them meat and drink. Though the blood of a murdered Prophet be upon their heads and the heads of their kind, let us show them that the Latter Day Saints do not desert the stranger in his hour of need, but, like the good Samaritan, pause and offer a helpful hand."

Murmured assent followed his speech, and the bishop hawked to clear his throat. Now his voice changed from the oratorical tone he had affected to his ordinary speaking voice as he announced:

"Prayer will be offered by brother Olaf Gunderson."

Brother Gunderson talked in a heavy Swedish accent, but he used none of the high-sounding phrases of the bishop. Rather, he prayed as though God were sitting in the front row and he were addressing Him personally.

There was singing that made a noise for Leo, no distinguishable words, for he was not listening for them. Then he became conscious of the bishop's voice again, breaking in on his consciousness like a snapped-on radio.

"And this woman, what of her? She had not accepted the truth; her eyes had not been opened. Does that mean that she is lost? No, my brothers and sisters, it does not mean that she is lost, but that the time appointed for the fulfillment of her salvation has been postponed by a greater judge than you and I. She will, one day, be numbered among the saints of heaven, just as we are numbered among the saints of this earth."

The Silver Springs cemetery was situated on a high strip of land east of the little farming community. It had one or two prosperous headstones, polished granite with deep-graved inscriptions, set in little fenced-in plots, but for the most part the graves had only simple white stones or pine boards that the weather had beaten to an anonymous gray, leaving no clue to the identity of the dead beneath them. There was no money to pay a caretaker, and weeds and sage had choked out the less aggressive grass, alien to this soil. Several large clumps of sage brush had been chopped out of the way to make room for Anna's grave. The undertaker had installed an automatic device for lowering the casket into the hole, and Leo was dully interested in this. He had never seen one of these contraptions before. The casket was placed upon two straps running from a framework about the grave, and when the tall young man pressed a lever with his foot the casket moved slowly downward, but halted when its top was flush with the ground level. Again the few bunches of flowers that had reposed on the casket in the meeting house were brought forward and placed on the casket. Mats of artificial grass, too bright for reality, had been spread all about to hide the raw clay.

As soon as everybody had gathered around the grave and the undertaker had lifted his foot from the automatic lever to allow Anna, her stillborn babe, and the box that enclosed them to sink into the earth forever, the little red-nosed man with the Cockney accent stepped forward and everyone took off his hat and bowed his head.

"Oh, God, our 'eavenly Father," he began. "A few of Thy children 'ave assembled ourselves 'ere this awfternoon to dedicate this grave to Thee and to the mortal remains of this dear sister to Thy earth. Bless and sanctify this ground that these mortal garments may repose in peace until they are called to reunion with the spirit on Thy great judgment day. These blessin's we awsk in the name of Thy son, Jesus Christ. Ahmen!"

Bishop Taylor's "amen" detonated above that of everyone else. Now she *is* gone, thought Leo, and why? Somebody's to blame for this. If it was a man and I knew who to look for, I'd choke his tongue out of his throat. She might have lived to be a grandmother and found a little ease in her old days after the bustle of raising a family. Did you kill her, God? If you did, you ain't got no idea of fair dealing. She never did anybody anything in her life but good turns, for everybody she had anything to do with. It wasn't natural or right for her to die in a ditch that way. There's nothing right about it, and if God's to blame, He's got a funny idea of what's fair and square.

Leo looked out over the wide plains on his right to where the snow-covered peaks of the Unitah Mountains floated along the horizon. The land on his left had been cut into grotesque patterns by the desert wind. Devil's Slide, Table Rock, Chimney Rock, and other descriptive titles had been given the phenomena, either by the original pioneers or the natives of a later day, and small sign posts along the highway pointed out the most curious of these oddities.

Leo seldom turned his head to look at these natural wonders. The atmosphere shimmered in the Wyoming heat, and the oiled road had melted until the tires picked up the sticky surface and threw it against the fenders with a rhythmic sound like that of small birds feeding from a tin plate. Terry was asleep and the children were silently regarding the landscape from the truck bed. Leo, stripped to the waist, had burned a dark brown. The hot air tossed his hair into his eyes, and he was continually wiping it away with a dirty forearm. They had left Cache Valley with five dollars and a tank of gas. The five had melted to three as the worn tires of the flivver had demanded patches. Twice they had been forced to buy more gas. During the night it had been possible to drain a little from unlocked hoses in the many small service stations they had passed. Their money would hold out till they reached Cheyenne and there was a chance that they'd make Denver, barring any bad luck. Leo had tried to make a few touches along the way, but service station attendants on the Lincoln Highway had been touched too often. They had become hard-boiled and suspicious. Leo hoped it would be different after they had passed Cheyenne.

As they neared one small town a sign beside the road told them they were nearing "The Home of Big Canyon Coal," and Leo hoped that there might be a chance to pick up a few days' work. Coasting down a slight incline into the town, the mines were plainly visible, and Leo made for them. It was not difficult to recognize the small, uniform frame dwellings on the south side of the town as being the "company" houses occupied by the miners. Each was colored a dirty, streaked gray, and many, Leo noticed, were deserted and run down. Near one of them a crowd had assembled and Leo pulled the flivver to a stop. The group was evidently excited, and before Leo and Terry were out of the car an ambulance had driven up and men in white clothes were forcing themselves into the crowd. A stretcher was laid out and a prostrate form rolled onto it.

"Why in God's name didn't you call a hearse and be done with it?" Leo heard one of the men in white say as he drew near the scene of the trouble.

A white cloth was thrown over the form on the stretcher, but as the men heaved a head almost rolled off and onto the ground. The man had been decapitated.

"What happened?" Leo asked a tall, thin man with a face like putty.

"Joe Gurtz come home and found his wife with that," said the thin man in a wheezing voice, indicating the ambulance.

"Miner?" Leo asked. He felt foolish with the sweat

popping out on him though his flesh was cold. Prickly chills ran over him as he saw the blood; his eyes blurred.

"Yeh," answered the thin man. "He was a queer one. Allus lived by hisself until last year when he married the ol' maid."

"You a miner?"

"Was until the damn quartz cut m' lungs into sausage." He tapped his hollow chest, and Leo thought of Monty Cass.

"Any quartz mines here?"

"Naw, that was out west fu'ther."

"Any work in the mines."

"Naw. Three men fer every job."

"No work at all?"

"Naw."

They heard this everywhere. Leo and Terry began walking back toward the Ford. The crowd had broken up into little clusters, discussing the Joe Gurtz affair. A large touring car drove by and Leo saw an angular woman sobbing inside. She must be the ol' maid, he thought. Lord, with all the trouble it causes a man, they still fight over it like cats and dogs. . . . The car was full of cops.

"Hey, you!" The wheezing miner had followed them and had Leo by the arm. "Hope you won't take offense, pardner. I've been on the road, and am jist two jumps ahead of the poor house now. But ef you don't find nothin', drop down to the Silver Moon Bar. I'll stake ye to a hand-out."

"Thanks," said Leo. "I don't take no offense when I think a man's got the right spirit. We'll be down, like as not. I don't believe a man could raise a dime in this burg."

Terry crawled in. His joints were twinging, and he anticipated rain because of this infallible portent. Leo cranked till the sweat coursed down his naked body. He hated to choke the engine because of the extra gas, but his arm soon ached and his breath failed him. He choked it cautiously, and at last the engine woke to life and Terry grabbed for the lever to cut down on the gas.

They decided they would save money by waiting an

hour or so and accepting the invitation of the thin man. They bought bologna and crackers for the children, but did not eat any of it. They were depending upon their miner friend. They drove to the tourist camp, a dry plot in one corner of the school grounds, parked the Ford under a scrawny tree, and stretched out on the grass to sleep.

When they awoke there was a slight breeze and clouds were covering the sky. They hurried down to the bar where their miner friend was working and ate two hot dogs apiece, washing them down with cold beers.

As the flivver chugged up a slight incline leading them from Big Canyon, Wyoming, so called because of its location in a hollow carved out of a low mountain by the Platte River, a full moon was rising over the eastern hills. Black clouds crowded about it, and Terry worried about his rheumatism. The speedier tourists zipped by them as the Ford labored along. Around the mountain peaks the thunder rolled and the lightning forked; the children were making small, frightened noises.

CHAPTER TEN

"Yes," said Alan Vass, "a busted leg, busted ribs, and, worse luck, my dear Uncle Russell's car practically demolished, splattered against a tree. It got to shimmying. You know how it is. You can't keep inside a forty-acre field." He wiggled his toes beneath the sheet. "I passed out cold, and Eunice ran back to the highway and hailed a coal truck."

He sighed and looked at Robert as piteously as a water-spaniel imploring pity. Robert knew that Alan wanted to tell him something more, but did not care to say it while Eunice, his bride, was in the room. She hovered possessively over the bed, swooping down on him to kiss him every few minutes. She patted his cheeks incessantly. Alan shrank, almost imperceptibly, but he did not say anything.

"Oooh! I was scared!" said Eunice. "I was running around like a chicken with its head off, and I guess I was squalling bloody murder. I tried to lift Alan, but I couldn't budge him, the big darling! But I got you home, anyways, didn't I, Sugarfoot?"

"Yeah," said Alan, with a tinge of sadness. "I'll bet I look like the wrath of God, don't I, Bob?"

"Don't talk like that, Sugarfoot. That's mockery to take God's name in vain that way," said Eunice, prettily laying her fingers across Alan's lips. "You ought to thank God every minute that we weren't both killed, and you will as soon as Father Riordan gets time to pay you another visit."

Alan's eyes flashed distress signals: I can't explain it

now. I can't tell you the whole story. But I'm certainly in trouble up to my neck.

"You do look used up," said Robert. "I was surely surprised when I read about the smashup and intended to come right out, but didn't get to. Then a couple of days later I saw that you were married."

"Yes, it was sudden," laughed Eunice. "But we had made up our minds a long time ago, hadn't we, Sugarfoot?"

"Yeh," said Alan, essaying a wistful smile.

"I asked at your Uncle Jingle ———"

"Oh, he was sore!" Alan broken in hastily. "Uncle *Russell* read me the Riot Act up one side and down the other, even with my ribs and legs busted he hung it into me. When I came to, I was lying in this bed, and here I've been ever since. It gets tiresome as the devil, though."

"Sugarfoot!" Eunice playfully sealed his lips again. "Nassy! Nassy! You want Eunice to get you some Lifebuoy for your naughty mouf and tongie?"

"He said you weren't there. Seemed rather gruff, I thought. But he did tell me where to find you," said Robert. He looked about him at the plaster casts of saints on the sideboard and the religious mottoes on the wall. There was a melancholy picture of Christ with the crown of thorns pressed on his brow and the blood trickling down his face, and another cheerful one depicting a profusely bleeding heart. Eunice saw Robert looking at the luminous crucifix, and snapped off the light to show how it glowed in the dark.

"Since I was just a little tike," she said, "I've always wanted that near me in the dark. It's *such* a comfort, 'specially when it's thundering and lightninging and I can see our Saviour so calm and loving up there. I sure squeal like a pig, don't I, Sugarfoot? He knows. I sleep on a day bed next to him here so I can wait on him, and one night when it was storming I reached over and grabbed his sore leg and hurt it. He yelped nearly as loud as I did, didn't you, Sugarfoot?"

"Uncle Russell is through with me for keeps," said Alan, ruefully.

"Let him be!" broke in Eunice, vehemently. "I told the old reprobate a mouthful over the phone, didn't I, Sugarfoot? When I told him Alan's leg was broke, he said it was a pity it wasn't his neck. Isn't that a swell way for an uncle to talk? So I just politely told the ambulance men to bring Sugarfoot here."

Robert saw that Eunice was going to do most of the talking, and Alan would not get a chance to unbosom himself. So he said that he had better be going, and that he would see Alan later.

"Don't rush off," said Alan. "I say! Come back a week from tomorrow and spend the afternoon, will you? Eunice's folks are going visiting, and we'll have the house to ourselves."

"All right," said Robert. "I'll do my best, but don't depend upon me."

The next week came, and Robert visited Alan once more. It did not appear that there would be any opportunity for confidential disclosures, for Eunice never moved more than a few feet away from the bedside. At three o'clock, however, she announced that she must run down to the corner grocery. She would be back in a jiffy.

"She will, too," said Alan rapidly, as Eunice closed the front door. "Well, maybe you've guessed that I'm in a pretty kettle of fish. Married! And the way it was, I could hardly get out of it. Not only that, they're determined to make a Catholic of me. The old man says he'll get me a city job, and I've been muzzled away from the flesh pots so long, it's a mighty temptation. I'll have to conform formally, anyhow. But that doesn't matter. I won't have it in my heart, and that's where it counts."

"You're certainly hard luck's little brother."

"You're telling *me*? I'm helpless as a babe, you see. Busted leg, busted ribs, and a long siege in bed ahead of me. Uncle Jinglebollicks has disowned me. I can never darken his door again, and Eunice spilled everything to her mother, who told her elephant-footed pa. He did some straight talking to me while I lay here on my spine. So what could I do but consent to the merry wedding bells?"

"You surely *are* in it to your neck. But what about the accident, though. That's when your troubles began, wasn't it?"

"And *how*! And you're to blame, indirectly, at least."

"I'm to blame? The hell you say! How?"

"Telling me about Leo's wife and the doctor forbidding her to ride in a bouncing truck. Well, you can guess the rest."

"But it didn't work for you?"

"Naw! I drove into a closed road, under repair, where I knew there were a lot of bad places in the concrete. Told Eunice I wanted to show her a sweet little bungalow that was the sort of dream house I had had in mind ever since her roguish eyes captivated me. I couldn't get her interested in literature other than sexy stories, and she's turned out to be a nymphomaniac. I guess she was repressed too long. And when she gave in to me she wasn't being a pagan, she was hooking me. She wanted to window-shop for furniture, and, after she knew she was knocked up, she began to ogle the cute baby togs in kiddie shoppes. So I gave up the idea of making a pagan of her, and, fact is, I wanted to shake her. But I had to make the bouncing ride a success—you understand—first. Destroy the evidence.

"Well, when I turned in that closed road and the going got rather rough, Eunice grabbed my arm, and that was playing right into my hands. I knocked over a gang of those smoking salamander torches and leaped in and out of holes like a mountain goat gamboling from crag to crag. Then I *did* lose control, sure enough, and the machine cracked up against a tree. Boy, O boy! That car climbed the tree like a squirrel. I woke up in this bed. Dear old uncle's car was reduced to junk, and what a time I had had borrowing it. It was the first and the last time.

Eunice joyfully assured me that the jouncing had had no ill effects on her. So," he shrugged wearily, "Kismet!"

"Another noble experiment gone to smash."

"Pipe down! She's due back. All right, laugh at me if you want to. You soon came back to your milk when you had decided to hole up down in Roosevelt Roost, didn't you?"

"I came back on my own terms. I didn't promise to kiss the rood or take the veil."

"You walked back on your own sound legs, too. You didn't come in an ambulance, out cold."

"I'm sorry, Alan. You win. I know how you were fixed. . . ."

"Miss me, Sugarfoot?" Eunice's voice ascended the stairs.

"Yow!" groaned Alan resignedly, laying the back of his head on his clasped hands.

As Robert waited on the corner for a street car, he remembered one of Leo's stories. It had to do with a speech expert who had been hired to cure a chap who stuttered. Patient and expert went off to the mountains, and when they came back the expert announced enthusiastically: "I-i-i-t's a-a-a-a c-c-complete c-c-c-cure." Reminded of Leo, Robert wondered if Leo and Terry were through working for Bishop Maroni Taylor, and when they would return to Green Valley, if ever.

Robert thought of Alan's plan, years ago, to write a novel about Kurt Leischer, *The Unvanquished*.

CHAPTER ELEVEN

The band, playing a funeral march, came first. The musicians were not uniformed, but wore overalls, cotton pants, and army breeches. But they made brave music, and stirring music, too. At times the marchers broke into chants, reverberating down the procession that stretched beyond the limit of Robert's vision. The hearse was banked inside with flowers, and an extra truck with the legend: "Ashs and Junks hawled Cheep" daubed in red paint along its bed was loaded with other wreaths. As the hearse passed slowly by, murmurs ruffled the crowd jamming the sidewalk. Most of the people around Robert were Negroes, and they were muttering indignantly or sorrowfully:

"*Ever'body's* gonna miss ol' Fatfolks, white and black!"

"Ol' Fatfolks done die game, boys, let me tell. Yassuh! He didn't back down nor scringe from none of 'em."

"Ain't it a shame! Ain't it a pity! Cullid people gonna miss ol' Fatfolks in dis man's town."

"*Ever'body* liked Fatfolks, white and black. Ol' Fatfolks he was a pistol! Yassuh! Dat boy was a pistol from way back yandah in a holler tree!"

"Dat's nex' big war, boys, sure as shootin'. Capital agin labor. Poor man agin rich. My ol' daddy tol' me dat ten years ago. I done laugh at 'im den, but damn if it don't look like it now, and dat's a fack, sure's you're born."

"Ol' Fatfolks made dem *po*leece holler fo' somebody help 'em let loose o' *him*."

Robert heard the steady whisper of shuffling feet. The march was silent, or gave the effect of ominous silence. There was the fading music of the band; and at intervals the marchers shouted timed chants punctuated by clenched and raised fists. He recognized Sol Abraham and Sally Vinson, and, near the hearse, Sunbeam carrying Fatfolks' stained shirt and a banner: "A Victim of Police Murder." But Robert was looking for somebody else among the grim marchers, and at last he caught sight of him. It's true! It's true! he thought in bewilderment. I mustn't look at him too hard. . . . There were several policemen in the crowd near Robert, and he imagined that every one of them had his eyes riveted on Leo and had recognized him, too. But none of the cops stirred from his tracks. The human river flowed by. "Twenty thousand, they say," one cop called to another. "Twenty thousand! Jesus Christ!" the other said, and shifted uneasily.

When Robert had seen the newspaper picture of the alleged leader of the unemployed in the riot at the city hall three days before, he had thought idly: That looks something like Leo. It was a fairly clear photograph for a newspaper. A smallish man with a revolver lifted above his head like a club, his face distorted with rage. The caption beneath the picture read: "Who is this man? This striking photograph of the alleged leader of the unemployed in the demonstration at the city hall yesterday was caught by a *Star-Record* staff photographer. A reward of twenty-five dollars will be paid by the *Star-Record* to anyone positively identifying this man. Address replies to 'Riot Editor,' *Star-Record,* Sixth and Main."

"Estimates as to the number of people in the mob vary widely," read the newspaper, "but the most conservative estimates place the number at at least ten thousand. The police department is to be congratulated on their admirable restraint in handling so efficiently what might have proved to be a serious situation. A committee, claiming authority to represent the horde of unemployed, was refused admittance to the mayor's presence. At this the mob began to attack with brickbats and other missiles, and the police were forced to employ tear gas to disperse the riotous crowd. A giant Negro, afterward identified as

Marvin ("Fatfolks") Jennings, a Communist agitator with a police court record, caught, with marvelous agility, a number of the gas bombs hurled by the police and threw them back among the officers, several of whom were overcome. An unidentified man, whose photograph appears on this page, appeared to be the leader of the riot. He carried a revolver, and police allege that he discharged it many times. At length the Negro, Marvin Jennings, fell, struck by a bullet which police assert was fired by some person in the mob, since it entered the Negro's back. The mob then retreated, carrying Jennings with it. Police were not able to apprehend the unknown leader who flourished his weapon throughout the *mêlée*, but the police department is inaugurating an extensive, city-wide search for him, and his arrest is expected momentarily. The whereabouts of the Negro, Jennings, has not been discovered, nor is the extent of his injuries known."

The next evening the *Star-Record* published in a box on the front page the information that the unknown leader of the mob had been identified as Leo Hurley, formerly an employee of the Foss and Arnheim Bridge Co. He had lived at 7398½ Warsaw Street until about six months previously. His picture had been recognized by a man who had been a shopmate of Leo's at the bridge plant.

Still Robert could not believe that the leader of the riot had been Leo, and he arranged to be near the curb when the mass funeral for Fatfolks passed by. Even then he could not credit the evidence of his eyes when he saw Leo treading somberly by. It just didn't make sense that Leo should do such a thing.

CHAPTER TWELVE

"Come on back, Hurley," called Sol Abraham. "Everything's okay. It's your brother."

Leo had been hiding in one of the back rooms of the Workers' Center, one near an outside stairway descending into an alley. He was brown as an Indian from the sun, and had lost a great deal of flesh. Robert had not noticed this so much in the excitement of recognizing him in Fatfolks' funeral procession.

"How are you, kid?" said Leo, warmly, shaking hands.

"Oh, so so. How's it with you? Where's Anna and the kids? And dad?"

"Anna's dead, Bob! She died in a ditch, bled to death with me tryin' t' stop 'er and almost goin' off my nut when I couldn't. The old man and the kids is in the old house. Ain't hardly a corner in that place you can keep dry in, though. Roof almost tee-totally gone."

"Gee, Leo, that's too bad about Anna."

"Yes. I can't help but think she might 'a' lived out her time if things had been better with us. There never was a healthier woman breathed than Anna when first I snuck back t' Green Valley t' fetch 'er t' St. Luke."

"I can't get over it. I hadn't seen Anna much lately, but it's different when you know a person's alive and you expect to see them again."

"We'll never see 'er again. Never! Never! As long as this earth holds t'gether. If there was a God that had any idea o' square dealin' and fair play He'd 'a' never served my Anna the dirty way he done."

"Well, Leo, I've been wondering about this demonstration business. Did you really lead that? If you did, it was a good job. I felt a kind of personal satisfaction, as though *I* had a part in it, when I read it and thought that you took such a prominent part. I'm getting convinced that the people will have to get their dander up before they ever get anything."

"It's a long story. I never intended t' be in that demonstration, but I ain't sorry now that I was. Maybe I can tell you what's what, but I doubt it. It ain't all straight in my own mind. But I had made up my mind that I'd be gone from this earth by this time. I was gonna make this old world sorry for the dirty way it had treated me and Anna, and I was gonna do some good fer the old man and the kids at the same time.

"I guess it was what happened when we made up our minds finally t' pull out o' St. Luke and go t' Green Valley—right after the New Year's Party the writer feller paid fer, you'll remember—I guess it was what happened after that that started me t' thinkin'. Ever'body was so nice and kind when we made up our mind t' take the trip, and they jumped in and helped us. Why can't workin' people allers help one another like this? I thought, when we was out on the highway, but I knowed that it wouldn't work when I thought it over. Poor folks don't have enough. Before we can help one another much we've got t' make them that's got it all in a bag and holdin' the string, besides parkin' their lazy butts on it, shell out. But that's ahead o' my story.

"Anyways, when we got back t' Green Valley after our trip through the west, and Anna under the sod out there in that lonesome graveyard in Utah, and the old man that disheartened and sick with everything that he bawled like a baby when he seen even that tumble-down shack that was a good house when we was little shavers. Five kids, and no mother fer 'em. No way on God's green earth o' keepin' their bellies filled, or feedin' my poor old father.

"So I doped it out this way: You're a back number, Leo, and you can't earn yer own keep, leave alone take care o' the old man and these kids. So I laid awake fer two weeks ever' night, thinkin', thinkin', and never gettin' a wink o' sleep till I could hear the roosters crowin'. Most of the time I couldn't get out of seein' Anna layin' there in the ditch with her life pourin' right out of 'er, and me not able t' do a thing. That was a hell of a way fer any woman t' die. You remember her like she was in Happy Hollow, so lively and full o' ginger. And in the first days here in St. Luke, it was the same. Ever' Saturday noon I cashed my check before comin' home and I allers come by the bakery or a delicatessen and fetched home a little special treat—a pie or box o' candy, or somethin'. I'd make her guess what it was. It was allers a treat for 'er, 'cause she didn't know what t' expect. And the little things we c'lected week by week in the ten-cent stores or the second-hand joints. Maybe an egg turner one Saturday night, or a vase or a purty pitcher fer the wall. Or a rockin' chair that was stylish and only a little wore. Then the children and the worry began t' take the sap outen her and ever' year she lost some of her ginger and get-up-and-go. She worked so hard and skimped and saved and patched t' keep things a-goin'. But life got t' be a worse hell for 'er afore she died in the ditch, after I couldn't get no work, and we went on that wild-goose chase t' the west."

He stabbed with his left hand in an inside coat pocket, but withdrew it empty. "I was goin' t' show you somethin', but I'm ramblin' too much. Seems like I could talk and talk and never stop sence my mind's got t' going like a sled on an icy slide. You remember how we used t' start at the top o' Walden's Knob and never stop till we coasted clean up and over the next hump? I was gonna tell you how it got out that I had led the riot. I didn't know nothin' about that till I got there and seen it, and that's a God's fact, and I didn't lead it. But after I seen it I'd 'a' been proud as a peacock if I had.

"I went there t' kill myself, and that's what I had the pistol fer. Yes, sir! Honest Injun, cross my heart and hope t' die! I was still as big a fool as when we was kids. You know how I used t' blow and brag that I'd kill myself so much that ever'body got used t' hearin' it, and tired of it, too, I guess. It was like the story in our school reader about the boy foolin' the woodcutters and hollerin' 'Wolf! wolf!' when they wasn't no wolf noways near, and he finally got eat up because he tried t' fool the woodcutters oncet too often and make a fool of hisself. So this was part o' the old foolishness creepin' out again, only this time I really aimed t' do it. And I had other reasons.

"I was gonna shoot myself right here on the steps of the city hall, where I'd be sure t' attract a lot o' attention, and I had some letters writ, pitiful as I knew how, after tryin' fifty and tearin' 'em up fer a week. I told all about my poor old father and my motherless kids in Green Valley, havin' t' beg till they're blue in the face fer enough t' keep their bellies from growin' t' their backbones. I told how Anna died, and all that—all the hard luck we'd had in our married life. I knowed the papers would make a big story outen this, they'd be full of it, and almost certain sure t' start the ball rollin' t' raise some money. I've seen that happen several times. You maybe rec'lect when that feller jumped off the bridge into the river and left a note beggin' people t' look out fer his wife and three hungry kids. They raised over five hundred dollars; I sent a buck myself. But that was in better times, and I didn't figger over maybe a coupla hundred.

"Anyways, I pulled out from Green Valley with a dollar and a pistol that must 've belonged t' the old perfesser, yer gran'daddy. It was in an old cabinet drawer in the liberry. It was old as the hills and a Civil War model, I guess, but it'd shoot after I polished the rust off and greased it slick as an eel in a bucket o' snot. I knowed that, 'cause I bought some ca'tridges and tried it out down in Happy Hollow, right near where the gypsy camp used t' be.

"I bet the old man and the kids thought I'd got it in my head t' go t' the North Pole 'stid o' St. Luke like I told 'em when I left, 'cause I took on so, somethin' I don't hardly ever do. I thought certain sure I'd never seen 'em again. And I aimed t' see you, too, but I knowed I'd have t' spill somethin' about killin' myself, and you wouldn't believe it, I'd said it so much. I had a note fer you amongst the others in my pocket t' be found on my dead body and published in all the papers.

"I slep' in one o' them two-bit hotels, where you have a little beaver-board cubby-hole with chicken wire over the top and a little army cot, and you can hear ever'thing that's said all over the place. I heerd one feller tellin' another one a joke, and thought—like I allers had before—I'll remember that one t' spring on somebody. You rec'lect I allers was a great hand fer jokes, and I used t' think I was a hell of a feller and smart as a whip because I could tell 'em faster and longer than the next one. So one of the fellers in the next cubby-hole says t' the other: 'You got any job yet?' and the other says, 'Naw! Nawthin' but promises, promises, promises, when times picks up. That's the song and dance they allers hand me. In a pig's butt! Times ain't *never* goin' t' get better. Speakin' o' promises reminds me of a tale I heerd about two little city sparrers. Come winter, one of 'em said adios, he was pullin' out fer the sunny south t'live warm and easy where the ground never froze up and the worms never dug in fer the cold weather. The other says that's where you're goofy. Stay right here at home and let the saps pull out and leave the gravy fer the wise birds. Horses eats more in winter than in summer, anyways. Well, these sparrers they meets agin in the spring, and, Lord, the stay-at-home is skinny as a fence rail; he's that ga'nt he has t' stand twicet t' make a shadder. "Wotta 'ell," says the fat and sassy guy that beat it south. "You look kinda under the weather, old palzy-walzy, old buddy. How come?" "Ha," pipes the stay-at-home, "they ain't a dozen horses left in this Godforsaken burg, and they're weanin' *them*. And the farmers follers 'em around with a shovel fer fertilizer. All I got done this winter was foller around after them little Fords goin' poop! poop!, and you know a guy can't live very fat jist on them promises."'

"I laughed and forgot about killin' myself fer a minute, but o' course it wasn't long till I was thinkin' how sorry I was gonna make the world fer the dirty way it had treated me and Anna, leavin' her die in a ditch, bloody as a hog-pen in butcherin' time. And how all the fine promises o' the New Deal had pooped out and left nothin' but a stink.

"When I got t' the city hall the next mornin' it was about ten, and damned if they wasn't cops ever' which way from Sunday. And this sounds comical, I know, but it's a God's fact. I was too skeered o' them cops t' yank out that pistol and kill myself. I thought I'd wait till they thinned out some.

"Then, afore you could say Jack Robinson, it seemed t' me, they was thousands and thousands of people there with signs and things that made me think they was all in jist as bad a shape as me. I don't know how it started, but first thing I knowed the cops was slingin' them gas bumbs, and my eyes and lungs found it out soon enough. A cop hit me on the elbow with his billy, and if they's anything makes me hoppin' mad and crazy, it's t' hit my crazy bone. I jerked out the pistol then and used it fer a club. I salivated more'n one cop with it, which I calls good work.

"But this colored feller, Fatfolks, the one that had the big funeral. He was the man! I first seed 'im when he was catchin' them bumbs and throwin' 'em right back at the cops. His hands was burned to a crisp, and his arms to the elbow, but he never stopped. His old blue shirt had ripped clean off his back and he didn't have on a sign o' underwear. He was the best-muscled man I'd ever' seen in my life. He'd been a river roustabout—a river rat, when he could get any work. And that sure puts the muscle on a man. It sure done my heart good the way he throwed them bumbs; he was a born ball-player. 'Attaboy, Fatfolks!' I could hear people yellin', and I started yellin', too. I forgot all about makin' people feel sorry fer me. All these people was down and outers, but they had a better way o' makin' the ones that's got plenty and too much and wants more shell out with it, too. They got poor old Fatfolks, and it was a policeman done it, too. Not like the papers says. I seen a cop aimin' from a window in the city hall jist as Fatfolks turned around t' pick up a bumb he'd missed. So that's how he got it in the back. But he done a heap more good than I'd 'a' done even if I'd 'a' got 'em t' pity me and fork over a few dollars on account o' my bumpin' myself off. I hadn't been thinkin' about the others in the same boat.

"One man can't do very much by hisself. And I'm gonna try the right way t' make 'em sorry. If I die, it won't be me that kills myself. It's gonna be somebody else killin' me, or sickness or an accident. As poor old Monty Cass used t' sing: 'If a tree don't fall on me, I'll live till I die.'

"Looky! It's like this. You take your hand with the fingers spread apart and hit somebody, and all you do is break yer fingers without doin' the one you're hittin' a mite o' harm. You gether it in a knot, in a bunch like all them people down there, and you got a fist that smacks anybody gettin' in its way a sockdolager.

"So I got a new job now and a steady one. I'm gonna try t' tell ever' livin' soul what I found out. We got t' get these factories back and open 'em up, and we gotta get these fields and orchards raisin' eats fer the hungry people. But they's only one way t' do it. That's take 'em and run 'em. When we was out in Californy we passed by a cannery that had a big pile o' green beans stacked out behind it, and nobody around watchin' it. Oh, boy! I thinks. We'll eat now. We was hungry enough t' eat a buzzard. But you know what? Them beans was all doused with old cylinder oil, and every bit of 'em ruined so's nobody could ever use 'em. The cannery didn't want t' use 'em up on account of lowerin' the price or maybe a strike or somethin'—ever' place we went we run into strikes— so they wanted t' be sure *nobody* got no good out o' them beans. And piles o' apples fifty feet high had rotted along the railroad tracks in Oregon the year before, we was told. It smelled like cider there yet, and the ground was a brown muck with gooey that looked like manure. And it's the same all the way down the line with them that's got more than they deserve, and more 'n they'll ever use. Like a dog in the manger, they can't eat the hay, but they want t' hi'st their legs over all of it t'keep anybody elset from gettin' any good outen it.

"Listen!" he explored in his pocket again and fished out a newspaper clipping. "Read that, Bob."

"It's about a speech that Mrs. Albertus Dean Fordyce, III, gave for the Elm Hills Young Matrons' Circle," said Robert. "Let's skip the part about what Mrs. Fordyce fed 'em and how she decorated the table with yellow chrysanthemums and yellow tapers. She gave the young matrons the low-down on 'Safe Guards for Maternity,' and said:

"'In this modern age child-bearing is no longer an excruciating or particularly terrifying ordeal, but a normal, healthful experience. The science of obstetrics has become so advanced that an accouchement is actually beneficial in every respect, and the young wife can approach it with joy rather than trepidation. But the pregnant mother should watch her diet carefully, and, above all, maintain a calm and tranquil spirit. She should be free from all worry, and turn all her household duties over to her housekeeper; her social correspondence and more personal matters should be taken care of by an efficient and tactful social secretary. The young pregnant mother must remember that the future of her baby depends upon her mode of life and mental attitude during confinement. Therefore, such matters as proper food, comfortable and appropriate clothing, serenity of mind, plenty of outdoor exercise—but not too much—and an abundance of rest in soothing surroundings, cannot be too emphatically stressed.'"

"Yeh!" said Leo. "So when I read things like that and remember how Anna died and how she lived when she was packin' her kids inside 'er, I see plain enough how the world is divided, and ever' year they been squeezin' the life outen us poor folks. Now we're gonna get our part back and make 'em give up all they got more 'n their share, besides.

"Some time we'll go down to the city halls ever'where,

and we'll go inside t' stay. We won't never come out no more, and then women won't have t' die in ditches like my Anna did. If she was the only one, I'd say it didn't amount t' so much only t' me and her and her children that's left without 'er. But they ain't nothin' just or right about a world that lets such things go on. But they's millions like Anna was and like I am, and we oughtn't t' never stop fightin' long as such things keep on. And we won't."

Robert stayed till nearly midnight in the Workers' Center. There was a kitchen in one of the back rooms, but the tin cups and plates did not look very appetizing to Robert. Sunbeam bustled about, brewing coffee. He peered in anxiously at the pulpy grounds in the dark pot, wondering if they would stand another boiling. He sniffed disapprovingly, but he felt that he must hoard the little coffee left in the cupboard. There was a large crowd, and they kept coming and going while Sunbeam stuck his head out of the kitchen door every few minutes to estimate the number of people for whom he would be expected to brew coffee.

"Dawgone!" he said disconsolately. "Couldn't *nobody* organize this coffee deal like ol' Fatfolks. That boy could bile them groun's till they was white as snowflakes, and he could get stren'th outen 'em when ever'body elset said they'd give up and was licked t' a standstill. Couldn't *nobody* in the Mississippi Valley fry fish like that boy. He could ketch 'em, too, and many's the time I he'ped 'im row down the river t' Dead Man Bayou t' ketch a mess, and then we'd all have a treat up heah. Po' ol' boy, I never *would* tell 'im that I done got that Lenin speerit he allers talked about, but I done got it long time sence, and ten times double over sence he done whut he did down thar' at the city hall. Wisht I could tell 'im that now. Wasn't *nothin'* I liked better n' argufyin' wit' that po' boy, but I won't no more. Done leave a empty spot in me won't *never* be filled."

The coffee had been boiled and re-boiled till it was rancid and pallid. Robert could not stomach it at first, but he saw that Sunbeam was pathetically eager to have him drink some—he was "company" here and everybody was trying to make him at home. So he swallowed a little with his stomach rebelling. He enjoyed being among the bright, earnest faces. And most of all he liked being with Leo. Even in the days when they had been driven apart by misunderstanding and antagonism, Robert had not forgotten his affection for Leo when they were boys in Green Valley. And now he felt that Leo had found a door and a road beyond it, and Robert thought wistfully that he'd like to be doing something more than frying bacon and eggs for himself and Nell. He had given up looking at the car-loading reports and stock market predictions long ago. He had ceased waiting for anything or anticipating anything.

But before he had reached Traders' Alley the coffee griped him more severely and he had to heave it up. When he opened the cupboard and rummaged around for something to eat, he wished that Leo and the others down at the Workers' Center might have some decent food like this. And he was glad that he did not have to drink coffee like Sunbeam's for breakfast in the morning.

CHAPTER THIRTEEN

During the next few weeks Robert spent a great deal of time at the Workers' Center. The news he heard there excited him as much as war dispatches coming in from a scene of battle. There were stories of fights for relief, against racial discrimination, messengers from the picket lines and the shops. Nell could not understand why he was staying away from home so much of the time. She accused him playfully of having another woman on the string. And beneath her bantering he could see that she was concerned and dubious. So he told her of his meeting with Leo, and his conviction that Leo was at last making something of his life. For some reason, he had hesitated speaking of this before. She had seen in the paper the photograph of Leo and its identification, but she had said little about it, only that it was "too bad that Leo couldn't keep out of trouble."

"So that's where you're going," Nell said, when he told her he had been visiting the Workers' Center. It was evident that she regarded him as a temperance fanatic used to eye a presumably reformed drunkard who had fallen into his old slough again. "You'll get your foot into it, just as Leo did. You stay away from there."

"I'll not do anything of the kind. I'll go where I please." And he was proud of his independent spirit.

"Well, all right," she frowned. "Only don't get into trouble. You know I can't stand the thought of trouble. I'd just blow up. I know how easy it is for somebody out of work to be misled by anybody with a slick tongue." She looked as though she might be wanting to say something about Mr. Harrison, but she thought better of it.

For a time she appeared to be sympathetic, asking about Leo and what he was doing, about what had happened at the Workers' Center. If I'm patient I'll get her to see that Leo's right, thought Robert. He kept talking about Leo as persistently as a press agent puffing a new movie star. One night he told her of visiting Leo's tiny room over Leslie's Radio Shoppe on Bridge Street.

"It's so small he says he has to go out into the hall to change his mind," said Robert. "He's afraid to stay at the Workers' Center. The cops have been there several times looking over the place for him. He's been organizing an unemployed council among the fellows he used to know in the bridge plant."

"Leo! Leo!" she said. "All I hear is Leo! You must think the sun rises and sets in his hind end."

"Well, why shouldn't I?"

"Well, I guess it's all right. Only I don't see what good he thinks he's doing always raising a rumpus. Bulldozing poor relief workers that have to live on starvation wages themselves. But I don't know anything about it; I'd better keep my mouth shut. Only don't you get into trouble, that's all."

It was the outcome of a meeting at Steve Felski's house, however, that caused her to deliver an ultimatum. She just could not stand her nerves being torn up as they were, and he'd have to quit sticking his head in the noose with Leo or give her up. It would be worse than death to lose Robert, but she just could not stand it, that was all. A person could stand just so much, and then something had to give way.

The police had never given up their search for Leo, and a stool pigeon had reported that he was going to attend a meeting of an unemployed council in Felski's home. The house was surrounded by a squad, two cops jerked open the front door, and tossed in a half dozen gas bombs, dashing in immediately after them. They were green at this sort of job, never having used gas before, and one of them keeled over instantly and struck his head on a heavy iron door stop. Leo and Robert were in the next room with a number of others, and managed to slip out of the house and escape. The officers who had escaped the gas by running back out of the front door were shouting and wheezing, and their fellows in the back and at the sides supposed the quarry was escaping and loped around to the front. When the officer who had been overcome by the gas died, either from the effect of his heart or from the fumes, it was charged that the ferocious Leo had bashed in his skull with some blunt instrument, and another crime was chalked up against him.

"Don't you see it's for your own good I tell you you'll have to stay away from him," pleaded Nell. "If you had been found in there, it would have meant a long sentence. Maybe a murder charge against you. You're too intelligent to mix with that riff-raff. You don't have to get down and grovel with them."

This sort of thing kept going on until Robert knew that some manner of crisis was imminent. . . .If she could only be persuaded that Sol Abraham and Leo and the others are not such blood-thirsty bomb-throwers, she'd be all right. It's Mr. Harrison that puts such ideas into her head. If she could see he's wrong, maybe she'd be converted. She might bore from within, and tell us all of the proposed activities of the America First Vigilantes. . . . But he could not persuade her to attend any of the meetings at the Workers' Center, and she became agitated every time Leo was mentioned.

"If he wants to throw his life away, let him do it. You've got most of yours before you, and you're not just a common pick-and-shovel man. You're competent enough to hold an executive position, or a good clerical one. I know it's tiresome waiting, but I want to tell you something I've been holding back. I talked to Mr. Harrison about you. . . ."

"Mr. Harrison again! I told you not to mention him around me. . . ."

"Aw, this is nothing about his political beliefs. Aren't you broad-minded enough to know that a person has a private life and a public life? So if he gives me work or would give you work, as he promised me he would soon, what has that got to do with the America First Vigilantes? After all, if a man is sincere, you can't despise him. And if he's anything, Mr. Harrison *is* sincere. If you'd talk to him five minutes you'd see that. I wish you could talk to him. . . ."

"So is a mule sincere, but that doesn't make him right."

"It's not much farther," said Robert to Nell. "The only place in St. Luke where you can get genuine octopus soup, and all sorts of Greek dishes. It's got more atmosphere per square inch than the Green Dragon ever had."

Robert knew that Nell still clung to this relic of her younger days; she doted on quaint and "different" restaurants. So he had painted a glowing picture of this eating house that existed only in his imagination, all in order to get Nell down to the Workers' Center. Once she saw what was going on, came into contact with the people there, she'd see things in a different light. He could not hope that she'd become a convert overnight like a Holy Roller in Pastor Epperson's church, but she might at least be impressed favorably enough to withdraw her objections to his association with Leo. He did not want to part with Nell; he remembered that he had been her first and maybe her only lover and he felt in a measure responsible for her.

"This is a crummy neighborhood," said Nell, canting her head disdainfully at the grimy shop fronts. "We must be getting near the stockyards to judge from the stink."

They were nearing the Workers' Center and Robert was beginning to feel fidgety.

"That makes it all the more picturesque," he said. "It's unspoiled by commercialism. The vulgar Philistines haven't discovered it and ruined it yet." He was talking in the old Green Dragon vernacular.

Then he halted abruptly; his breath catching in his throat as though a grain of corn had lodged in his windpipe. He saw a policeman emerging from the hallway leading to Leo's room, and behind the policeman came Leo, handcuffed. The pair started up the street toward

Robert and Nell. They've got him! They've got him! Robert thought. And he said to Nell: "Jesus, they've got Leo! They may railroad him to the chair!"

"Keep your head," she muttered. "Don't let the policeman see you or recognize you or they'll have you in court. They'll sweat it out of you about that meeting where the officer was murdered. . . ."

"You mean where he fell and busted his head and inhaled a lot of the gas he'd thrown in there himself."

"Oh, no difference. I hope the little fool has sense enough and consideration enough not to bawl out and beg you to help him or find bail for him. That's about what he'll do."

"He won't do that."

"Well, you'll get into plenty of trouble, anyhow. Don't say a word. It wouldn't do him a speck of good and they'd be sure to summons you and probably indict you for something or other. Mr. Harrison told me how many charges they can bring up against such meetings, all perfectly legal and water-tight."

"Damn Mr. Harrison!"

"Shhh! Dry up!"

They passed by Leo and the policeman. Leo kept a poker face without even rolling his eyes. The policeman was making for a phone on a lamp post a block away. He was going to call a patrol wagon, and once they had Leo in jail they'd fight to keep him there, and would. Murder! Look what they did to Mooney. It doesn't make any difference how much evidence we'd try to dig up, they'd have him behind those bars. He turned about and stared wildly after Leo and the patrolman.

"I won't see him railroaded," he said. "I'm going to coldcock that flatfoot and let Leo take a run for it. It's going to be easy. He won't suspect. Go on. We'll both get away. Go back home. I'll see you there."

"You fool!" said Nell, so loudly that Robert was afraid the cop would catch on. "You get your foot into that, and I'm through. You hear me? I'm through. I humbled myself to beg you back when you went off in your other tantrum and pouted down in Roosevelt Roost. You want me to lose my job, I guess. Don't you think for a minute they won't find out where we live, and all about us. And I'll have no more job. It'll be a good thing for you when he's gone, then you'll stay with me sometimes of nights. I'll be glad when he quits pouring foolish ideas into your head, and maybe you'll come to your senses again."

"How'd the cops find out where he lived? You told Mr. Harrison!" he said, but he didn't really believe it was true. She flushed angrily, and averted her eyes.

"I *did not*! Why should I tell him? Leo's nothing to me one way or other."

"You did!" He grasped her by the shoulders and shook her vigorously. "You can't lie to me! You were jealous, and wanted him out of the way. Nobody else'd tell." In spite of his accusation, he could not bring himself to believe that she would do such a thing.

"Turn loose of me!" She wrenched herself free. "You're pinching a piece out of me, you big bully! What if I *did* tell? It'd be the best thing that ever happened to you. You don't know how to take care of yourself; you've always been like a big baby. You and your unemployed councils! What business have you got in them? You'd better be grateful *you're* not on relief."

"So Mr. Harrison is a stool pigeon for the police."

"He *is* not! I don't see why you've got any call to crab about him. If it weren't for him, you'd live a lot leaner."

This thrust severed cleanly the umbilical cord that had bound their lives together. He could not be sure whether or not she had told Mr. Harrison where Leo was living, but that made no difference. Their orbits must swing apart now, never to impinge again. A gigolo! He'd been a gigolo, as Leo had hinted once during the strike at the bridge plant. She had kept plenty for him to eat, and she had a warm and loving body. These things had bound him to her. He could see that now.

"You'll not come back! Don't think you'll come back this time!" she screamed as Robert made off rapidly toward Leo and the policeman. The policeman was unlocking the telephone box.

"I don't want to. Good-bye, good-luck, and God bless you, Mother Machree!"

"I've still got the Lysol. I'll sure make you wish you'd never been born when I drink it and you're exposed—you'll be to blame."

He was not moved by this threat. . . . If only she doesn't think to warn the policeman what I intend to do. . . . But she was too wrought up about her own injuries. He came close. The policeman was pulling out the phone, regarded Robert with faint interest and a flicker of amusement.

"Gettin' you told, ain't she, sport?" said the cop.

"Yeh," said Robert, grinning, but nervous. His legs began to shake—visibly, he was afraid. "She gets spells like that when she comes around. Lots of women do. You're a married man yourself, I guess. Just got to walk away and leave her. She'll cool off. She'll get over it."

"Officer! Officer!" squealed Nell, her high heels clicking on the pavement. She caught one of her heels in a crevice, it twisted off, and she sprawled on the sidewalk.

"Aw, forgive and forget. Pick her up, kiss her, and make up," suggested the cop, as he turned half about to expose a splendid target under the side of his jaw. Robert struck him so suddenly and savagely that he was down before he had known what hit him. He grunted and shook his head like an angry bull, resting on palms and knees. Then he pawed for his revolver, his fingers all thumbs and his head still foggy as he tried to pull his gun out of its holster.

"The alley, Leo!" yelled Robert. "Come on, boy!"

"Good boy," said Leo. "Let's shake ol' brown and they'll never ketch us."

They dived into the alley before the policeman had a chance to fire. His whistle shrilled blast after blast. The shadows of evening were dimming the canyons between the high blank walls of the buildings. They ran swiftly and silently until they had gone two blocks and more.

"I'm among friends here," said Leo. "I know all these people here. But you've buggered yourself, boy. You'll be a marked man."

"Never mind that," said Robert. As they raced along doors opened and heads were thrust out of windows.

"Jump in here, Comrade Leo. They won't never think of lookin' for you here," said one.

"Hey! What's the rush? Come in and tell us about it," called another.

"It's funny with these handcuffs. Like runnin' with yer hands tied. If I was t' fall down I'd sure bust myself. Couldn't use my hands t' save myself. It's a funny feelin'."

"We've got to get a file to take off those handcuffs."

"That's easy. I was invited t' supper and that's where we're goin'. But I thought fer a while I'd take supper on the city."

The business houses thinned out and they descended a hill at the foot of which were the small, dark houses of factory workers, smoked like herrings from the continuous belching of the stacks. Leo opened a gate and stood on a front stoop, knocking at a door. "It's me, Joe," said Leo. "It's Leo."

A Hungarian with heavy black eyebrows and a sadly drooping mustache flung open the door. His eyes were twinkling merrily.

"Bracelets, Joe," said Leo, holding up his hands.

"Ha, I feex 'em up! Wassa matter, bum, no comin'? I tell you come early, Leo, help peel spuds. Lazy like hell, Leo. Das no gude. Goulash all feexed now. All you gotta do now eat 'em."

"I had an appointment with the police, Joe."

"Ha, I know!"

"Where's the goulash? I can smell it. Can't nobody make goulash like Joe."

"Goulash comin'," said Joe. "Wait. I feex 'em up." He returned with a file and set to work on the handcuffs. "Dees style bracelet no gude, Leo. You like?"

believe it, I'd said it so much. I had a note fer you amongst the others in my pocket t' be found on my dead body and published in all the papers.

"I slep' in one o' them two-bit hotels, where you have a little beaver-board cubby-hole with chicken wire over the top and a little army cot, and you can hear ever'thing that's said all over the place. I heerd one feller tellin' another one a joke, and thought—like I allers had before— I'll remember that one t' spring on somebody. You rec'lect I allers was a great hand fer jokes, and I used t' think I was a hell of a feller and smart as a whip because I could tell 'em faster and longer than the next one. So one of the fellers in the next cubby-hole says t' the other: 'You got any job yet?' and the other says, 'Naw! Nawthin' but promises, promises, promises, when times picks up. That's the song and dance they allers hand me. In a pig's butt! Times ain't *never* goin' t' get better. Speakin' o' promises reminds me of a tale I heerd about two little city sparrers. Come winter, one of 'em said adios, he was pullin' out fer the sunny south t'live warm and easy where the ground never froze up and the worms never dug in fer the cold weather. The other says that's where you're goofy. Stay right here at home and let the saps pull out and leave the gravy fer the wise birds. Horses eats more in winter than in summer, anyways. Well, these sparrers they meets agin in the spring, and, Lord, the stay-at-home is skinny as a fence rail; he's that ga'nt he has t' stand twicet t' make a shadder. "Wotta 'ell," says the fat and sassy guy that beat it south. "You look kinda under the weather, old palzy-walzy, old buddy. How come?" "Ha," pipes the stay-at-home, "they ain't a dozen horses left in this Godforsaken burg, and they're weanin' *them*. And the farmers follers 'em around with a shovel fer fertilizer. All I got done this winter was foller around after them little Fords goin' poop! poop!, and you know a guy can't live very fat jist on them promises."'

"I laughed and forgot about killin' myself fer a minute, but o' course it wasn't long till I was thinkin' how sorry I was gonna make the world fer the dirty way it had treated me and Anna, leavin' her die in a ditch, bloody as a hog-pen in butcherin' time. And how all the fine promises o' the New Deal had pooped out and left nothin' but a stink.

"When I got t' the city hall the next mornin' it was about ten, and damned if they wasn't cops ever' which way from Sunday. And this sounds comical, I know, but it's a God's fact. I was too skeered o' them cops t' yank out that pistol and kill myself. I thought I'd wait till they thinned out some.

"Then, afore you could say Jack Robinson, it seemed t' me, they was thousands and thousands of people there with signs and things that made me think they was all in jist as bad a shape as me. I don't know how it started, but first thing I knowed the cops was slingin' them gas bumbs, and my eyes and lungs found it out soon enough. A cop hit me on the elbow with his billy, and if they's anything makes me hoppin' mad and crazy, it's t' hit my crazy bone. I jerked out the pistol then and used it fer a club. I salivated more'n one cop with it, which I calls good work.

"But this colored feller, Fatfolks, the one that had the big funeral. He was the man! I first seed 'im when he was catchin' them bumbs and throwin' 'em right back at the cops. His hands was burned to a crisp, and his arms to the elbow, but he never stopped. His old blue shirt had ripped clean off his back and he didn't have on a sign o' underwear. He was the best-muscled man I'd ever' seen in my life. He'd been a river roustabout—a river rat, when he could get any work. And that sure puts the muscle on a man. It sure done my heart good the way he throwed them bumbs; he was a born ball-player. 'Attaboy, Fatfolks!' I could hear people yellin', and I started yellin', too. I forgot all about makin' people feel sorry fer me. All these people was down and outers, but they had a better way o' makin' the ones that's got plenty and too much and wants more shell out with it, too. They got poor old Fatfolks, and it was a policeman done it, too. Not like the papers says. I seen a cop aimin' from a window in the city

"Yeh, like you do. Joe's bull-simple," he said to Robert. "You'll learn what it is t' be bull-simple. You get it from bein' beat across the kidneys and havin' a hose stuck in yer mouth, and sometimes yer pratt, and the water turned on full force. Then they got other cute little ways, ain't they, Joe?"

"Go' damn right! Hell, yes!" said Joe. "I know."

"When you get bull-simple, ever' time you see a bull you can't hold yerself from shakin' like jelly in a bowl. So Joe won't open the door till he knows who it is. He jist done a stretch o' six months fer leadin' a strike at the Carson Packin' Company. So he's bull-simple."

"Same like you, bum," said Joe, returning with two steaming bowls of goulash.

"Yeh, same like me," said Leo. "He's an outlaw, too. My brother." He jerked his thumb toward Robert. Joe was pouring the amber coffee.

"You remember how we used t' play outlaw down in Happy Hollow, Bob?" said Leo. "We're real outlaws now. We'll have t' remember how we used t' dodge old King Brady and Old Sleuth when they come gunnin' fer us. I was allers Jesse James and you was the whole Quantrell gang at oncet."

The brothers ate with relish, regarding one another with admiration and affection.

"Eat hearty," said Leo. "You don't find grub like this ever'day. This coffee ain't been boiled but oncet, has it, Joe?"

"Das all. Sometimes once, sometimes lonk time," said Joe. "Some day we all eat roasta pork, pie, kek, drink anyt'ings we want. What you say, Leo? Okay?"

"You bet," said Leo. "We'll make you commissar of the goulash."

They sat enclosed warmly in the comradeship of sorrow and weariness and anger, fellows of the men and women—fighting, laboring, seeing—who cry out relentlessly and passionately at factory gates, who mass in thousands on the steps of city halls and in the streets to reiterate endlessly and inexorably their harsh questioning of those who batten on the flesh and blood of the inarticulate and the submerged. Their breath a whisper that will not die—the prelude to storm.

It is good to be here, thought Robert. It will be good to move. My body and my mind have been numbing from disuse, like a foot planted on the floor too long. It will be good to feel the blood tingling and circulating once more.

And to walk, no matter where I go.

University of Illinois Press
1325 South Oak Street
Champaign, IL 61820-6903
www.press.uillinois.edu